Contents

Series Editors' Foreword

The Chapman & Hall Series in Tourism and Hospitality Management is dedicated to the publication of high quality textbooks and other volumes that will be of benefit to those engaged in hotel, catering and tourism education, especially at degree and postgraduate level. All the authors in the series are experts in their own fields, actively engaged in teaching research and consultancy in hospitality and tourism. This is a distinctive feature of the series and each book comprises an authoritative blend of subject-relevant theoretical considerations and practical applications and illustrations prepared by experienced writers. Furthermore, a unique quality of the series is that it is student oriented, offering accessible texts that take account of the realities of management and operations in the hospitality and tourism industries, being constructively critical where necessary without losing sight of the overall goal of providing clear accounts of essential concepts, techniques and issues. The tourism and hospitality industries are diverse and dynamic industries and it is the intention of the series to reflect this diversity and dynamism by publishing quality texts that embrace topical subjects without losing sight of enduring themes. In this respect, the Chapman & Hall Series in Tourism and Hospitality Management is an innovative venture committed to quality, accessibility and relevance. The Series Editors are grateful to Chapman & Hall for supporting this philosophy and would particularly like to acknowledge the commitment, expertise and insight of the Commissioning Editor, Steven Reed, whose contribution to the realization of the series has been invaluable.

C.L. Jenkins
R.C. Wood

The Scottish Hotel School
University of Strathclyde.

Interpersonal Skills for Hospitality Management

Mona Clark

**School of Food and Accommodation Management,
University of Dundee, UK**

CHAPMAN & HALL
University and Professional Division

London · Glasgow · Weinheim · New York · Tokyo · Melbourne · Madras

Published by Chapman & Hall, 2–6 Boundary Row, London SE1 8HN, UK

Chapman & Hall, 2–6 Boundary Row, London SE1 8HN, UK

Blackie Academic & Professional, Wester Cleddens Road, Bishopbriggs, Glasgow G64 2NZ, UK

Chapman & Hall GmbH, Pappelallee 3, 69469 Weinheim, Germany

Chapman & Hall USA, One Penn Plaza, 41st Floor, New York NY 10119, USA

Chapman & Hall Japan, ITP-Japan, Kyowa Building, 3F, 2–2–1 Hirakawacho, Chiyoda-ku, Tokyo 102, Japan

Chapman & Hall Australia, Thomas Nelson Australia, 102 Dodds Street, South Melbourne, Victoria 3205, Australia

Chapman & Hall India, R. Seshadri, 32 Second Main Road, CIT East, Madras 600 035, India

First edition 1995

©1995 Mona A. Clark

Typeset in 10.5/12pt Times Ten by Photoprint, Torquay, Devon
Printed at Alden Press Limited, Oxford and Northampton, Great Britain

ISBN 0 412 57330 X

A catalogue record for this book is available from the British Library

♾ Printed on permanent acid-free paper, manufactured in accordance with ANSI/NISO Z39.48-1992 and ANSI/NISO Z39.48-1984 (Permanence of Paper).

Foreword

It has always amazed me that the hospitality industry always puts so much emphasis in product, buildings and all the latest technology, but fails to recognize how much is invested in its people. People have to be our principal strategic asset and the recruitment, training and development of our people have to be every manager's most important responsibility. How these people communicate, whether with colleagues or the external customer, will determine the success of the business.

The businesses that survive in the future will be those that are able to deliver service standards that always meet the customers' expectations as a minimum and exceed their expectations as often as possible. Every single instance of failing to meet the customer demand or expectation is measured as a failure. Those failures are measured in hundreds of thousands of pounds in poor public relations, loss of future business and the cost of replacing that business. Investment in our people, and the improvement, on an on-going basis, of the ability to listen, read situations and communicate, has a far greater return on investment in the long term than anything I know.

This book clearly establishes that each person must take responsibility for their part in communication and each organization must support everybody within it in these developments. The book has a very practical approach, identifying key areas of interpersonal skills development, together with techniques that support the reader in developing their ability to communicate effectively. The exercises contained within the book and the language used throughout reinforce good practice and can be used on an individual basis for self-study or by groups in more structured sessions.

I am delighted to endorse the publication of this book. Its subject matter is of key importance to everyone at a professional and personal level. I commend this book to you and hope that you enjoy it but more importantly that you use it. There is absolutely no question that in today's business climate, with new organizational structures and absolute focus on our internal and external customers, the ability to communicate effectively will determine both personal and business success.

Peter J. Lederer, OBE, MI, FHCIMA,
Managing Director and General Manager,
The Gleneagles Hotel, Auchterarder

Acknowledgements

My sincere thanks to all those who contributed in some way or another to the task of writing this book, especially those whom I probably bored to death with the whole project but who still asked regularly and kindly after its progress and my sanity.

My particular thanks must go to the following.

To Roy Wood, Reader, The Scottish Hotel School, University of Strathclyde, who gave me the courage to take up this challenge.

To my colleague Colin Doherty, School of Food and Accommodation Management, University of Dundee, for his regular and intensive questioning of my assumptions about the 'teachability' of interpersonal skills, which helped enormously in clarifying for me how I would tackle the challenge.

To my colleague Steven Gregory, post-graduate researcher at Leeds Metropolitan University, whose experience in training in this area produced so many valuable observations on and suggestions for the practical exercises.

To my students, Morag Thirlwell and Tracy Muir, who read parts of the manuscript, and commented so usefully on its 'readability'.

To all my other students from 1990 onwards who, willingly or unwillingly, knowingly or unknowingly, allowed me to use them as guinea pigs for my ideas.

Finally, thanks to my Head of School, Adam Clark, for his interest and support in this project.

Mona Clark

Introduction

To speak agreeably with him with whom we deal is more than to speak in good words or in good order. (Francis Bacon)

I do not imagine anyone would deny that in 'people-centred' occupations, communications and interpersonal skills are of key importance. In any service industry, the human element – the smiling face, the thoughtful words, the warm voice, the welcoming posture – is the 'added value'. This is arguably even more so in the hospitality industry, where the very essence of the concept of 'hospitality' suggests a special caring relationship of the sort we share with family and friends, far more so than the service relationship we might share with a hairdresser or bank clerk. Indeed, a recent article in the *International Journal of Hospitality Management* (Brownell, 1992) stated that 'hospitality managers' communication competence is particularly important ... social interactions are part of the "product" itself'.

Therefore it is not at all surprising that if you want to succeed in the hospitality industry specifically, and the wider tourism industry in general, where the idea of welcoming someone to your region or country has connotations of welcoming someone to your home, you are encouraged to acquire highly sophisticated and effective communications and interpersonal skills in order to enhance these social interactions. The practising and enhancing of interpersonal skills is thus of key significance in courses for students planning to go into the hospitality and tourism industries.

An appreciation of the scientific studies of human behaviour, and the intensely human element which affects all communications processes, formal or informal, helps us choose the most effective communications tools and develop the most effective interpersonal skills to achieve the objectives of the process. Therefore the approach herein is to encourage you to think about communications and interpersonal skills firstly at a theoretical level, so that you can base your awareness of the deeper and more complex aspects of social interaction on pertinent psychological and sociological theories and evidence, and then to apply these ideas at a very practical level through being actively involved in a number of supporting exercises designed to help you think about, develop and assess your own skills of self-presentation and interaction with individuals and groups.

If you are reading this as a student new to this area of study, you will probably share the initial view of the subject matter of each new cohort of students I teach. That view is that it is all 'screamingly obvious', merely 'common sense', which by definition is shared by everybody and thus not open to debate, let alone as part of the content of higher education. After all, we can all communicate and interact perfectly well with each other. We have no problem getting on with each other, living together, being neighbourly, working and playing together, very amicably.

But do we actually get on with everybody all the time? And as effectively as we might? Just think about it. If it is all so easy, if it **is** 'common sense', then why do people ever fall out with one another? Why do we often talk about someone not being on the same 'wavelength' as us? Why have many of us at some time in our lives not got on with someone because we perceived that person to be boring, thoughtless or aggressive?

Why are we not all as eloquent and confident as our favourite TV presenter or public speaker? Why can't we all act like an Oscar-winner when we need to perform a particular social or professional role? Why do negotiations between individuals or groups break down? Why does a simple disagreement end up in a full-blown conflict? Why do wars break out? Yet, if 'common sense' (or experience) **does** tell us anything about social relationships, it is that most of us most of the time do appear to **want** to get on with one another, to like one another, to agree with one another and to live with one another amicably. So human relationships, social interactions, are obviously not so simple, so clear-cut, and so easily managed.

I am sure that you could add indefinitely to the above questions, each of which is directly to do with how effectively we communicate with one another. So we have to recognize that this 'common sense' is not as common as we might think. There's a lot more to communicating, to social interaction, than meets the eye – or ear! And as Sparks (1994) points out, the uniqueness of the hospitality industry is that it relies heavily on the sale of 'intangibles', like the service encounter–customer interaction, where the service provider could be said to convey the 'personality' of the service offered to the customer.

To illustrate this point, why **is** Meryl Streep considered to be a better actress than Madonna, Dustin Hoffman a better actor than Sylvester Stallone? Because winning Oscars for acting in the movies is almost entirely about good communications techniques. There is far more to performing than merely learning a script, however good that script is. Great performances are about the ability to communicate moods, personalities, feelings, attitudes, through a number of cues, to the audience, with which they can identify, and which makes the characters' actions and behaviour meaningful in the context of the scene and story. In the same way, winning and keeping customers are achieved through the communicative aspects of the receptionist's or head waiter's role as it is perceived by the customer.

This book is about the study, understanding and application of these communications skills, and although it is a 'textbook', it is not about theorizing as a purely academic exercise for its own sake. Even if you feel you already have this 'common sense', the book is specifically written to encourage you to **enhance** your communications and inter-personal skills actively and continually.

Such skills are not just a question of smiling at the right time, answering the phone in a particular way, writing a report, or giving a short oral presentation. They are also about the far more complex, more subtle, more elusive, more sophisticated interpersonal skills required by potential leaders in the hospitality industry. The book is a response to demands placed upon you by the hospitality and tourism industries. For example, a survey of 118 practising hotel managers in the UK and USA (*International Journal of Hospitality Management*, 1990) revealed that they believed six out of the top eight **essential** competencies required by hotel managers were the ability to:

1. manage guests' problems with understanding and sensitivity;
3. communicate effectively both written and orally;
4. achieve positive working relationships with employees;
5. demonstrate professional appearance and poise;
6. develop positive customer relations;
7. motivate employees to achieve desired performance.

And first of the competencies listed of **considerable** importance is the 'possession of needed leadership qualities to achieve organizational objectives'.

I am sure you will recognize that these competencies all require high-quality application of communications and interpersonal skills. These views reflect an increasing amount and range of evidence from the industry and from educators which suggests that we ought to think about these skills in a more structured and analytical way, because if they were so generally or easily available then such attention would not be drawn to them.

Hopefully by the conclusion of the book, you will have built up a deeper understanding of the skills of individual self-presentation and social interaction, through to skills of leadership, skills with groups, negotiating and conflict-resolution skills. The text offers a range of ideas and methods as to how to think about, practise, and assess your own interpersonal skills.

It is divided into eight sections, each covering a specified group of skills. The heading for each section consists of a question, or questions, to be answered relative to the particular skills discussed in that section, accompanied by a brief scenario or 'snapshot' reflecting an associated communications issue or problem. There is a certain amount of sup-porting theoretical material in the sections, which I hope you will find is pitched at an appropriate 'user-friendly' level, with jargon kept to a minimum – a communications skill which we lecturers often find quite difficult to sustain!

So that you do not lose sight of the core material in each section, you will see that it is summarized periodically within sub-sections called Keynotes. Each section is accompanied by a number of exercises, which you can attempt on your own, with fellow students – or even friends – or in the classroom. There is no 'one right answer' given for the exercises; by its nature, the study of human behaviour and social interaction has an in-built unpredictability, and what works for one person, or in one situation, or on one day, will not necessarily work again. That's why understanding the **process** of communicating helps us to some extent to be capable of **controlling** it.

There are references for further reading at the end of each section, and an extensive general bibliography should you want or need to delve more deeply into ideas or applications. I have tried to make the contexts reflect as much as possible situations within the hospitality industry, but you can also test their appropriateness in quite different contexts, including of course your role as a student and within your own personal relationships.

My experience of students suggests that they could do with some lessons in negotiation and conflict-resolution skills if they want to persuade me to accept a late essay! You will also find that reference is generally made to the reader as 'manager' or future manager, but that is indicative of my reading of your potential, rather than that which you might have in mind for yourselves! One of the key academic findings of motivation theorists is that people behave according to the expectations we have of them.

To conclude, a highly respected academic writer on management, Rosemary Stewart (Stewart, 1980) established through her research that managers spend approximately 80% of their time communicating through the oral or written word. It seems superfluous to suggest that if they can't communicate effectively, they are failing in the key component of their day-to-day task. To support that thesis, you might like to have a look at the following analysis of the various roles which a manager has to play, as classified by another very prestigious management theorist, Henry Mintzberg. Mintzberg (1980) points out that the formal or operational position and status given to a manager by the organization is enacted through a number of responsibilities, activities and skills.

Have a really good think about these. How much of a manager's success in fulfilling these roles depends upon highly developed communications and interpersonal skills, as the hospitality industry becomes more and more internationalized in terms of its workforce and its customers, and the rapid changes in demands.

The Manager – a position with formal authority and status – interpreted through the following roles:

Interpersonal role
figurehead
leader
liaison

Informational role
monitor
disseminator
spokesperson

Decisional roles
entrepreneur
disturbance-handler
resource allocator
negotiator

I hope the above allows me to say, as a lawyer would, in advocating this book 'I rest my case!'

Postscript

You may feel that I undervalued the significance of a smile in this introduction, because the smile is the one thing that distinguishes us from the animal kingdom; it is the one form of communication which is common to every human being, and its positive message is one which is understood by every human being, whatever his or her culture. So perhaps the following, which I first read in the Staff Induction Manual produced by the international contract caterers, Gardner Merchant, will retrieve the situation!

THE VALUE OF A SMILE

- It costs nothing, but creates much.
- It enriches those who receive, without impoverishing those who give.
- It happens in a flash, but the memory of it sometimes lasts for ever.
- None are so rich they can get along without it, and none are so poor but are richer for its benefits.
- It creates happiness in the home, fosters goodwill in a business, and is the countersign of friends.
- It is rest to the weary, daylight to the discouraged, sunshine to the sad, and nature's best antidote for trouble.
- Yet it cannot be bought, begged, borrowed, or stolen, for it is something that is no earthly good to anyone until it is given away.
- So if at any time others should be too tired to give you a smile, can we ask you to give one of yours, for nobody needs a smile as much as those who have none left to give.

Communications and interpersonal skills – their nature and characteristics

1

The interest in life does not lie in what people do, nor even in their relations to one another, but largely in the power to communicate with a third party ... which one may call life in general. (Virginia Woolf)

Question 1: What are 'communications and interpersonal skills'? How can we examine and enhance our interpersonal skills? Why should we?

Snapshot

Kate, the Public Relations Manager, and Andrew, the Banqueting Manager, are discussing their first impressions of the new Restaurant Manager, Ross, over their morning coffee.

Kate: 'Funny guy, isn't he? Don't see he's got the right personality for a restaurant manager.'
Andrew: 'What do you mean?'
Kate: 'I can't really pin it down – it's just that if I were a guest and not very sure about what wine to order, I don't think I'd ask him. He's so superior – and sort of threatening.'

What exactly is it that Kate 'can't pin down'? I'm sure you have quite often heard similar comments about individuals. The importance of her message for us is that it shows that when we are talking about communications and interpersonal or social skills, we actually may have great difficulty in defining what we are talking about, and therefore identifying exactly what we are trying to investigate or study. We know the good communicators, the socially skilled people, when we meet them, but it is much less easy to articulate the components of the behaviour, the activities or abilities which have led us to label someone as 'socially skilled', although that phrase itself is not often used in everyday conversation – Kate's comments above are a more likely format for such a discussion.

This is probably because one of the factors which we, consciously or unconsciously, use to judge people as good communicators or socially skilled is that they appear to be so 'natural' in their social interaction. Perhaps the very reason we like them is because they are so 'genuine'. This makes it difficult for us to appreciate that the ability to interact effectively with others in social situations is indeed a **skill**, or, more accurately, a package of skills. That is because by definition a skill means an ability which we acquire through learning and training, like making an omelette – and which can be improved upon – like making a better omelette!

Just as Kate uses the concept of 'personality' to discuss Ross's behaviour, we often talk about someone having a 'sparkling personality'. Someone who is well-liked, who can get on with everybody, is very interesting, lively, great fun to be with. There are many occupations and careers, including that of hospitality management, in which a 'sparkling personality' is right at the top of the list of required assets. But many people believe that an individual's personality is basically the consequence of certain qualities or traits one is born with, certain patterns of behaviour which are considered to be innate, and one is just lucky – or unlucky – with one's inheritance. Thus it is nothing to do with a skill, or learned ability. Alternatively, being able to get on with people is just 'common sense', which, by definition, we all have. So what's the point of an academic course which claims to enhance our social skills – isn't it in fact a bit of an affront? After all, none of us is inclined to believe other than that we have a 'sparkling personality'.

But communications and social skills can and need to be thought about analytically. Just as we can and have to analyse what is needed to market a new function suite successfully, or a new type of Special Interest holiday, so we can analyse our social skills. We then know exactly what we are trying to develop or enhance in order to market ourselves more effectively, in whatever social role we are playing. If your place as a student had been partially dependent upon your performance at an interview, then you certainly understood the concept of marketing yourself! So if we can identify where and why it is not just about 'common sense', whatever our personalities, from 'plonk' to 'vintage', however sparkling, we can learn to be even more sparkling. There are champagnes – and vintage champagnes – and there's no limit to the quality of the bubbles!

Firstly, let's emphasize the point that social skills are something we **acquire**. They are learned, they are not instinctive. Michael Argyle, the social psychologist who has probably done more work in this field than any other academic, stated that 'a skill is an organized, co-ordinated activity in relation to an object or situation, which involves a whole chain of sensory, central and control mechanisms'. Translating Argyle's definition into a process of social interaction in the hospitality industry, you might have something like the following:

> Working towards persuading a guest to try an unusual wine through carefully assessing the needs, motives and on-going responses of that individual, choosing one's words and tone of voice in a manner which will encourage the guest to take the chance, and recognizing through a number of verbal and non-verbal cues whether the feedback from the guest – his refusal to try the wine – is because of insecurity or lack of money.

In other words, one knows whether to give up the attempt or whether to continue by finding another social technique which will deal with the insecurity!

This is rather a laboured interpretation, but I hope it makes the point. But if you still have a 'gut reaction' that certain abilities and aptitudes must be 'natural', you are not entirely wrong. Research indeed shows that skills acquired do depend upon some existing basic potential. I referred above to the example of making an omelette; perhaps a better example for our purposes is that of learning to drive a car. There's no doubt that some of us have better eyesight than others, or quicker reactions, or more sophisticated spatial ability, or more 'nerve', and these do appear to be a consequence of the luck of the genetic draw. So it is unlikely we could **all** be Grand Prix drivers, even if we wanted to be!

Thus the ability to detect slight variations in body language, or in the tone of someone's voice, which in turn then gives us a clue as to that person's mood, could be due to the fact that we have better eyesight or sharper hearing than others. This has enhanced our **perception**, and therefore how quickly and effectively we can interpret the mood. But at least the recognition that it is to do with perception, the **cues** we get through our senses and how we read them, allows us thereby to be more aware of the cues to look for, and to practise and thus improve our skills of **interpreting** what we see and hear. Whatever their innate creative talents, painters or musicians have to practise the tools and techniques of their art in order to realize fully these talents. The concept of perception will be referred to regularly in the text as it is the basis of our understanding of the world around us, and how that world 'works' – or how **we** can 'work' the world!

Are you still feeling I am talking about common sense? Well, of course we all have a common sense about how we interact with our fellow human beings. Our whole experience of growing up, our socialization process ensures that. 'Socialization' is by definition about 'common' sense, or shared knowledge. We are brought up and shaped according to the rules, roles, norms and values of a particular social group. It is the process whereby we become fully fledged members of that group or society. As socialized individuals we learn the appropriate ways to act in different social situations.

We learn to speak 'politely' to someone because that person is in a position of authority relative to us, or has the advantage of age over us. We learn the appropriate gestures and body language to encourage the communication process with someone we fancy, someone we're introduced to at a party, or someone we don't like – the persistent unwanted suitor. And we soon learn that other social groups expect other patterns of communication, which might be quite different from our own. Being 'polite' is a **label** for behaviour; that behaviour can take a number of different **forms** of behaviour in different cultures.

You may have heard the story of Captain Cook, the explorer, who was killed by natives he approached on one of the South Sea Islands he visited. He stretched out his hand in a non-verbal gesture of friendship recognized by our culture, the handshake. To the culture he was visiting, the stretched-out hand was a threatening gesture, it implied an attack might be forthcoming. So the natives decided that the best form of defence was to attack first, and Captain Cook suffered the extreme consequences of his lack of understanding as to how to communicate with a different social group!

Within our own social or work groups, our reactions over the years do become almost automatic. We don't consciously think through the social rules and norms when we are first introduced to our future in-laws, or to the managing director at the company Christmas party. We seem to do the right things instinctively. Just as when driving a car we change gear, or make an emergency stop, or employ many of the other skills of driving without consciously thinking about it. Have you ever tried to teach someone else to drive? It can be very difficult to unpack in detail what is necessary. Thus we have to recognize that these skills are not really instinctive in the sense that we blink when we get a speck of dust in our eye, or sneeze when pepper gets spilt.

This implies that good communications and interpersonal skills mean being particularly sensitive to the attitudes and beliefs, rules and norms of social interaction with others, and especially so in situations with which we are not familiar, or in situations which unexpectedly change during the interaction. That sensitivity comes from perceiving, picking up, cues faster and interpreting them more quickly and more effectively than others might, like highly skilled drivers reacting not only to what is happening in their immediate vicinity, but also reading what is happening perhaps two or three hundred metres away, and, furthermore, what is likely to happen.

The socially skilled restaurant manager reads the cues put out by a prospective customer when he hears the initial estimate of the cost of his daughter's wedding reception, the content of the communications process which shows the conflict between the customer's wanting the best for his daughter but not wanting to appear to be mean. The thoughts may not be spoken in so many words, but the manager deftly holds on to the customer by negotiating alternatives to the formal six-course dinner without the customer's 'losing face', losing his self-esteem because he does not want to admit he can't afford the best.

To recap, social skills may be defined as

> those aptitudes and behaviours which allow one to interact with others in all social contexts through goal-directed and controlled procedures which further personal objectives while maintaining the process in a mutually beneficial manner to a mutually beneficial conclusion.

In other words, 'How can I persuade him to give me this job?'; 'How can I convince this disgruntled guest that the bar service is normally excellent?'; 'How can I discipline the Personnel Manager for mis-reading that employment legislation without destroying her self-esteem?'; 'What's the best way to explain to the chef that behaviour could be considered to be sexual harassment?'; 'How can I present a cheerful mood to that unexpected coach load demanding bar lunches?'

Keynotes

1. Being 'socially skilled' means that we have learned to interact effectively with our fellow human beings in a range of social situations.
2. This is partly as a consequence of a shared or 'common' sense as to what the social situations expect of our behaviour.
3. The highly socially skilled person has developed an **uncommon** sense which allows him or her to establish the required behaviour more speedily and implement it more effectively in a greater variety of social situations.

Now let's think about that phrase 'mutually beneficial' in our definition above. Just as we know it takes two to tango, so we should understand that it takes at least two to communicate! In other words, the very nature of communicating is that we cannot do it on our own – although we could **practise** some aspects of it in front of a mirror, or with an audio-cassette recorder or videocamera. The best way to think about this idea of mutuality is through the key concepts of **feedback** and **transaction**.

The communications process can be presented by a **loop**, a loop which can be broken at any stage. Well developed communications and social skills ensure that there is constant feedback ('I know what he's getting at; he knows what I'm getting at') so that the loop is not broken. Or if it is, then it is done deliberately in a manner which allows it to be reconnected very easily if and when necessary. This can be shown **diagrammatically**. A diagram is a **technical** method of communicating which furthers understanding, because it links up words, ideas and their relationships in a visual form, thus enhancing the ability of the mind to interpret the information, which in turn keeps the communications process going. We will be identifying and assessing these technical or operational methods in a number of activities.

Thus the transmitter (speaker) puts the message into a form which s/he believes to be the most effective for the purpose **(encodes)**, the receiver (listener) **decodes** (if it was in the most effective form) and through some cue or cues (a head nod, a phrase or sentence) gives the transmitter **feedback**. This tells the transmitter whether s/he has achieved the purpose of the communication, and, of course, how to follow it up, or keep the loop going if necessary.

Another way to think about the communications process is of it being **transactional**. If the process is to be effective, then a transaction, or exchange, is negotiated between the transmitter(s) and receiver(s). Negotiation implies that both transmitter and receiver have something to offer, and both hope to see the communications process ending in mutual benefit. The socially skilled person tries always to ensure that the process does end this way – everyone in a 'good mood' – with the loop being disconnected only when and how the participants wish.

An example of this is the dissatisfied guest who feels he has been able to make a fair point about poor service in the restaurant and goes away with a story to tell his friends about he got the restaurant manager to apologize, thus ensuring special attention on his next visit, while the restaurant manager is equally satisfied at having soothed a very difficult guest sufficiently to ensure he will return. (We have all been there before!)

The emphasis in the communications process always has to be on the human element. For instance, facts may be on our side, but when

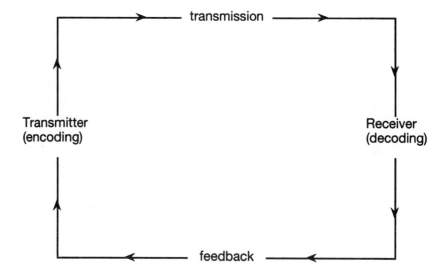

Figure 1.1 Hospitality management

attitudes, values and emotions have to be dealt with, the facts may be irrelevant. That is why we label these skills as 'social', as opposed to technical, or intellectual. You may have come across the incredibly clever tutor whose standing as an academic is first-class, but who cannot impart that knowledge in a lecture to mere underlings. He has not acquired the appropriate communications skills, despite his intellect. There's no mutual understanding between you and him.

How often do you hear the phrase, 'I just don't see it that way'? Meaning that the speaker interpreted the facts as he perceived them to be, not necessarily as they were. Or how often have you heard someone say to another, 'You're not listening to me!' That's another good example of the breakdown in that mutual process. We 'hear' automatically with the physical organ, the ear. But we need actively to 'listen' to make psychological or linguistic sense of what the ear picks up as pure waves of sound. And being a 'good listener' is certainly considered to be a sophisticated, highly developed social skill which we will be looking at in a later chapter.

Listening is about **reciprocity**, meaning there has to be involvement from both or all parties, and a **mental set** in the communicators which encourages the creating of meaning and purpose in the communication. And possible barriers to that process need to be picked up if it is to continue, for example, being able to perceive and interpret the **cues** which suggest to the 'good listener' that an emotion is surfacing which is affecting the speaker's apparently factual statement. Or being able to control your own emotions if the social situation demands it in the face of listening to something you don't want to hear.

There must be occasions in a hotel manager's career when he would like to tell a particular guest never to darken his foyer again, but dare not because the person concerned brings good, regular business to the hotel. So the manager pretends to listen sympathetically, because he realizes that the guest just requires to 'sound off' every so often to reinforce his self-esteem.

Things happen to us when we are in the company of the good communicator. We learn, we are motivated, we are comforted, our self-esteem is boosted, our understanding of our role or status is enhanced. We form a closer and more positive relationship with others, a closer and more positive understanding of ourselves. This is what the 'transaction' is all about. Encouraging the 'feel good' factor in others is part of the stock-in-trade of those who desire, even require, to be the greatest communicators of all – politicians!

So it is not by chance that the phrase often used to describe someone who appears to interact very effectively in an organization is that she is very good at 'playing politics', or very good at appreciating the 'politics' of a situation, meaning, for example, that there could be the human elements of power and status underlying what looks like the breakdown of a communications process, an argument which on the surface looked like a conflict over facts.

There is not just a practical reason for being a good communicator, having the technical skills and abilities to write a succinct business letter or report with clarity and authority, or to construct a visually exciting flow-chart or present statistical information in an accessible visual manner. Even these very formal means of communicating have to reflect an element of social skills in their construction, because social skills emphasize the 'human needs' aspect, to be constructive rather than destructive of feelings, attitudes, values, and this always influences both the content and the context of the communications process.

There are ways and ways of writing a letter of complaint, or a report which lays blame for a business problem at a particular individual's door. Social stroking is an analogy derived from the behaviour we exhibit towards a cat or a dog, or any other pet, when we want to calm it down, make it feel good, make it feel we are interested in it, and that it deserves our attention. It seems to me that phrase encapsulates a lot of what we are investigating. And as medical experience has shown, the effect on the person who does the stroking is just as positive as it is on the animal being stroked – so there's a lesson there for us all!

Keynotes
1. Communicating is a **process**, a series of actions which produce a desired change or development through a period of time.
2. Communications are **transactional**. That is, those involved negotiate meaning from the process. The socially skilled person ensures that the meaning negotiated is both understood and desired by all concerned.
3 The ability to do this depends upon highly developed **perceptual** abilities – perception being the process through which we detect and interpret information from the external world by means of our senses.

Finally, given that skills can be identified and **can** be learned, how do I involve you in that learning process? Can I get you to accept that you have anything to learn? Can I persuade you that you need to practise something you think you have been doing all your life – or you would not be here in the first place? Will you at least embark on an 'awareness-raising' exercise?

Let us try another analogy, draw further upon a skill mentioned at the outset of this section – the making of an omelette. Now that may seem a very routine and mundane exercise and not up within the top ten managerial skills! But in terms of the understanding of what we need to know in order to acquire skills, then being skilled at omelette-making requires much the same **learning processes** as becoming skilled at communicating. We can define and describe an 'omelette' and we know what a perfect omelette tastes like. We can listen to lectures which inform us that its creation depends upon the appropriate use of various theories of physics, chemistry, biology, metallurgy, etc.

One of the reasons you come to college or university on a hospitality management course is to understand how these various theories contribute towards the perfect omelette (or any other dish you may have to step in to provide for a guest if the chef walks out on you) and to practise their application in sheltered surroundings. If things go wrong for you, and the omelette does not fold over in the perfect half-circle, ends up like scrambled eggs or the sole of an old boot, then only you, your tutor or fellow students know. No lost customers, no lost business, no lost money. You may even have been able to make an omelette before – so now you can learn how to make an even better omelette. But your capacity to **make** an omelette, or make that better omelette, comes from your practising in the kitchen.

So just as training in that particular culinary skill takes place within this sheltered environment, so also can training in social skills. There are appropriate theories, appropriate tools, appropriate techniques, appropriate criteria for evaluating a communications objective or output achieved. You can practise these on yourself, or in conjunction with fellow students, or even friends. And if a particular exercise in social interaction doesn't work the first time, and you have to think of other ideas, other techniques, there are no lost customers, no lost business, no lost money . . .

Keynotes

1. The intellectual exercise of recognizing the nature and characteristics of social skills is not sufficient; the real importance and objective is to be able to apply them in a vocational situation or context.
2. The social skills training classroom or workshop could be compared exactly with the experimental kitchen or food technology laboratory.
3. Each individual possesses skills or dimensions of ability which are infinite in their capacity for improvement, from wherever one starts. This can be illustrated diagrammatically thus:

Table 1.1 'Skills are dimensions of ability to behave effectively in situations of action.'

Situation:	Interview
	Meeting
	Talk
Dimension of ability:	Using appropriate words and symbols
	Covering up nervousness
Effective behaviour:	Increasing credibility
	Keeping control
	Creating empathy

Dimensions of ability

Low ability			High ability
Ineffective	Behaviour		Effective
	Present	Desired	

Of course, there is not much point in just **reading** about ways of thinking about social skills, or the techniques which we might employ in order to achieve our communications objectives. We are not interested in a purely academic or intellectual exercise, however fascinating or challenging it might be. You want to be able to assess your ability to implement these ideas. After all, 'the proof of the pudding (omelette?) is in the eating!' So the six exercises, or **activities**, which follow each section of the book, illustrate and develop the theories and concepts in the sections, and set you tasks which test your understanding and application of the ideas.

Each activity has a follow-up, a discussion on how you might have gone about the task, and shares with you my ideas on the subject matter. Thus the 'sheltered environment' to which I was referring above could even be the solitude of your bedroom or study. But it's much more interesting, much more fun and much more informative if you can work your way through the activities with others. You will find in doing so that there are numerous ways of developing one's interpersonal skills. Adding these to your repertoire enhances not only your own understanding but also your ability to pass on such skills to your staff. Good communicating. Good luck!

Activity 1.1

Think of a fellow student who you would say has a 'sparkling personality'. Why do you think that? What is it about him or her that makes you say it? Jot down what it is, isolating as many factors as you can. Try to identify the 'personality' in terms of things you see, or hear, not things you feel, emotions you might have about the individual. It's the **behaviour** of the individual we are interested in. Do you think he or she has the 'right personality' for a front of house manager? Or a tourist information officer? Or human resources manager in a big organization? Are there personality factors which these positions share, or do they require a 'personality' which is specific to the role and position?

Thoughts on Activity 1.1

Did you jot down words like 'vivacious' or 'bubbly' or 'lively'? Or 'he makes me laugh' or 'she makes me feel good'. Or 'he's always so enthusiastic about things'. It's not surprising if you did – most people respond to that question in that way. You can test this by conducting your own little experiment by asking friends or fellow students the same question. The responses will almost certainly support the fact that most people do not make a clear distinction between words which **describe** behaviour, as opposed to what actually **is** behaviour. Yet it is the behaviour that we really want to establish.

If our role demands that we have a 'sparkling personality' then that is really about what we are seen to **do**, how we are seen to **behave**. And behaviour can be learned, copied, reinforced, enhanced. So have you jotted down things like 'he looks at you as if you matter', 'she doesn't interrupt me when I'm trying to say something', 'she's very good recognizing when I am feeling low and gives me a hug', 'he always seems to have a happy expression on his face'.

When we actually put into words what it is people are **doing** when they are praised or criticized for their social skills, then we can see that it should be possible to acquire through practise those behaviours which achieve positive effects in the people we communicate with, and we can try and 'unlearn' those behaviours which create negative effects. Can you guess what behaviour could have made Kate and Andrew in our opening scenario label the new restaurant manager as 'superior' and 'threatening'? Was it what he said? How he sounded? The manner in which he moved? The expression on his face? Perhaps when you were interviewed for your place as a student, you might have been asked if you thought you had the 'right' personality for the hospitality industry. Meaning in fact, could you 'behave appropriately'.

Activity 1.2

Now link up the reflections in the previous activity with some further thinking about personality and role. Consider four lecturers you have had in your time as a student, who are as different as possible in personality, style and behaviour from one another. Jot down some words to describe how these factors relate to communications and interpersonal skills. Can you link up your findings with positive and negative aspects in their performances? Try and be specific – don't just record that 'A communicates well', 'B communicates badly', 'C is a bit of a pain', 'D's good to work with'.

If you indicate the **consequences** of the behaviour for you, then it is perhaps easier to identify the actual behaviour. For example, 'A fires me with enthusiasm.' 'B bores me to tears, even although the subject is quite interesting.' 'C is so patronizing – he always makes me feel as if I'm pretty inadequate intellectually, whereas D at least treats me as an adult.' What **are** the behaviours which have these consequences? What do they say about the lecturers' communications and interpersonal skills, given their role and objectives in the organization?

Thoughts on Activity 1.2

This is another activity which asks you to concentrate on thinking about words and phrases (like 'firing with enthusiasm') which, when analysed, clearly involve **behaviours** which are **observable**. To re-emphasize, they can be copied, learned, practised, if they produce the effects you want – and unlearned if they don't! You are picking up and interpreting cues which you see or hear, which indicate attitudes or moods, which in turn elicit responses or actions on your part.

Lecturer A, who 'fires with enthusiasm', is not performing a trick with a cannon in the circus ring! This is about an individual who is using his or her voice, facial expression, body language, to transmit interest and motivation to an audience. The pitch and tone of the voice (a sense of excitement), its speed (faster than normal), the amount and type of eye contact (direct, with wide open eyes), the use of hands and arms (movement inviting involvement, response), body posture (leaning forward, ready for action), all contribute.

But Lecturer B 'bores to tears'. The exact opposite cues to those given off by A (no eye contact, a monotonous tone of voice, body language which indicates disinterest) plus some others, which are to do with the construction of the lecture – certainly a communications skill, but also a social skill. No identifiable key points to encourage you to listen, or make it easier for you to remember. No attempt to draw out what is so interesting or useful about the subject matter. No attempt to take into account the needs of the audience, their level of attention (a lecture at 4 pm on a Friday?) or their understanding (using jargon you are not yet familiar with).

Lecturer C is 'so patronizing'. A tone of voice which you perceive to be threatening your self-esteem, a use of language which does not take into account that you are a student without the range of knowledge and understanding of C. Poor listening skills; no sign that C is attentive to what you are saying, or reflecting that it is important.

Whereas Lecturer D 'treats you as an adult'. Again the exact opposite behaviour from C, probably. Communicating in a manner which assumes that although you do not share status, level of knowledge or understanding with D, you have a right to be treated as an equal human being. The sort of lecturer who would arrange the furniture in his or her study in a way that invites you to sit and talk to one other as equals – not confronting you from behind a formidable desk with you in an uncomfortable chair!

Learning is not just about the actual quality of the academic knowledge delivered to you. It requires a positive social and psychological environment, and that's about good communications and interpersonal skills, And although I have been getting you to think of your experiences as a student, I have no doubt that you will see its significance for your future role as a manager in terms of training staff or giving talks, or indeed to skills you will require as a leader, which are over and beyond that of a manager, as we will be discussing in Chapter 6. After all, what we have been talking about in this activity is a form of 'academic leadership', is it not?

Activity 1.3

On page 6 you looked at a diagram which showed the elements in the communications process. That diagram talked about **encoding** and **decoding**. Encoding means putting a message into the appropriate **code(s)** and transmitting it through the appropriate **channel(s)** to a receiver. Decoding means interpreting the **feedback** (what the receiver is transmitting to you).

Examples of **codes** are :

• the English language, used either colloquially or formally, diagrams, charts, drawings, photographs, mathematical symbols, style of dress, all body language.

Examples of **channels** are:

• a letter, a memo, a telemessage, a meeting, a notice board, the telephone, an overhead projector, a video, the press.

And **appropriate** in this context means that the transmitter and receiver must **share the meanings** of these codes with one another, interpret the use of these channels in the same way. Not as easy at it sounds! At the most obvious level, that means I would not generally give a lecture in Gaelic, you would not generally present your ideas to staff as to how to deal with the queue at the fast-food restaurant through the mathematical formula of queuing theory (yes, there is one!) and the front of house manager would not generally arrive at the reception desk in her jogging gear! Nor is a telemessage generally the best channel for telling a member of staff he is to be made redundant, or a formal meeting the best channel to deal with someone in the organization who is alleged to have sexually harassed certain colleagues.

Let's think of a simple application of this thinking. As by chance I am writing this on 14 February, let's think of communicating in the form of a Valentine card. You want to transmit to the object of your passion how much s/he means to you, with the desired effect that the feeling will turn out to be mutual. You buy the card, on which the message is encoded through written words and visual images. Presumably you will have already taken into account whether the receiver would like romantic poetry and hearts and flowers – or whether s/he prefers the witty, cheeky or bawdy symbolism – another form of coding, taking into account the needs of the receiver. You send the card through the post, the channel of communication. People generally like getting mail, and the receiver might consider it a bit of a slight if the card is delivered by hand. ('Am I not worth a first-class stamp?')

The feedback? Well, it may be that the receiver phones you (another channel); an immediate response and a delighted tone of voice which suggests that you have achieved your desired objective. Or you may have to wait for further cues when you next meet. Because you have to consider the deeper symbolism, or coding, attached to the use of the Valentine card. The surface message is supposed to be that the receiver will not guess whom it is from, but the coded message usually ensures the transmitter is identified!

Always remember that the example of the Valentine is only appropriate if you come from a culture which understands the symbolism, or the code, of a Valentine card as a means of showing a desire for a closer interpersonal relationship! Now evaluate the various communications channels and codes, with their associated psychological and symbolic connotations, in terms of their use in the following situations. What would you choose and why?

1. You have a new leisure facility to market to the public, but at the same time you wish to be fairly selective about the clientèle who will use it.
2. An irate guest, who had a meal in the hotel restaurant on a night when you were not on duty, has written to you with her complaints.
3. You want to explain to staff a new regulation concerning food hygiene.
4. You have a group of Japanese businessmen staying in the hotel while on an 'incentive' holiday to Scotland. You want to make them feel especially welcome.
5. Your Head Office wants to know exactly what you intend doing about poor occupancy rates in the low season.
6. You have been brought in to take over a big catering contract because the present manager has shown himself to be extremely inefficient. He and the rest of the staff will continue in the job, although now under your command.

Thoughts on Activity 1.3

It is important to remember that the code, reflecting a cultural or social context, and the channel, the technical means whereby information is transmitted, do not function independently of one another when a message is transmitted. Each can influence the effectiveness of the other. Keep these points in mind when you assess your responses. Here are my suggestions.

1. **Marketing the new leisure facility** A leaflet drop in a particular area or areas. Coded in the language which the group(s) you want to target will relate to, which is short and to the point and which uses a variety of presentational skills (pictures, diagrams) to catch attention, remembering that many people cannot be bothered with junk mail.

2. **The irate guest** An initial phone call if possible, as soon as possible, followed up by a letter. The channel of the phone showing you are reacting fast to her complaint, so she will be likely to be soothed temporarily, thus giving you time to investigate the complaint and construct an appropriate response to go through another channel, the post, which both registers her complaint formally (you are taking it seriously) and is also a protection for you (she cannot misquote you).

3. **The new food hygiene regulation** A short meeting, an oral presentation supported by something on paper, perhaps a brief outline of the key details. This allows for questions which may reveal lack of understanding or misunderstanding. Even better, an acetate on an overhead projector, so that staff can write down details, an action in itself which reinforces learning. Finally reinforced by specially prepared notices which staff can read fast – not the original legal or technical jargon.

4. **Japanese businessmen** A welcome notice in Japanese. A video on the hotel network which shows local places of interest. A leaflet in Japanese in the bedrooms which explains local customs. Your waiting staff trained to say 'good morning' in Japanese, and to show some understanding of Japanese body language, in some respects quite different from ours. For example, the degree to which a Japanese will bow helps identify the relative status of individuals.

5. **Poor occupancy rates** A perfectly prepared and presented report, in clear and concise business language, with all the appropriate data (words and figures) in a format which can be easily and speedily processed.

6. **The new manager** An immediate informal meeting of all staff, you **looking** at your most formal, but **speaking** in a relaxed manner. Nothing on paper, no new lines of authority spelled out, merely a request that staff individually come and see you some time about the new arrangements, after you have spelled them out at this first meeting. This is **not** a situation in which you want to come over as the 'new broom which will sweep clean', but rather more as leading a smooth transition with everyone co-operating and no self-esteem lost. At your meeting with the former manager, you and he negotiate, on paper, a

new role and responsibilities for him, on paper because it then acquires the status of a contract, if not formally.

Of course, if you have difficulty establishing the Japanese for 'good morning' or you do not have access to an overhead projector, then you will have to investigate other codes and channels. Remember, your effectiveness as a communicator is measured by your achieving what you want to achieve, so one channel or code may be more appropriate than another for you. My suggestions only relate to what I think I might do to achieve the purpose of the communications process. You might think that teaching these Japanese businessmen a little of the local dialect would be a far better way of making them feel welcome. You only need to see the success in selling dish towels with, for instance, well-known Yorkshire sayings printed on them!

Activity 1.4

On page 2, I quoted Argyle's definition of a skill as 'an organized, co-ordinated activity in relation to an object or situation, which involves a whole chain of sensory, central and control mechanisms'. I then translated that into a process of social interaction within the hospitality industry, which I hope helped you understand what Argyle was getting at. If you did have problems with the idea of a 'chain of sensory, central and control mechanisms', then think of that rather abstract language saying that skills involve using relationships between what we see, hear, etc. (our senses), how we interpret these messages, and how we then use our thought processes and resultant activities in a purposeful manner.

To use the car analogy again, when we are driving, we are aware of symbols which warn us, say, of an obstacle or problem ahead. These symbols are not necessarily in words, but coded diagrammatically and often very stylistically, in a very simplified manner, so we need to have had experience of them to decode them (the sign for a slippy road, or men at work).

Once we have decoded them, we consciously think of slowing down, applying the brakes, looking more carefully to see how to negotiate the problem. And unconsciously, we co-ordinate our right foot on the brake with our left foot on the clutch. The action of slowing down has become so 'second nature' that the driver does not need to think about it. But the learner had to – those of you who are drivers will no doubt remember as I do just how often one stalls the engine while learning.

That's the way it is with social skills. Behaviours practised become organized, co-ordinated, to achieve the effect one wants in the communications process almost effortlessly, as 'second nature'. But that does not mean that they do not need to be thought about very carefully in the first place. Now construct an example from the hospitality industry of Argyle's definition in action, this time perhaps a manager–staff situation or relationship.

Thoughts on Activity 1.4

I have come up with two examples of Argyle's definition in action. One is a situation which you might be involved in as a human resources manager, the other as the domestic bursar for a student hall of residence which is hosting Americans at a summer school on the campus.

1.   Working towards trying to establish through appropriate questioning and listening skills (**organized**, **co-ordinated activity**) whether a member of staff is having an alcohol problem, something you suspect because of subtle cues from his verbal and non-verbal behaviour (**sensory mechanisms**). Choosing one's words and tone of voice so that youdo not sound threatening or judgemental (**central and control mechanisms**), and interpreting through his verbal and non-verbal behaviour during the interview whether your suspicions were correct, or whether his occasional inability to fulfil his role as head waiter is due to the physical effects of alcohol, or due to some psychological, social or motivational problem (**sensory mechanisms**).

   This is a delicate situation because alcohol-dependency can be a 'sackable' issue, and self-esteem and status come into the equation because the individual concerned may perceive as a disciplinary session what is intended to be a counselling session. The **chain of mechanisms** must come together for you to achieve your objective. That is, identification of the problem, and solution of the problem with a mutually beneficial outcome.

2.   Working towards giving American tourists their best possible experience of British hospitality and customs (**organized**, **co-ordinated activity**), while recognizing that their expectations of accommodation may be more up-market than a hall of residence normally offers, that the 'traditional' food they are expecting is not so traditional (Scots do not eat venison and salmon all the time) and that the 'traditional' food that they do get (haggis) is generally only eaten by the Scots on one night a year and requires to be served with a certain amount of social skill because the content of a haggis can be somewhat off-putting if one knows of it (**central mechanism – knowledge and understanding of another culture**). Then assessing from the feedback whether your guests are quite happy with the limited accommodation and the odd food habits (**sensory mechanism**).

   Have you managed to convince them through your communication skills that they are privileged to have such an opportunity – or should you forget about marketing to the Americans altogether? Have they really enjoyed the experience – or are they just being polite? Your skills in using the **chain** will tell you that.

   The **organization and co-ordination** of your activities and your reading of the situation through your **sensory, central and control mechanisms** in the second situation depends on your understanding of how the social and cultural context affects the outcome of the communications process. That situation is worth reflecting upon for another reason. The skill of handling complaints! The situations in which one would 'be polite' are themselves socially conditioned. The British as a group are less likely to complain when they are unhappy. They just won't come back. The continental European and American will complain, but having done so, can be soothed!

So you as a hospitality manager should practise the skills of identifying and dealing with complaints in a way which maintains the communications process. Mars and Nicod in their book *The World of Waiters* (1984) record some lovely examples of how waiters develop sophisticated strategies for defusing complaints. No lack of social skills there, customer satisfaction being the name of the game! But what do you do about the guest who does not return? That is a form of feedback – but how can you decode it? A complaint can be very constructive – and at least you are still communicating!

Activity 1.5

Have another, closer look at the diagram in the keynotes on page 10, which gives us another definition of skills, which encourages us to think further about the process. 'Skills are dimensions of ability to behave effectively in situations of action.' Now think about the following 'situations of action' and work out what communications and interpersonal skills you would require to behave 'effectively'.

1. A counselling session with a member of staff whom you suspect has a financial problem.
2. A talk to a group of foreign hoteliers on the British tourist industry.
3. A meeting with suppliers to negotiate a bulk order for furnishing fabric.

Identify the key dimensions of ability and what you would consider to be the effective behaviour in each case.

Thoughts on Activity 1.5

As always, there are no definite and correct answers to these questions. There are an infinite number of ways in which one might construct a perfect meal, but we use the basic, tried and tested theories of cooking, of meal presentation to offer us ground rules as to what is likely to be successful. So your answer in all the activities starts from what are most likely to be the appropriate communications skills in terms of objectives or desired responses, but then depends upon your perception of the situation, your judgement as to what you see to be the key factors to be taken into consideration, and your evaluation of your personal abilities and strengths in a range of communication skills and techniques. A weakness in one ability can be compensated for by a strength in another.

1. **The counselling session**   Dimensions of ability could include the use of language appropriate to the delicacy of the situation and the one-to-one informality of the discussion, language which does not imply any judgemental stance at this initial stage, language which suggests the listener can empathize with the speaker, imagine what it feels like to be in such a situation, even if you are not.
2. **The talk to foreign hoteliers**   Dimensions of ability could include avoiding language which was colloquial English and therefore likely not to be fully understood; the knowledge to be able to make comparisons with their own hospitality and tourism industries which would aid understanding; and the ability to show an appreciation of cultural differences in attitudes towards the requirements of tourists.
3. **The meeting with suppliers**   Dimensions of ability could include the skill of not revealing the strength – or weakness – of your hand too soon, to prevent non-verbal leakage which suggests that you might feel you are going to get the worst of the deal, and the capacity publicly to keep one's 'cool', despite privately being full of tension and uncertainty.

Now what about the 'behaviours'? In other words, those social skills you need to employ in order to achieve your objectives?

1. THE COUNSELLING SESSION

How easily can you construct and control a dialogue which shows you are sympathetic to the problem, have no personal moral view on it, and which keeps the atmosphere as that of friend to friend rather than employer and employee? What sorts of words and phrases do you think you could use? What body language?

Now assess yourself: 0 ————————————————— **5**

2. THE TALK TO FOREIGN HOTELIERS

Can you encourage understanding through your command of formal English? Will they go away with a reasonable amount of knowledge which you have worked out is useful and interesting to that specific audience? Have you left them with an appreciation of your ability to understand their culture?

Now assess yourself: 0 ————————————————— **5**

3. THE MEETING WITH SUPPLIERS

Can you, through your eloquence and bargaining tactics, achieve the best possible value for yourself in this deal? Can you manage to do that in a manner which strengthens the other side's respect in your negotiating skills?

Now assess yourself: 0 ───────────────────────── **5**

By analysing communications situations in this way, we can identify fairly accurately those interpersonal skills which each requires. Not only does this help us assess our own weaknesses and strengths as communicators, but it also allows us to identify skills within others, and thus ensure that the skills, or dimensions of ability, are available for each situation. If not all there in one individual, then they may be distributed among the team.

──────────────────── *Activity 1.6* ────────────────────

We have looked in the text at the idea of communication being a **transactional process**. Or to give it its rather less academic label, **person-building**. Just as a good lecture should make you feel more knowledgeable, more interested, so should a successful piece of social interaction make you feel a happier person, a more involved or sociable person. So communication is not just about merely transmitting information or passively receiving it. The notion of its being a **process** implies a series of actions which produce a change or development.

All successful social interactions should result in both parties getting something of positive value out of the process. So your social skills should be geared towards keeping the communications process going in a manner which leads to satisfaction or person-building for both parties. Now think about this idea in the context of a pub or a restaurant which you frequent, either for business or pleasure, and consider your answer to the following questions. The first question relates to a factor we have only briefly touched upon but will develop further in Chapter 4.

1. What sort of impact does the physical or spatial setting have on this communication process, one we might call a 'host-guest transaction'? For instance, the seating arrangements, the lighting, the number and appearance of the staff? Do these factors encourage a positive outcome for the process?
2. Part of the person-building process comes from a shared **meaning** between you and others in this communications. That meaning depends upon your having within your own mind some idea as to what to expect from the social context and the communications process. In this context we are talking about those who are communicating with you as a customer, offering you hospitality. What does that mean to you, what are your expectations of the process?
3. Finally, the management and staff's expectations, interest, in the outcome of the communications transaction. What sort of feedback do they want? Is it purely economic? Or may there be for them other 'valuable' consequences of the transaction?

Thoughts on Activity 1.6

You may have recognized that the answer to **question 1** is to do with that notion of 'atmosphere'. How often have you heard the phrase 'it's got a great atmosphere' about a particular bar, or perhaps a disco? And if we unpack that notion, then we are thinking about the way seating is arranged to encourage communication, the image suggested by the decor, the impression given by staff through their appearance and body language – all of these are forms of non-verbal communication. There are 'exciting' colour schemes and 'restful' colour schemes; staff uniforms which suggest a formal approach or an informal approach to the service. There are 'theme' restaurants or pubs, which suggest the age group which would be the most comfortable or most welcome there. The 'mood' of the communications process is encouraged from the outset.

Question 2 suggests that you think about what the experience means for you and to you. Firstly, in the sense of what you think it **ought** to mean, how you **expect** to be treated. You would find it a very strange process of transaction if you went to a very up-market restaurant and the staff responded to you in the same manner as they would in the High Street Burger Bar! You would be very uneasy, because the social rules and norms would be being challenged, the meaning of the experience was obviously not shared, with the likely prospect that the outcome of the negotiation would be unsuccessful – a somewhat dissatisfied guest.

Remember Ross, the Restaurant Manager, in our opening snapshot? His 'superior' manner could easily result in a guest's not coming back because that guest expected to be treated with a certain deference in such a situation.

When a customer turns up in what is considered to be inappropriate dress for a smart restaurant – no tie, or no jacket – the customer and the establishment apparently do not share the same understanding of what that particular atmosphere, food and service are supposed to engender.

There has been a breakdown in the negotiation of meaning of the customer's dress, dress being a form of non-verbal communication. Angry scenes may follow – not much chance of person-building coming about here! What social skills would you employ to achieve a mutually successful outcome here? Mars and Nicod's, *The World of Waiters* (1984), has a particularly interesting description of how restaurant managers deal with customers who are considered to be inappropriately dressed!

Finally, **question 3**. If you were a member of staff in this establishment, then you would also have expectations as to how you should be treated, communicated with. The person-building for you is that you are likely to be far happier and more motivated in your work if you feel that you and the customers have a shared understanding of your role and theirs, the social rules and norms that govern your interaction, and that both parties appreciate the negotiation and transaction of service is a two-way process, in which each gets added value beyond that of the formal and technical proficiency resulting in a better tip.

It is said that one of the problems of the UK hospitality industry arises from the concept of 'service' being equated with being 'servile' – which is not a very person-building concept! As a consequence, unlike our North American and mainland European competitors, insufficient pride is taken in good service. Therefore the successful transaction in the process of communication between restaurant staff and customers necessitates that both parties show appreciation of the other's value.

The final test of the effectiveness of this transactional process, this person-building, is that you would go back to that restaurant or pub and recommend it to friends. Why? You came away from it feeling good and well looked after. The atmosphere was friendly. The staff seemed to enjoy their work. And they have gained by getting your repeat custom. But perhaps the transaction failed. Was it an 'uncomfortable' experience?

Andrew and Kate think a visit to their restaurant might be if Ross seems 'threatening', that he might make a guest feel an idiot if she does not know what are the appropriate wines to have with her meal. Ross might feel good because he is showing off his knowledge. But the customer does not want to leave feeling inferior. Thinking of the communications process as a transaction, a negotiation, with each party wanting to get something of value out of it, is a very good first step towards being better at it.

FURTHER READING

Argyle, M. (ed.) (1981) *Social Skills and Work*, Methuen: a very good set of articles on different aspects of social skills, if somewhat 'academic', with more of an emphasis on the theoretical studies which underpin the practical applications. However, it does reinforce the fact that social skills are rather more than just 'common sense'.

Guirdham, M. (1990) *Interpersonal Skills at Work*, Prentice-Hall International: a constructive, down-to-earth approach, in an easy-to-use format. Lots of practical examples for discussion, and fairly general in its coverage. An undemanding book for initial reading.

Stewart, J. and D'Angel, G. (1988) *Together: Communicating Interpersonally*: an extremely 'user-friendly' book, very easy to read, with lots of interesting ideas and tests for the reader. As the title suggests, the concentration is more on the personal than the work situation, but a stimulating and engrossing book for those new to the subject.

The components of interpersonal skills: the context and the content

2

The art of conversation is the art of hearing as well as the art of being heard. (William Hazlitt)

Question 2: What do we find when we unpack the components of interpersonal skills, analyse the behaviour, investigate the content and its relationship with the contexts?

Snapshot

Michael, the General Manager, Moira the Personnel Manager, and Andrew, the Banqueting Manager, are having a quick word about the very busy afternoon ahead of them.

Moira: 'Pity these interviews for Joanna's replacement are taking place today. I've got a session trying to deal with Jenny's health problem, and then another looking at that issue of sexual harassment in the kitchen. I'm not going to be in the best mood for sussing out which of the candidates is the one we want.'

Michael: 'Yes. The trouble is that they're all very good on paper, so it looks like we shall be depending upon their performance in front of us. Although I hate having to assess someone purely on their 'gift of the gab', or their 'power-dressing'.

Andrew: 'Well, I'm sorry I'm not going to be there, given that they do seem to be a good final selection of interviewees. I'm meeting with the executive committee of the local Rotary Club to try and charm them into making more use of our new conference facilities. Then I need to be back to give our American guests an appropriate welcome to British hospitality.'

Just a day in the life of . . . ? No wonder it has been said that the best training for a hotel manager is a course at a drama school. Can there be any other occupation which demands that you have to be capable of communicating and interacting at so many levels and in so many roles and contexts? Colleagues, subordinates, superiors, guests from a diversity of social backgrounds and cultures, other professionals, to name but a few.

There is no difficulty whatsoever in constructing scenarios which reflect your having to slot into every one of these communications contexts in one day. So let's get down to brass tacks. Given the number and variety of contexts, what are the implications of this for the communications process? Indeed, what exactly are we doing when we are 'communicating'? **We are selecting and transmitting symbols between people with the purpose of achieving desired responses.**

What was that about 'brass tacks'? That phrase in itself is 'symbolic'. We don't actually mean what we say when we use it. We're not in reality going to kneel down and hammer in some brass tacks together. The phrase was first used in an article in the *New York Sun* in 1926, as a symbolic way of communicating: 'now we must try and identify exactly, at the simplest possible level, what it is we are talking about'.

But my using the phrase also says something else, is symbolic in another way. It is supposed to communicate something about the relationship between you and me, one I intend to be a friendly, rather than formal academic relationship, in which I am not going to inflict too much of my professional jargon on you in case you do not get the message I am transmitting. So the phrase has a particular **style** and **tone**, which together comprise its **register**.

The **register** of a communication describes the overall impact of the language used, and in good communications should be appropriate to the situation and context, and should recognize the linguistic constraints which apply to that situation and context. An example of a linguistic constraint is that one would be unlikely to respond to a letter from a guest complaining about the cost of a bottle of Château Margaux 1975 being £85 by calling him a 'daft bampot' because he should have known that a wine of that type and vintage would cost that much. You might want to take some time to find words which meant exactly that – but did not put him off returning to your restaurant and buying another bottle!

'Getting down to brass tacks' is a symbolic communication in another way, as it's a phrase used in our society which reflects our history, culture and particular figurative use of language. Each society and culture has its own share of 'sayings' which are not necessarily understandable by those outside the culture, and indeed if used in the wrong context can lead to very dramatic breakdowns in communications!

So if I am encoding a message for you, I have to know that you can decode it, that you have an understanding of my society – or I of yours – because the meaning of words can go far beyond that of the formal knowledge of the English language, or in this case the dictionary definition of 'brass' and a 'tack'. Otherwise, I will not be communicating with you, although you will be hearing what I say. In that case all I might get in return would be a blank look, instead of the desired response – an agreement that we should get more speedily to the objective of the discussion.

But communicating is not just about words – written or spoken (which we will be looking at in more depth in Chapter 3). It's also about the register for other forms of communication, the symbols employed there. It's about the tone of voice. Will Michael be decoding confidence, enthusiasm, drive, as he listens to the candidates for Joanna's job? And it's also about **body language**. Might Moira's attempts to sift out the poor candidates include her judging that someone is 'too laid back', not taking the exercise seriously enough? Being perceived as 'laid back' is more than just the words and phrases one uses. It is also about behaviour, about what we see. The way one might sit in a chair (as if watching the telly after a relaxing pint?) or the way one might dress for the occasion (in Levis and Doc Martins for an interview for the hospitality industry?)

So the socially skilled person is adept at recognizing the appropriate register for different occasions, purposes, audiences, subject matter, and adept at slipping easily from one register to another. In our snapshot, Moira is going to be discussing sexual harassment with two of the kitchen staff at one stage of her day, then revising her register to counsel one of the receptionists, and further revising it to put the appropriate questions to prospective candidates for a high-powered position within the company.

There is quite a different style and tone for each of these examples of the communications process, switching from the questioning to the sympathetic to the authoritative to the challenging. And Andrew will certainly not go to meet the executive of the Rotary Club in his pinstripe trousers and black jacket. This may signify his important position and particular expertise in the Banqueting Room, but these same qualities and abilities are signified by a rather different outfit at a meeting of businessmen in another setting. And he will certainly switch his 'act' from being the hard-headed, financially aware businessman with the Rotary Club to performing the much more informal, yet just as carefully constructed, role of genial 'mine host' for the American tourists.

Keynotes
1. 'Communicating' is the selection and transmission of symbols between people with the purpose of achieving desired responses.
2. It requires these symbols to be encoded and transmitted in the appropriate style, tone and register.
3. It requires a shared understanding between the people concerned of what these symbols mean, otherwise the receiver of the transmission cannot decode it.

Perhaps it would be helpful to illustrate these ideas further if they were to apply to an hotel in which you were involved with the architect at the first stages of planning. Let's say a four-star hotel in the centre of a city with a historic past, somewhere in the north of England, perhaps Yorkshire. You are very clear here about the appropriate style or styles you want the architect to consider in the design.

The context and purpose of the building would be all-important. An historic town, with buildings still standing from the great Victorian heyday of magnificent public edifices, leafy squares and terraces built in the eighteenth-century Georgian style, and even a few Elizabethan timbered houses from the sixteenth century. Plus, of course, some Roman city wall left! So you would be consulting with your architect as to the style which would fit in best with that heritage, which is what will be attracting your guests.

You will also want to think about what is the house style of your company, one which is part of its corporate image, or personality. Can it be reconciled with this context? Then you would be thinking about the tone, the emotion or feeling you would like the building to foster in your guests. Does it convey luxury? Does it convey a professional approach to customer care – the sort of customers, or market segment, you wish to attract? Does it also convey a sense of the past, the traditions in the city, if that is mainly why people come to it?

Just as you and the architect have to think about the tone of your new hotel, so you have to consider the vocabulary and code appropriate to the context. The vocabulary of your building can be interpreted as the materials you use. Outside, local York stone, inside velvet, brocade, real linen tablecloths, porcelain and crystal tableware. The code, Georgian silver cutlery instead of chopsticks! Just as in the main we use the code of the English language with our guests rather than Chinese.

We all recognize the importance of the tone in what we say, both as interpreted through the words used and the sound of the voice; the tone, or message, your appearance conveys to your guests. We know what is meant when someone says, 'I don't like the tone of his voice.' Or 'The waiting staff's uniform doesn't convey the expensive image the company would presumably like it to.' And what about 'register'?

Well, the vocabulary you would use with the high-powered design team with regard to the proposed new menus, place mats, information sheets, brochures, etc. for the company employs quite a different range to that you might use to train the new young waitress, or make the slightly insecure guest feel at home in your palatial dining room. The encoding and decoding process with the designers is the English language, but the vocabulary could be so specialist, no one other than the specialists can communicate in it.

How many among your relatives or friends could decode 'mise en place', even if they could speak French? Or would we talk about the number of 'covers' if we were working how many guests to have for a meal one evening? Or take the code of 'the business suit', the medium whereby we communicate efficiency, formality, the social role we are playing. The British view of what constitutes a 'business' suit can be quite different from that of the Italian or the American. What about the feminine version of the business suit? We've all heard of the concept of 'power dressing' in women.

Consider the process of thought of the female executive deciding what to wear for a high-powered presentation she has to give. She muses: 'In our society, status and authority are often seen to be reflected in a certain way in dress. I will therefore wear my black pin-striped suit – I am transmitting that I want to be seen as having status and authority. However the suit will comprise a skirt and jacket. As far as I am concerned, trousers are not appropriate for the business-woman in this company. And I'm not very happy about wearing a tie, but I am quite prepared to wear a feminine version of the crisp white shirt!'

In the previous paragraph we referred to a 'social role'. Let's consider again the view which suggests that the effective hospitality manager has to be, among other things, a very good actor. This is because your daily relationships demand that you have to be able to play a number of 'social roles'. The role of leader, trainer, counsellor, mediator, team-worker, group manager, host/ess, businessperson, the 'marketer' of the image of the organization to various individuals and groups outside it, etc., with all the myriad of communications and social skills that implies.

Just as playwrights construct the appropriate language for the context of their idea, and the actors then communicate that idea as they interpret it, so you have to play out your social roles. For instance, it is very likely to include being able to control the communications process to pretend emotions you do not feel, something which we can let slip with our friends and family, but which could have crucial consequences for our professional role.

'Good morning, Mr Brown. I'm so pleased to see you still consider we offer the best facilities in town for working lunches.' ('Unpleasant little man – no wonder the staff hate waiting on him')

Or contain emotions you do feel: ('Unpleasant little man – I can hardly bring myself to be polite to him – even if he is a local dignitary and an office-bearer in the Rotary Club.')

If only it were as simple as that! We also have to be able to decode the response, or feedback we get. An expression on the face, a tone of voice, a shrug of the shoulder. No wonder Michael was slightly worried about selecting a new member of staff on the basis of his or her oral and visual presentation. People put on an 'act' for an interview. They know that they are being judged, among other things, on how they might act out the role the position demands. So we have to train ourselves to be as perceptive as we can when we decode messages. If we are interviewing for prospective staff, we have not necessarily to take people at 'face value', a significant phrase indeed in this context!

Recent research at Surrey University showed that the credibility of witness statements in court depended more on the witness's looks and how confidently he or she spoke than on the content of the evidence. Just as the wine waiter should cultivate his/her sense of taste, his perception of the subtleties of the Chardonnay compared with the Semillon grape, the distinction between a good and bad claret, or an Australian claret and a French claret, so the senses we employ most if we are socially skilled should be trained. That is, what our eyes and ears tell us. 'Why am I sure that chambermaid is not listening to what I say?' 'What makes me think that Andrew should be dressed slightly differently if he's meeting Rotary today? In what way do I think he should look different?'

We are now back to looking for these behaviours, or cues, which give away feelings and reveal the social constraints we see a communications situation presenting us with, and how quickly we can decode the behaviour or cues sent by others which either enhance the communications process or cause it to break down. Research has shown that those people who are most popular, or most influential, have very highly developed perceptual sensitivity, are very good at identifying those subtle shifts of tone in a voice, the range of expressions on a face or movement of the body, which can reveal, often without the individual concerned being aware of it, a mood, or a change of mood, a requirement for a particular response from the other engaged in the social interaction.

Goffman, the academic who has probably been the most influential in the study of social roles, described how we 'give' information about our feelings consciously, but may also **give off** information quite unconsciously. He talked about 'giving off' as **leakage**, a nice metaphor – profits are 'leaked away' from a bar – and it's nothing to do with a bottle not being sufficiently tightly corked!

Keynotes

1. The communications process involves a transmitter, a receiver, an encoding and a decoding of a message.
2. To achieve the desired response, the transmitter must ensure that the transmission takes into account the social role(s) considered to be appropriate to the context.
3. 'Perception' is the mental process whereby we decode the messages we receive through our senses about the outside world. The socially skilled person decodes interpersonal communications more speedily and more accurately than most, and is aware of the importance of perceiving subconscious as well as conscious cues.

Earlier, I referred to someone appearing not to be 'listening'. You will remember the distinction between 'listening' and 'hearing'. It may seem strange to talk of 'listening' as being a skill, an ability acquired by training. But you soon try to learn it when you are required as a student to take notes in a lecture if you want to do well – although some of us may never really acquire it in that context! On average, during a communications process, we spend as much as 45% of our time listening. That is, combining hearing what person says – the sound waves coming to us – with involvement with that person talking – the manner in which we decode what we are hearing and then give feedback to the person with whom we are communicating.

The 'listening' required in a lecture is what we call **deliberative**. Its purpose is narrow, specific and does not necessarily require interpersonal skills, or any recognition at all of the 'human' element in the process. Unless, of course, you wished to enhance the lecturer's perception of you as a student who is highly appreciative of his or her sense of humour, so you smile and laugh at appropriate moments in the lecture. (Yes, it has been said that good interpersonal skills are about manipulating people!)

The listening skills we are interested in for the purpose of improving interpersonal relationships, however, are those which are labelled as **dialogic**, those we employ when we talk to friends or at work in a context where we must not only get the 'facts' right, but also have to decode the emotional content of a message. In other words, the 'poor listener' may get the facts right, but fails to recognize the feelings involved, which may even contradict the facts, and may be more important than what are said to be the facts.

If Moira is a 'good listener' she will soon realize that Jenny is in fact stressed over a problem with a personal relationship, not a health problem as she first claims. Andrew has to assess the truth of the negative response of the Rotary Club treasurer to his proposed charges for the new conference facilities. Does the treasurer really mean the club cannot afford them, or is he playing a negotiating game?

So what is the good listener doing that makes the difference? What behaviour are you indulging in? The skills involved are grouped in **clusters**, covering those which show you wish to keep the communications process going, such as **attention** and **following** skills, and those **reflective** skills, which show you are empathizing and understanding the feelings of the speaker.

For example, you are showing you are attending to what is being said by looking at the person who is speaking, by leaning forward, by purposefully ensuring the environment is not distracting. You are prompting for useful responses by asking encouraging, although not frequent, open-ended questions – good listening is not just about hearing! Moira listens to Jenny's personal problems in attentive silence; Jenny decodes Moira's behaviour – her body language – a gentle pat on the shoulder – as offering sympathy and feels therefore she can unburden herself further.

The good listener shows she can understand the feelings and emotions. Moira's hand is saying, 'I sympathize.' Her words reflect Jenny's feelings 'I appreciate it must be difficult just now to devote yourself 100% to your job. Can we do something about it from our end?' Moira is linking up the content of the communication from Jenny with the feelings, the insecurity behind it, the real reason for Jenny being there – after all, Moira is not her doctor. And in Andrew's case, he needs to be able to use exactly the same skills in order to put the Rotary Club treasurer 'off his guard', at ease, for much the same reasons – to get to the truth of the reaction, to assess where and when the treasurer might weaken in his resolve to beat down the cost to the club to its minimum, to assess where compromise might be possible.

In 'listening', silence, at the appropriate time in the communications process, can be surprisingly effective, even when you feel you should be talking! As Bing Crosby, the great crooner, said, 'Listen a lot and talk less – you can't learn anything when you are talking.' Just as learning from a lecture comes more easily if you are a good deliberative listener, so does learning about people and good human relationships come from being a good dialogic listener. And it's a skill which can be acquired and practised just as one can practise taking notes when someone is talking at the rate of 500 words a minute and you can only write at the rate of 60 words a minute!

What was that about good communications having to be encoded in symbols to which the receiver relates? 'Bing Crosby' and 'crooner' are symbols you may not recognize. Pity I couldn't have quoted instead something said by Michael Jackson or Madonna. But no doubt by the time you read this, there will be new symbols of popular music . . .

Keynotes
1. 'Listening' is an active, not a passive, exercise.
2. Listening skills can be said to be grouped in clusters.
3. These clusters are about attending skills (e.g. eye contact) following skills (e.g. occasional open-ended questions) and reflective skills (e.g. identifying feelings and meanings)
4. Listening can often communicate more to us about another person's views and feelings than can talking.

Activity 2.1

We have tried to identify the 'yardsticks' whereby we judge communications and social skills in others. Can we do the same for ourselves? Just how clearly do we recognize what we are good at – and what we would like to be better at? It's not very easy to 'see yourself as others see you'. People tend to view themselves in a positive light – it's necessary to do so for our self-esteem. Indeed, that understanding should make us more aware of the expectations others have of the way they should be treated.

But it does help if we can 'stand back' from ourselves, and try to assess just how socially skilled we are, and where we think we might improve our ability to handle human relationships. So how would you answer the following questions? They further unpack these 'dimensions of ability' we looked at in Activity 1.5, and all relate to those social skills we shall be analysing throughout the text.

1. Do you think you are a 'good listener'? Why? Can you think of a situation in which you know you were a 'bad listener'? Why? What stopped you 'listening'?
2. How would you feel if you were asked to put out a short talk on local radio about the tourist attractions in your area? What factors would determine these feelings?
3. Can you identify those cues which would tell you that a colleague was very unhappy about something, but appeared not to want to talk about it?
4. If you had to step into the Banqueting Manager's shoes at the last minute and construct and lead a team to deliver a very special function, do you think you have the necessary social skills?

Thoughts on Activity 2.1

1.   If you think you are a 'good listener' it's very likely that you are thinking about two very obvious skills or behaviours. Firstly, good listening is usually characterized by not interrupting, and secondly, by **looking** as if you are interested, using the appropriate amount of eye contact. It also involves more sophisticated behaviour – for example, the effective use of other types of non-verbal communication, in the form of body language, perhaps. But good listening can also depend upon your actually **speaking**, but at an appropriate time and in an appropriate manner, or **register**, and your ability to do that brings in your ability to read the **cues** given off by the person to whom you are listening. We will look at an example of this later. So any one of these factors being ignored could have caused you to be a **bad** listener – plus others to do with the spoken word. Switching off can be brought about because certain words or phrases become a barrier to communication, and we will also be looking at that further on, in Chapter 3.

2.   You may feel very happy about such an exercise. But it is more likely that it will terrify you – at least the first time! And again it's about self-esteem. Some people worry about what they sound like, about talking to a microphone as opposed to a human being. Or they worry about the messages they give off through their accent (perhaps a regional or class-based accent) and pitch and tone of voice (high-pitched through nervousness). Some worry about the lack of feedback from the audience – because they cannot see or hear them, we cannot judge whether what we

are saying is going down well. These factors reflect the human element in the communications process. We trust the technology, we have the facts in front of us – but the 'human' factors are interfering in the formal communications process through the airwaves.

3.   Initially, you probably would be saying that you had perceived she was not behaving 'normally'. There had been cues from her tone of voice, the expression on her face, the tilt of a shoulder, which suggested unease of some sort. But the real skill here is the skill of **questioning**, not in the 'hit or miss' manner of everyday conversation, but in a manner which allows the other person to see that answering your questions is a way for you to help her.

Can you do it in a manner which allows the other person to respond in the manner she wants to, but also gives you the information you require? If you don't get the answer you want, then perhaps you have asked the wrong question, or the question in the wrong way. Questioning is a sophisticated social skill in itself; one that you will want to develop to a high level when you are interviewing. Again we shall be looking at that skill in a bit more detail later on.

4.   Now we are talking about a **cluster** of social skills. You know what is to be done, the goal to be achieved. You know, in practical and operational terms, how it should be done. But how strong are you on the techniques which get this team to work for you? What is involved in leading and motivating people, in maintaining group cohesion? Are you sufficiently articulate to spell out your plan? Can you speak confidently to the team? Does your body language give off an air of authority? Do you think you have leadership qualities? Or do you believe that you can do what leaders do, whatever your personal qualities?

The above are only a few examples which reflect the skills we will be discussing. Perhaps you felt quite confident of your talents in the above areas, perhaps quite diffident. Whatever your position, such assessments identify for us our range of capabilities and how we might extend it.

——————————————— *Activity 2.2* ———————————————

Opposite is a diagram which suggests there are a number of groups or individuals with whom you, as a hospitality manager, could be communicating in any one day. The diagram represents your **social environment**, meaning that however you might be connected to these groups geographically (in the next room, or an office down the road) or technologically (at the end of a phone or a fax machine) the communication must be undertaken in the context of the human relationships and motives involved in the process, and the human elements which have to be taken

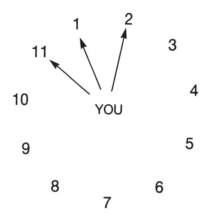

Figure 2.1

into account if the communications processes are to achieve their objectives.

See if you can identify those groups I am thinking about, and then, having done so, jot down one or two human elements which you would consider were important when you were encoding your communication to a particular group.

Of course, you may be able to think of other groups – if so, you get extra Brownie points!

Thoughts on Activity 2.2

The manner in which this diagram is presented perhaps suggests that you are likely to be communicating an equal amount, or on a regular basis, with all those groups. Obviously this may not be the case; of course you will be communicating with your colleagues rather more than you would be with a local councillor. So those communications and interpersonal skills which are required to lead people or work with them in groups, and to deal with customers or guests, will be of the most importance to you.

However, the supporting communications skills you need will reinforce the core skills, and as they both depend upon the same body of knowledge and understanding ('know your audience; know your objective') then it is not too difficult to transfer the thinking and the techniques. In many of the Activities, we will be looking at specific examples of this range of skills; this is just an initial 'signposting' of the complexity of the matter.

1. **Your colleagues – the management team** You share a 'language', your share a goal, you share a culture – hopefully.You want the communications skills to lead from the front – but in today's culture, it is better your are perceived to be leading from behind! Otherwise you could be seen as being autocratic, patronizing, dismissive of specialist knowledge and abilities. In fact this is an example of a situation where traditional leadership skills are no longer those which are required. We will look at this issue more fully in Chapter 6.

2. **Your staff – your subordinates**   To re-emphasize the point made in this chapter, the hospitality industry arguably has a more varied social mix within its workers than has any other major industry. The cultural, educational and socio-economic background of your employees could be such that your communications skills are stretched to the limit, each group or individual requiring a particular register and code. The new young commis chef from a minority ethnic group, and new to the UK, is quite a different 'receiver' from the female undergraduate on work experience with you, and the assistant manager who worked his way up through the industry and is much older than you.

3. **Your superiors – top management at head office**   Perhaps some geographical distance from you. You do not often meet them face to face, so most of your communication is by phone, letter or fax, a limitation which serves to intensify the demands on communications skills and techniques which can be used. Putting ideas, issues, problems on paper, means constraints which do not exist in regular informal day-to-day discussions. The written word means that language is likely to be more formal, the written word can be irretrievable, and the human relationships which build up through face-to-face contact are not there to manipulate.

4. **The professionals – the lawyer, the accountant, the architect**   Each with his or her own often inaccessible jargon, ready, understandably, to claim that 'they know best' – which is why you employ them. But you want to maintain your authority as client, so you perhaps do that through acquiring some of their jargon, so that you can communicate with them, and can keep control of the process. You learn to question, to challenge, to look for alternatives, which will not threaten their self-esteem, because at the end of the day there are areas in which your social skills are no use, and you need the professional, however arrogant s/he might be!

5. **The suppliers of goods and services**   Another 'language' to learn, and another interpersonal skill, that of negotiating. Negotiating prices, quality, delivery dates, completion dates. Sometimes from strength, sometimes from weakness. The language and techniques of the skilled negotiator are among the most difficult of interpersonal skills to acquire. The history of the world is full of disasters which have come about through negotiating failures.

6. **The trade unions**   Most likely if you are working in the public sector or in a large hotel company. Negotiations again, but more likely to be in a climate of distrust, or starting from such a base. 'Us and them' is generally the context of industrial relations, a factor which does not affect negotiations with the brewers supplying your real ale, or the textile company replacing your curtains. Building up trust is a interpersonal skill, involving a complex pattern of behaviour. Test that by thinking about someone you **don't** trust, whatever he or she says or does, and work out why!

7. **The governmental apparatus**   Local officials and central civil servants. To communicate with them, you need to have access to their

'official' language, often highly legalistic, and within the context of what is considered to be the public interest, the often slow processes of democracy, accountability, and myriads of petty regulations or restrictions. Just think of arguing your case in a planning appeal, or to a Licensing Board. To do so effectively, you have to understand the constraints within which they communicate – the law as they have to apply it, and breathing down their necks their political masters who made the law, and do not want it to be seen to be an ass!

8. **The political apparatus**   Your local councillors, your local MP, your MEP. The context here is that they will bring to the communications process factors like 'How will coming out in favour of this building proposal or tourist development affect my support in my constituency? When am I next up for election? What is the party line on this?' So you communicate with them in the light of the fact that they need to be persuaded that it is in their self-interest or their party's interest to respond to you. Thus you would frame a request to your local councillor for support which would take into account the philosophy of the particular political party to which s/he belonged.

9. **Pressure groups**   Conservation and environmental groups, animal rights, Real Ale campaigners, Action for Smoking and Health – all those organizations with their own special interest you might have to respond to in order to persuade them either not to attack you or to support you on a particular issue. You have to develop the communications skills to 'buy off' opposition, to argue your case against theirs if necessary, to be on top of facts and figures which might be thrown at you, and to debate at a fairly sophisticated level in the public arena, where emotions and values are often more important than facts.

10. **The mass media**   Coping with the inquisitive reporter looking for a story, or using the media to gain helpful publicity. The language of the press release, or the local radio or TV interview is quite different to that of the business letter or report. We shall be looking at what's sometimes called 'journalese' in Chapter 8. And by way of the media, the general public, who may write letters to the press or be involved in radio 'phone-ins'. You may not like what they say, but they may be prospective customers.

11. **Your guests and customers**   A select group, who present no problems when it comes to the communications process. Or is that always the case? Hotels which cater mainly for businessmen and women during the week may also cater for short break holiday-makers at the weekends, or for British tourists most of the time, but have a regular influx of foreign visitors. Different sub-cultures acquire different interpersonal skills. You could be involved in communicating with every one of these groups in one single day. This Activity was to test your thinking about the more far-ranging and generally more complex communications skills you need to develop if you are to be successful in the hospitality industry. Have you thought of further

groups you could add to this list? If so, what particular communications and interpersonal skills do they require?

Activity 2.3

The way we 'see' the world and the way we make 'sense' of it comes through the process of **perception**. Perception is the selection and interpretation of the information we get through our senses (sight, hearing, smelling, tasting and touching). They give us our **frame of reference**, which allows us to come to judgements about people, situations, actions, events, organizations, and therefore how to behave. The selection and interpretation relates both to the uniqueness and to the similarities of our experiences. It does not necessarily relate to an objective 'reality'.

A particular food commodity may be rejected by an individual or group for reasons which are nothing to do with its nutritional value or the quality of the cooking. Sheep's eyeballs, prepared by Anton Mossiman himself, would most certainly not be my choice for starters! But the culture which find these a great delicacy would almost certainly reject roast pork with crackling, which is one of my favourite foods, and a very good source of protein. Thus perception is a highly **selective** process.

If we apply this understanding of the social and cultural factors in the process of perception to its role in the communications process, then it helps us appreciate why, for instance, dressing up in a particular way for an interview is important. The interviewer selects visual information which suggests the interviewee fits in with the conventional (meaning social and cultural) perception of how a prospective hospitality manager should dress.

In terms of interpreting what we hear, a guest might perceive a waiter, or a manager might perceive an employee, as sounding insufficiently deferential. Because of our psychological need to see the world in a way which does not threaten our self-esteem, values and beliefs, we are inclined to ignore evidence that does threaten that need.

'He only sees what he wants to see' is in fact a very meaningful phrase – we are all subconsciously inclined towards seeing only what we want to see. (If a student of mine fails to understand what I am saying, then do I see it as my flawed teaching, or her lack of concentration?) We have to take that tendency into account when we are constructing a communication which challenges conventional ways of thinking or doing something.

A second important factor in terms of communicating is that this tendency towards selective perception often leads to **stereotyping**, another human tendency which can have adverse effects on the communications process. Stereotyping comes about when you have some general assumptions about, or expectations of, an individual or group, based on past knowledge or understanding, or on social and cultural expectations which in themselves may be invalid. 'Sexist' and 'ageist' behaviour is often about stereotyping.

In your human resource management studies, you will have read about MacGregor's Theory X relative to workers' motivation. If the employer perceives employees to be Theory X types, then the way s/he communicates, leads, them will be to some extent determined by that stereotype. So now let's test two aspects of these findings. Firstly, let's think about the labels we might attached to someone's behaviour, which reflect our judgement of that behaviour, and which come from our interpreting language, tone of voice, and general demeanour or body language.

Here's a list of adjectives, describing individuals as I perceive them. These adjectives all suggest negative qualities. But you see things differently. The very same behaviour **as observed** you have perceived as positive, because you start out from a different frame of reference. Like MacGregor's Theory Y managers, you give people the benefit of the doubt!

Frivolous .... you see as .... ?
Foolhardy .... you see as .... ?
Snobbish .... you see as .... ?
Authoritarian .... you see as .... ?
Fussy .... you see as .... ?
Arrogant .... you see as .... ?

Now let's think about the **stereotyping**. This might be interesting to do with two or three of your friends, although to test the validity of the concept, try to select them from roughly the same social and cultural background as yourself.

Fill in the blanks in the following sentences, as fast as possible – it's important that it is your immediate reaction which is recorded.

1. Italian men are ....
2. Rugby players are ....
3. People born to wealth are ....
4. Students are ....
5. Politicians are ....
6. Blondes are ....
7. Germans are ....
8. Chefs are ....

Thoughts on Activity 2.3

The first exercise on 'opposites' would be interesting to experiment with through discussing the actual behaviour which takes place when someone is classified as 'timid' – a negative label – and then just see how much – or how little – it varies from behaviour which could be classified as the opposite – as positive and commendable. What are the nuances, the cues, even the single cue, which determines the positive or negative perception?

So 'I see him as **timid**; you see him as **cautious**'; 'I see her as **frivolous**; you see her as **light-hearted**'; 'I see him as **foolhardy**; you see him as **brave**'; 'I see him as **snobbish**; you see him as **shy**'; 'I see her as **authoritarian**; you see her as **authoritative**'; 'I see him as **fussy**; you see him as **fastidious**'; 'I see him as **arrogant**; you see him as **confident**.'

And just to illustrate the wider social context which can condition such perceptions, think about the 'authoritarian–authoritative' spectrum. Lady Thatcher, when Prime Minister, was often attacked for being 'authoritarian'; occasionally these attacks were the consequence of a perception as to what was appropriate **female** behaviour, which she did not appear to subscribe to! The same behaviour in a man might well be classed as 'authoritative' – a very positive perception. Now what about the stereotypes?

1. Italian men are musical, excitable, romantic.
2. Rugby players are 'macho', beer-drinkers.
3. People born to wealth are privileged, don't know anything about the 'real world'.
4. Students are lazy, into drink and drugs, spongers.
5. Politicians are corrupt, power-mad.
6. Blondes are dumb, sexy, bimbos.
7. Germans are hard-working, highly organized, have no sense of humour.
8. Chefs are temperamental, volatile, autocratic.

Now I did not invent these stereotypes. The national ones came from research done some years ago; the others from my asking students what they thought were stereotypical images of groups. The interesting fact is the general consistency of the views, which shows that being part of a group or culture does to some extent condition our behaviour. But the lesson for the good communicator is that we must not start out by **assuming** that everyone in a group will exhibit similar attitudes and behaviour.

The communications process may soon break down if we let a stereotype dominate the way we frame the communication rather than continually evaluating the feedback. There is a lot of evidence which suggests that the main reason few women achieve top managerial status is to do with male attitudes, which result from what they think are stereotypical 'female' personalities and capabilities, and secondly, what they see to be stereotypical managerial skills, which are presumed to be lacking in women. The 'women don't make good bosses; they're too emotional' syndrome!' (And there's research which suggests that the hospitality industry is the worst culprit in this area!)

So how about assessing just how much **your** stereotypical views of certain groups might affect how you communicate with them. I suggested that the exercise on stereotyping should be carried out with fellow students or friends who are of the same social and cultural background as yourself, because stereotypes are passed on through our socialization process, and it is therefore far more likely that we share stereotypes if we share cultures.

And stereotypes can help us in that they give us somewhere to start from. But it can be a mind-broadening experience to ask others of a different culture or social background to yours to do this exercise, asking them to produce **their** stereotypical responses to hearing where you come from, what you are. For example, I am a Scot. What stereotypes does that conjure up? And how might these stereotypes condition how you expect me to behave, or how you perceive my behaviour?

Activity 2.4

In this chapter we discussed the importance of **shared symbols** in the communications process. Being socially skilled implies that, among other things, you are skilled at selecting the most appropriate and most effective symbols in order to transmit your message. Words are symbols, in that they transmit ideas, values, emotions, as well as literal facts. Figures are symbols, diagrams may be symbolic, three-dimensional models are symbols.

Body language is generally symbolic; think of the variety of ways in which we greet someone with our bodies, or insult them! If you are having a discussion with your accountant, or architect, you will not be able to communicate with one another unless you understand the significance of the figures as presented ($2 + 2 = 4$ does not always do so in these days of creative accounting!) or the significance of the two-dimensional plans and elevations for your three-dimensional building.

At the time of writing, there is some debate about the symbols used to classify hotels in the UK, because they are causing confusion for foreign visitors. Stars, crowns, roses – there is even a difference between Scottish and English classifications, and we are supposed to be one country! In fact the whole of the communications process, because of its dependence upon social and cultural contexts, is surrounded by symbolism, meaning something that represents or stand for something else, by convention or association. The barrier to communication, or the breakdown in communication comes about when that representation is not understood or is misunderstood.

We will keep coming back to this idea because it is so important, but just now have a shot at this example of symbolic communication. It is extremely basic and simple, but shows just how complex the issue can become. The 24th letter in our alphabet is the letter X. It represents a sound like ks or gs. How many other messages does the letter X communicate, or symbolize? And would they all be understood universally?

Thoughts on Activity 2.4

Well, how many different symbolic meanings of the letter X did you think of? Here's what I came up with – and I am not saying that these are all the meanings which exist. Indeed, individuals and groups often construct their own symbolic language which is shared only within the group, and which serves as a 'social cement', a means of group cohesion. This can be deliberately used to communicate that those who do not have access to the symbolism are excluded from the group. The Masonic handshake is an example of this; the 'in-joke', or the use of professional jargon, are other ways in which the same message is being communicated. So it would not be surprising if you came up with some less 'public' meanings for X.

X = the Roman notation for 10
X = the mark of an illiterate person
X = an unknown quantity
X = a gas, xenon
X = a ray, an X-ray
X = an abbreviation for 'Christ' in Xmas
X = a kiss
X = marks the spot
X = (used to) signify a film which must not be shown to anyone under 18 years old
X = a choice on a ballot paper

So without some understanding of the culture and the context, the particular meaning of the symbol would not be necessarily be obvious. How many of the above meanings do you think would be decoded in the same way outside our Western culture?

Activity 2.5

'What's in a name? That which we would call a rose by any other name would smell as sweet.' This time I think Shakespeare got it wrong. I am sure you are already very well aware of the importance which is attached both by ourselves and by others to our names, both first and surnames. We feel that names are a key part of our identity; they help define who we are and what we are.

To be on 'first-name' terms with someone, or to have to call someone 'Mr Bloggs' instead of 'Joe' implies particular relationships, and in certain social or work situations, woe betide us if we get it wrong. First names very often give us clues as to someone's age, class, religion, regional or ethnic background. We associate particular qualities with particular names, which can lead us into the trap of stereotyping.

If you receive a written request from someone for a room booking, and it is signed 'Sashti Ahmed', you will form some idea in your mind as to 'who' that person is, just as you would if you knew that the new baby next door was to be called 'Seonaid' instead of Janet, Seonaid being the Gaelic version of Janet. There is no logical reason why we cannot name a baby boy 'Anna' – and 'Shirley' and 'Marion' used to be male names – yet on being given no other information about a baby other than its name, we then respond to him/her in gender-specific ways. And forgetting some-one's name when he or she thinks you should have remembered it can be perceived as far more than just a social blunder; it is as if you have forgotten their existence.

Thus yet again a social skill comes into action – we consciously try to get names right, to remember names of important guests in order to show we appreciate their status, to learn the names of new members of staff as soon as possible in order to show that we appreciate them as having an identity as a human being as well as an identity as 'Jonathan', the new head porter. Many people have their own techniques for remembering names, for example, associating a particular fact about the person which rhymes with the name, or is an alliterative statement. For example, 'Postman Pat', or 'married Carrie'.

As this ability to learn and remember names fast is a basic social skill, I am going to suggest a way of speedily remembering the names of a group of people. And the form I am going to present it to you will endow you with another skill which might be legitimately also claimed to be a social skill – that of being able to impress with your knowledge. I wonder if you have that knowledge in the first place to undertake this exercise? How well have you studied the food and beverages input in your course? What are the names traditionally attached to the various sizes of champagne bottles, and more importantly, if a guest asked you to tell her the progression of sizes before she ordered, could you do it?

Thoughts on Activity 2.5

I don't need to tell you that having this information at your fingertips can in itself be seen as a social skill. It impresses upon others that you are on top of your job, which increases their respect for you – and your own self-esteem! And at a very practical level, memory techniques such as these can be very useful in training staff – or for rote-learning of the sort required in some of the more basic parts of your course! So the value of this exercise goes far beyond that of purely remembering someone's name, and I have suggested a couple of books on memory training in the book references. There is also an extremely useful book for extracting this sort of information called *Inquire Within: The Ultimate Problem-Solver*, by Moira Bremner.

What then are the names or labels for the champagne? After the most common size sold, the ordinary 75 cl bottle they go as follows: **magnum, double magnum, jeroboam, rehoboam, methuselah, salamanzar, balthasar and nebuchadnezzar**, each being equivalent of twice the size of the previous one.

Now these names are difficult enough in themselves, and I have no quick solution to that problem. So keeping the order right is an additional hurdle to get over. I chose the example of champagne bottle sizes because it was relevant to your profession, but the object of the exercise is actually directed towards remembering names, which are very unlikely to be quite as unusual as those above, given that 'magnum' is a Latin word (for big) and the others are ancient Judaic names from the Old Testament.

But even remembering initials can help prod your memory. So we have eight names, or words, to remember, **and** in order. Well, as there is no obvious 'sense' or reason for that order, one way to remember is to create an order to aid our memory. let's take the first letter of each. M, DM, J, R, M, S, B, and N.

The easiest way to make sense of these is to connect them to new words which **do** make sense. Here's my attempt. 'My Dear Mother Joined Many Social and Business Networks'. Or 'Many Delightful Meals Just Relish Munching Slowly, Beautifully and Nicely'. Perhaps not quite the sort of phraseology you would normally or easily use, but at least sensible enough for you to remember. You could have a competition among your fellow students to see who can come up with the wittiest or cleverest sentence. And the same technique could be used to remembering the ingredients of a recipe!

Now you should have no problem whatsoever with remembering not only individual names, but a whole group of new names of people, or objects, for that matter. Yet another technical skill which has a 'social' pay-off, and therefore can be labelled a social skill. Is this not an example of what we referred to as 'social stroking' in Chapter 1?

('How nice – he's remembered my name – I am obviously a very important/interesting/amusing person!')

Activity 2.6

In conjunction with good listening, questioning, or drawing out and handling the flow of information in more personal and less formal dyadic communications situations, for example, in appraisal, counselling or interviewing, often involves dealing with a considerable human element of unease – through fear, or suspicion or inability to communicate strong emotions. Your style, tone and register of communication for these purposes must elicit useful and essential answers, but it is often difficult to do so without appearing aggressive. There are several basic rules to follow here.

1. Make sure that you are aware of and can use the distinction between **closed** and **open** questions. A **closed** question invites a 'yes/no' answer; an **open** question encourages expansion, allows for feelings, attitudes, to be expressed. But don't let an open question expand into several questions pretending to be one. You will just confuse the receiver.
2. Pitch the question at the level the receiver can understand. Watch out for the jargon; the receiver may only pretend that s/he has understood the question rather than lose self-esteem by asking for meaning.
3. Rephrase questions which seem to have been misunderstood or not responded to in a useful manner.

4. Avoid leading questions which indicate your preferred answer ('I don't suppose you would ever do such a thing, would you?')
5. Aim for precision in your questions. Frame them to draw out exactly what you want to know, be it a clarification of facts ('Can you give me examples?') or of feelings ('In what way does working with Jenny depress you?')
6. Finally, create a mood within which the questioning process is not seen as an interrogation, but as a partnership in which it is in your mutual interest to talk about the issue or problem.

Below are a number of questions or statements of different formats and types, and a number of purposes for which these questions might be used. After thinking about the guidelines suggested above, can you link up each question with its appropriate purpose, and suggest the label you might attach to each type of question?

PURPOSES

1. You want to introduce a topic and encourage a fair amount of general discussion.
2. You want to open up discussion of someone's views or values.
3. You want to signal that you are interested in further information.
4. You want to draw out further information about a particular issue.
5. You want a smooth transition from one topic to another which you have chosen.
6. You want precise information.
7. You want to confirm or verify a point or an idea.
8. You want to move the other person on to thinking of a new area or idea.
9. You want to signal 'carry on speaking – I am listening'.
10. You want to draw together the key facts in a discussion, and encourage a pledge to action.

QUESTIONS

1. 'Just how long did it take you?'
2. 'How would you have tackled it if . . .?'
3. 'I think we've exhausted that point, so let's move on to. . .'
4. 'Ye-es, go on . . .?'
5. 'Would you try and describe for me . . .?'
6. 'Would you agree that what we have debated and settled so far is . . .?
7. 'Yes, but it seems to me . . .?'
8. 'Can you tell me a bit more about . . .?'
9. 'What do you see to be the relative worth of . . .?'
10. 'What I understand you to be saying is . . .?'

Thoughts on Activity 2.6

Here are the answers – the question which links with the purpose specified. In each case the question has been classified as one of a specific **type**. So do more than just tick off or think about the correct answers. Construct another question or phrase of that type which you could use in order to achieve each purpose. Test it out on a fellow student, or a friend, and see if you do achieve the intended purpose. Indeed, you might also like to experiment with using the wrong type of question, and seeing what happens!

Purpose 1: Example 5: an **open** question, used if you do not want simple 'yes' or 'no' answers

Purpose 2: Example 9: a **comparative** or **evaluative** question

Purpose 3: Example 7: an **inhibitive** or **restraining** statement

Purpose 4: Example 8: a **probing** or **investigative** question

Purpose 5: Example 3: a **linking** or **connecting** statement

Purpose 6: Example 1: a **closed** or **restricted** question

Purpose 7: Example 10: a **reiterative** statement

Purpose 8: Example 2: a **hypothetical** or **speculative** question

Purpose 9: Example 4: a **lubricating** or **encouraging** statement (although you might call this a 'noise', rather than a statement! Academics would call it a paralinguistic communication – a word, or words, that are in a sense meaningless)

Purpose 10: Example 6: a **summarizing** or **reviewing** statement

Questioning skills are of vital importance in forming opinions and judgements about the individuals with whom we interact. Drawing out information and managing its flow depends greatly upon the use of language which is designed to ensure that the person leading the conversation guides it along the desired lines while remaining neutral and uninvolved. The skill is to **prompt**, rather than to contribute.

FURTHER READING

Murdoch, A. and Scott, C. (1993) *Personal Effectiveness*, Institute of Management/Butterworth-Heinemann, Oxford: a good book for laying the 'ground rules' and range of objectives to be achieved, although not necessarily set within a management or vocational context. Explains well how interpersonal skills fit in to and are a part of a broader spectrum of personal transferable skills.

Rasberry, R. and Lemoine, L. (1986)*Effective Managerial Communication*, Kent Publishing, Boston: a good introduction to the subject matter. Emphasizes the practical, operational aspects, rather than the reflective or psychological, but is nonetheless effective. The American background gives added interest.

Wood, R. C. (1994) *Organisational Behaviour for Hospitality Managers*, Butterworth-Heinemann: this textbook is right up to date in terms of understanding and discussion on leadership, motivation, group dynamics and other aspects of organizational behaviour within the context of the hospitality industry. Although communications within organizations is only a small part of its content, the direct relevance of the issues and examples make this very useful supportive reading.

Words and their meanings – social and symbolic

3

First learn the meaning of what you say and then speak.
(Epictetus)

Question 3: Is having a good vocabulary anything other than an academic exercise? Why should we take such care over the language we use in social interactions?

Snapshot

Michael, the General Manager, and Moira, the Personnel Manager, are discussing an incident which took place in the staff restaurant.

Michael: 'I can't believe that Gerry could be so touchy as to object to being called "Paddy". It's almost like a term of affection when talking to an Irishman.'

Moira: 'Maybe, but in today's climate of "politically correct language", it could be considered as offensive as calling the new Head Office guy, Sanji, a "Paki". Anyway, it doesn't do any harm to remind the staff that they need to be that more careful about what could be interpreted as racist or sexist language, given the number of foreign guests we now have – and the number of women we employ.'

Michael: 'Well, I think it's all gone too far. What with "visually impaired" instead of shortsighted, and not being able to talk about a "manhole cover" any more, it's just laughable. What about the old saying, "Sticks and stones, will break your bones, but names will never harm you."'

Moira: 'I don't agree. If you call me a "bimbo", then the impression that gives to others of me could certainly harm me.'

'Stop sweet-talking me.' 'I don't like his bad-mouthing.' 'If you pay peanuts, you get monkeys.' Most, if not all, of you will know what these slang or idiomatic expressions mean. That is, if we belong to an English--

speaking Western culture. Their meaning is one that you might not get in a conventional dictionary. You might have to go instead to a reference book such as *Brewer's Dictionary of Phrase and Fable*. That's because words can mean much, much more than the dictionary tells us.

They often also have a **social context**, and thus in the communications process require to be 'translated' into or encoded within that social context in order that they can be then interpreted, or decoded, by the receiver. We have already referred to this social context in Chapter 2, when we discussed the meaning of **register** in communications. This is one reason why a foreign language can be difficult to learn, as the skill required is not merely that of being able to translate from one language to another in the linguistic or literary sense.

I wonder if you are familiar with the word 'hen' which is used as a term of endearment in the west of Scotland. The literal translation of that into French is '*une poule*' – which also happens to be a colloquial French word for a prostitute. Lots of possibilities for misunderstanding there! So we have to think about the colloquial, or symbolic meanings of words and phrases, as well as their literal meaning, in order to communicate truly in a foreign language.

I chose the example above of 'paying peanuts' and 'getting monkeys' because I had a Chinese student who, when she sat her examination for me, spent a considerable amount of her precious writing time trying to understand what 'paying monkeys with peanuts' actually meant. The fact that she was allowed to use an English dictionary to help her with her examinations was of very little help – what had the dictionary definition of a peanut to do with a case study on organizational behaviour which she had to interpret?

But there is much more to this idea of a social context for language than simply its usage in colloquialisms, geographical variations or slang expressions. The language we learn and use can profoundly influence the way we perceive and experience the world. Words are not always **neutral**; in addition to their **denotative**, or dictionary definition, they may have a connotative meaning. The **connotative** meaning is the one which has the emotional, cultural or symbolic content. There is a whole academic study around the connotative meanings of words, called **social semantics** or **sociolinguistics**, which relates verbal communication – words spoken or written – to history, geography, class, sex, age, status, ethnic group and context.

For example, we know that the use of 'slang' or local colloquialisms can be a means of identifying someone's socio-economic group, and thus suggest further avenues for, or barriers to, communication. Think about the language of 'rap', and the whole social and cultural context that suggests. Think about what used to be called 'BBC' or 'Received English', that which was spoken by the 'upper class', those who had power and influence in society, and therefore were in a position to dictate 'standards' – **their** standards!

One of the most interesting attempts to categorize language's relationship with class was that of a novelist rather than an academic.

Nancy Mitford, in 1956, classified words and phrases was being 'U' – used by the 'upper classes', and 'non-U' – used by the rest of us. If you were 'U', you talked about 'writing paper', 'table napkins', 'looking-glasses' and 'drawing rooms'. If you were 'non-U', you talked about 'notepaper', 'serviettes', 'mirrors', and 'lounges'! We have a strong tendency to assume that those who do not 'speak' like us are unlikely to share our perceptions, values and attitudes, thus a barrier to communication is created which exists independent of other assumptions which might be based purely upon our accents.

Without perhaps realizing it, you will have come across the application of sociolinguistic studies in the debate about 'politically correct' language. Although a lot of jokes are made about some of the wilder flights of fantasy attached to this new label for language, it is in fact an important way of thinking about how and why people use certain words, and the manner in which words can significantly structure our perceptions, emotions, values and attitudes. In addition, the use of particular words can lead us into categorizing, or stereotyping, individuals and groups, and into reinforcing prejudices.

So having that appreciation, we can understand why, whatever the dictionary definitions may be, the connotations, or emotional and symbolic content, of certain words, and the messages drawn from them, may convey far more than the transmitter knows or intends. For example, language can be perceived as patronizing, impertinent, perjorative, dismissive, or uncaring, when it may not be intended to so be. Not just the tone of voice but the words themselves can have positive or negative connotations.

There are several good examples of the linking of language with perception from your industry. The 'hospitality' industry sounds much more 'user-friendly' a label, and more embracing of the talents and skills it requires of those who work within it than does the 'catering' industry. Think of the distinction we employ between using the word 'guest' for someone to whom we sell a room, whether there is food involved or not, and 'customer' for someone to whom we only sell a meal. What extra connotation does the word 'guest' have in our minds? And think about the meal itself. The wonderful stretches of imagination used to describe what has been done to a piece of dead cow! The extra taste sensation which is supposed to come from 'baby' carrots or 'garden-fresh' peas, or 'morning-gathered wild' mushrooms.

I personally think that one of the simplest and best examples to illustrate the impact of the connotative meanings of a word is that of the use of the word 'home'. My dictionary defines 'home' as where one lives, or 'a family or group living together in a house'. An ostensibly neutral definition. How often in the hospitality industry is food advertised as 'home-made', or 'home cooking', an hotel as having a 'homely' atmosphere, of guests being made to feel 'at home'. All highly positive attributes. (Mind you, I have often wondered about that phrase being so used by the industry – when I am off on my holidays, I don't really want where I am staying to be like 'home' – especially if I have paid rather a lot of money to live quite differently from when I am home!)

Yet think of the other side of the coin. Would you like someone to tell you your clothes looked 'home-made' – or that you had a 'homely' face? Care has to be taken with the use of even that simple word.

Our formal verbal communications skills, meaning a command of language in the dictionary sense, allows us to express ourselves through a wide range of words in a variety of contexts, and enables us to choose between words which may have similar meaning, but different connotations in different contexts. When we label someone as being extremely socially skilled, it is often because they always seem to have the 'right turn of phrase', 'the right words for the occasion', whether we are talking about the spoken or the written word.

At a very practical level, before we pick up again the point about the social context of language, the skilled communicator is someone who can communicate with others any level of literacy or learning abilities. This, for managers within the hospitality industry, is an extremely important skill, given the diversity of educational backgrounds and attainment which we know is present within employees in the hospitality industry, and that of our guests and customers. Indeed, a 1993 study by the UK Adult Literacy and Basic Skills Unit reported that some six million adults cannot read well enough to cope with daily activities. Yet we expect all staff to be able read and understand complex health and safety legislation, changes in employment or licensing laws.

Therefore having a wide-ranging vocabulary is a very powerful communications tool in itself – or should we say 'bag of tools'.

This is not say that you should cram your business and professional correspondence with long, obscure, or overly formal words and phrases, just for the sake of showing your command of language! As the cliché goes, time is money, and no body wants to spend it reading letters and reports which say in 500 words that which could be said in 50. You can be taken seriously as a professional without having to communicate in a special business 'jargon'. It also takes up more time to type 500 words as opposed to 50; and it costs more in paper and ink, and it costs more in physical effort, or electronic effort, to type and print out! One of the most succinct business 'letters' I have ever seen was that sent by one Egyptian civil servant to another at the time of the Pharoahs. 'Zeno to Amenhotep. You did well to send the chick peas to Memphis.' Full stop!

The above are in the main practical or operational points. Now think about the human element in this. What can the use of excessive business or unnecessary technical jargon tell us about the writer? I am sure you can work out an answer to that. One of the twentieth century's greatest philosophers, Ludwig Wittgenstein, stated that 'The limits of my language are the limits of my world.'

He was saying something much more important than the fact that it is to our advantage as communicators to have a large vocabulary in order to express our thoughts adequately, and indeed we will come back to his thinking on language further on, but certainly we are limited in our capacity to communicate with the world if we do not have sufficient words in our mind to allow us to pick and choose to suit the context and objective of the communications process. Imagine being restricted in your response if a member of staff, or a group to whom you are speaking, asks you to explain something, and you have to conclude with a waffly 'you know what I mean'. And even the simplest words can have a multiplicity of connotations. The word 'set' has no less than 195 meanings, depending upon how it is used.

So having a good formal command of language does not necessarily mean we are socially skilled. We need to enhance our awareness of the symbolic or emotional content of words, and why and where the use of certain words, in certain contexts, are seen as quite inappropriate, with the consequence that barriers to active listening are raised, or the whole communications process breaks down.

Keynotes
1. A word may have both a denotative (literal or obvious) meaning and a connotative meaning (a symbolic association or idea).
2. Words are not 'neutral'; they come about, exist, and have these connotative meanings through their social contexts.
3. We have to ensure that these social contexts are taken into account when we encode and decode messages, in order that unnecessary barriers to communication are not created.

Most of us are now well aware of the attention drawn to what can be construed as sexism and racism in language. We have seen how legal cases involving charges of racial or sexual discrimination often have a particular use of language as the issue. The little scenario at the start of this chapter actually mirrors a real instance, where a publican in the north-east of England a year or so back was taken to court by a Scottish customer because he objected to being continually addressed as 'Jock'. The case came about because it was argued that always addressing a Scot as 'Jock' was just as insulting and racist as calling an Afro-Caribbean male 'Rastus', when his name was actually David.

Given our multicultural and multi-ethnic society, we have to be aware that problems in inter-ethnic interactions are more subtle than a lack of knowledge of each other's languages. And with the increasing number of foreign visitors to our shores, we have to be even more careful about the meanings of words, and even more appreciative of the different connotations certain words might have for cultures other than one's own. Will the language you are using transmit the message as you want it to be, or might quite a different message to that which you intended be decoded?

The importance of this cultural understanding cannot be under-estimated in a world which is becoming 'smaller' by the day. As the academic and social commentator, Marshall MacLuhan, said, we now live in a 'global village'. More and more organizations are becoming international or multinational, and managers have to understand and cope with processes of communication and decision-making in cultures which can be quite different from our own, even although the organizational structures may be similar, or even identical. Already there has been considerable research undertaken into managerial leadership styles, which are very much about how one communicates with and to subordinates, in different cultures.

One recent study on negotiating skills compared the communicating styles of pairs of US, Japanese and Brazilian negotiators. The findings revealed that the Japanese looked at each other less, said 'no' less often, and had longer and more frequent periods of silence. Their major priority was to establish trust, which could take a considerable time, but would then smooth the way in the long term. This style made for impatience in the US negotiators, who were more interested in concrete decisions made for the short term, and thus communicated to further that end. The direct versus indirect communication styles initially caused barriers, until a mutual style was agreed.

But there is more than ethnicity to take into account in terms of the cultural impact or social context of language. 'Sexism' and 'ageism' as ways of thinking, or attitudes to certain groups, can each be reflected through language which appears to be patronizing or offensive or demeaning. We may personally not be offended, or feel threatened by certain emotive words, but we have to be sensitive to the possibility that others could or would be. For example, talking about a female as a 'dolly bird' or 'chick' is distasteful to a number of women. Indeed, some women object to being talked about as **females**. And just as with racist language, legal action can be taken if it is felt that certain language amounts to 'sexual harassment'.

You may not personally object to using words like **manpower** planning, **manning** the organization, work**man**like, or chair**man**. But a number of people feel that examples like this, where the language used seems to exclude half of society, serves to reinforce exclusion in social reality. It is far more than the fact that we have generally considered certain language to be inappropriate in mixed company because it is 'coarse' or would not be used by a female because it is considered to be 'unladylike'. It is argued that certain language both reflects and reinforces power structures and social inequalities.

These points may seem to be rather more to do with academic debate than social reality, but a very nice test of the above theory is to think about the historical place and perception of black people in western societies, and then think of the number of words or phrases in the English language which use the word 'black' to suggest a negative rather than a positive situation or idea. (I have counted seventeen!) Indeed, I initially used the word 'denigrating' above instead of 'demeaning'. If you are one of those people who is interested in the etymology of language, you might like to think why I chose not to.

Dale Spender, author of an important book which looked at sexism in language, identified 287 words for a female of questionable morals and only 13 for a similarly inclined male, drawing the inference that in our culture a 'loose woman' is far more to be criticized and labelled as such than a 'loose man'. Indeed, it even sounds odd to talk about a 'loose man'. We do not need to agree with Ms Spender's hypothesis to accept that it is the basis of a very powerful movement, which we can already see having an enormous impact on how we frame written and spoken language.

We can extend this thinking to age and 'ageism' in language. There has been a move away from talking about 'old age pensioners' to 'senior citizens'. 'The elderly' is no longer acceptable (in any case, when does someone become 'elderly' – it is easy to see that can be a very subjective or emotive label). 'Elderly' is seen as depersonalizing and distancing, with connotations of dependency and frailty. 'Older people' is more generally accepted. And as that group in our Western population is not only the fastest growing age group but the group with perhaps the most disposable income and leisure time, then the hospitality industry certainly should be thinking of the most appropriate language with which to communicate with them.

What about the language of 'disability'? Roughly 15% of our population are classed as 'disabled'. It has been estimated recently that there is within the European tourism market potential earnings in excess of £22 billion, if those with special needs like the elderly or disabled were better catered for (Tourism for All Advisory Committee, 1994). It is in the interests of the hospitality industry to accommodate this group, both literally, through easier physical access and facilities (which is becoming a marketing feature of many hotels) and symbolically, through the use of appropriate language.

Have a look at how facilities for the 'disabled' are identified in hotels, restaurants, or bars. We use the word 'disabled', or we present a symbol, a wheelchair (despite the fact that only 4% of the disabled are wheelchair users). Think instead about the phrase 'people with disabilities', which suggests a society which should accommodate **them**, rather than stigmatizing them by the condition itself. By using

Keynotes
1. Language which one culture or social group perceives to be appropriate may be perceived as totally inappropriate by another culture or social group.
2. Language which reflects a relationship in which one group is labelled as inferior to another is considered to be particularly inappropriate.
3. We must consciously adapt the words we use to the social context within which we use them.

language with care, you can relate to all your audience, whoever they are, rather than alienating groups within it through thoughtlessness.

But there is far more to being socially skilled in this area of communicating than merely using the 'right words'. The concept of **register** also implies the appropriate phrases and sentences. There are messages and **metamessages**. A metamessage is a message which comes through in more subtle forms than that which is suggested by the transmitter's actual words and phrases, either consciously or unconsciously. Think how you might decode the very common phrase 'Please yourself'. Does it always means literally that you should please yourself? Or the phrase 'with all due respect, chairperson'. Is the metamessage not that in this instance you actually have **no** due respect for the chair? We will pick up the importance of understanding the role of metamessages in the communications process in one of the activities.

So learning to use language is more than just learning a vocabulary and the grammatical rules; it is also about learning the speaking practices of a culture and the way social interaction is organized. This is a social skill as opposed to a purely linguistic skill.

I had an interesting discussion not so long ago with an American and an English woman as to whether a waiter who served us over dinner in a smart restaurant was being too 'forward'. The English customer said he was; he had made some slightly jokey remark about her menu choice, and had then asked the American if it were true all Americans in the hospitality industry went around saying 'Have a nice day.' The American customer however saw this as the waiter being friendly, extravert and trying to relate to the customers – all of which he expected from staff in such a position. The disagreement between the two revolved around the concept of the **language game**, a concept created by Wittgenstein, referred to above, to explain how we learned, used and evaluated language in terms of its appropriate **style**, **tone** and **register**.

Wittgenstein saw language as an activity just as a game is an activity. Language has rules which define the game itself (we are playing tennis or we are playing football) and it has rules which define how the game is played (a 'line ball' or an 'off-side'). If we are truly socially skilled, we are specialists at playing the game according to the rules, no matter what the game is!

So the 'language game' can be that of the rules governing the way the hotel manager deals with foreign visitors, the housekeeper deals with staff, the receptionist deals with an angry guest, the barman deals with the businesswoman. And woe betide us if we get the rules wrong! Greeting someone for the first time? In our society the phrase is likely to be something on the lines of 'Hullo. I'm very pleased to meet you.' I'm sure you will all know that well-worn phrase, 'Do you come here often?' It is extremely **un**likely that in developing a new relationship with a member of the opposite sex the opening 'serve' or 'kick-off' is 'Hullo, can I go to bed with you?'

Indeed, one of the first signs of someone suffering from certain mental conditions is that they appear to have forgotten the conventional language game rules. An extremely interesting study (Spradley and Mann, 1975) was undertaken of a very simple example of the language game – or 'speech act', as the study labelled it – that of asking for a drink in a bar. The study showed that asking for a drink can be done through any number of speech acts, but on analysis customers tended to select those that would achieve certain ends. In addition to asking for a drink, the speech act was used to convey something about themselves to the bar staff, or to others.

For example, to demonstrate their prowess with females generally, to show they were adults, to establish status or authority, or that they were regular customers and knew the 'scene'. All through the skilful use of language; merely asking for a drink set in motion a number of social processes and interactions.

It is not surprising that conversation is often referred to as an 'art', and in recent years there has been some fascinating research into conversation which suggests that it can reveal how power and dominance comes about in social interaction.

For example, in analysing speech styles of men and women, it has been noted that men on average talk more than women (despite the stereotype of women as chatterboxes!), interrupt more, and that there are distinct variations in the use of certain adjectives, adverbs, pronunciation forms and intonation patterns, all of which seemed to reflect the different private and public roles played out by men as opposed to women. Other studies of this sort suggest that those who are good leaders, who appear to have the power to persuade and influence others, do it to a great extent through the use of language, how they organize words and phrases, what sort of speaking style they use.

These ideas have been used to analyse the speeches of successful politicians, and they do reveal what appear to be effective rhetorical strategies. If you are interested in developing your talents in public speaking, then you might like to follow up these ideas in the work of these researchers (Atkinson, Goffman, Thorne, Heritage and Greatbatch) as it certainly supports the argument that we can all **learn** to be good leaders, because it's about communicative styles, not just having been fortunate to be born with charisma.

Thus we are obliged not only to be highly conscious of the words we use, but also of the way in which we combine the words into phrases and sentences. Even in the simplest communications process with our nearest and dearest we play the language game, well aware of the emotional content and social context of the words we use. In interpreting the range and number of social roles you may have to play during one day in the hospitality industry, your awareness of the language game should be honed to perfection. Otherwise, your careers, the jobs of our staff, your personal and professional bank account, may all suffer.

We shall be looking at the implications of this thinking in the activities, but meanwhile think about one activity you may hear regularly in an hotel, that of the 'after-dinner speech'. Every audience has different characteristics. A good after-dinner speaker will deliberate on these characteristics (age, sex, social status, culture, educational background, mood, attitudes, values, beliefs) and frame his or her speech accordingly. The message contained in an after-dinner speech to, say, members of the Institute of Civil Engineers, may be the same message as that put over in an after-dinner speech to members of the Ladies' Circle. But the tone and register of the language used is likely to be quite different.

Finally, you might like to thing why there is an on-going and very heated debate within the information technology professionals as to whether a computer, even although it can be programmed to use perfect grammar and sentence construction and have a human-sounding voice, could ever be programmed to engage in genuine 'social interaction'. Those who argue that that can never be base their view on the fact that the communications process in which humans are involved depends for its effectiveness on highly subtle and complex verbal and non-verbal cues, and an infinite variety of combinations and permutations, many of which are interpreted intuitively or in a creative manner which is denied the computer, however sophisticated its technology.

The ultimate test of whether a computer has 'interpersonal skills' is supposed to be that you could engage in a conversation with a computer – and never ever guess you were not talking to a human being! At the time of writing, no computer programmer has come remotely near achieving this. What does that tell us about the nature of communications and interpersonal skills?

Keynotes
1. Using language appropriately is far more than just the correct use of grammar and a wide range of vocabulary.
2. The written and spoken words both create and reflect an underlying social context and thus we have to be aware of the meta-message which is given off at the same time as the message.
3. The communications process can be compared to a game, the 'language game' in which we recognize certain rules apply, depending upon the nature and objective of the game, or communications process.

Activity 3.1

Before we begin to think about **what** we say, the continuation and effectiveness of the communications process is just as dependent upon the **way** we say things. A professional actor would tell you that a great deal of his/her skill revolves around the simple concept of **voice control**. Meaning that the sound of the voice alone can transmit so many messages, including the attitudes, moods and personality, status, culture or socio-economic background of the speaker. So in any oral communications context, the more skilled we are in using our voice to reinforce the message of the words we use, then the more likely we are to achieve our objective when communicating.

Phrases like 'I don't like her tone of voice', or 'He sounded very approachable', are important indicators of the likely success or otherwise of a communications process. So what yardsticks or criteria would you lay down for assessing the quality of your voice, and thus what if anything you need to do in order to use it to best effect? To help your thinking, think about a yardstick you might use to test the quality of a restaurant. It could be its colour scheme (does it 'jar' in any way?). Or the size of portions (too large or too small portions can be 'off-putting', for quite different reasons). Concentrate on thinking of the **criteria** – don't get caught up in thinking of examples. 'His voice is too loud' is an example of what yardstick or criterion?

Thoughts on Activity 3.1

Those of you who are musical perhaps will have found this exercise easier than others, because some of the labels we looking for are also used to evaluate the quality of a piece of music. Indeed, we often talk of someone having a 'musical voice', generally considered to be a compliment.

What I would expect you to have identified is the following:

1. Tone – would you consider the voice to be **harsh** or **gentle**, **strong** or **weak**?
2. Pitch – is it **high** or **low**?
3. Volume – is it **loud** or **soft**?
4. Pace – is it **fast** or **slow**?
5. Enunciation – is it **clear** or **slurred**?

Now have a go at testing your own voice relative to these criteria. Tape it. Listen to it on an answering machine. If you feel uneasy about hearing your own voice (and most of us do – even experienced lecturers) try and establish which particular factors worry you. With women it is often the **pitch**. 'Shrill' or 'penetrating' may be the words used. Alternatively, 'sexy' is a word often used to describe a low-pitched voice in a woman. In the man, the low-pitched voice is considered to reflect masculinity.

It is interesting to note, however, that our individual voice range has to some extent been 'socially constructed' to reflect male/female norms, because research suggests that we have a range of tone and pitch which is very much wider and more controllable than we think. I wonder if you put down **accent** as part of voice quality? Of course you are right in that an accent can help or hinder the communications process. You may have been thinking of a regional accent you find difficult to understand. But the reason you cannot understand it is likely to be far more to do with **enunciation** or how the words are **articulated**, rather than the sound of the accent itself.

Although certain accents may be more melodious than others, accents in themselves are more likely to be thought of as valuable in giving off cues reflecting social factors related to the speaker. The individual components which make up the tone and quality of our voice are quite separate from the tone and quality of the **language** we use. The skill is to match the two to good effect, and make sure that the voice itself is not a barrier to communication. Thus whatever the innate qualities our voices have, we know that, like good actors, we can learn to **manipulate** our voices in order to enhance their ability to communicate mood, attitude, personality, role.

The 'monotonous' voice to which we referred in a previous activity has by definition only one tone. This does not inspire interest or involvement. The high-pitched voice indicates excitement or fear; the too-fast voice indicates nervousness. Poor enunciation means that the listener may have to ask the speaker to repeat what s/he has said, thus setting a possible scene for a communication barrier. The speaker may be insulted; the listener will only ask once for fear of embarrassing the speaker and prefer to miss out on understanding rather than ask again. The communications process grinds to a halt!

And if there are no other cues to help the listener interpret the communication, then it is even more important that the voice is used effectively. For instance, on the telephone or radio. So get a few of your fellow students and practise saying the following sentence in many different 'moods', or reflecting as many different 'personalities' as possible. For example, you are sad, or nervous, or angry, or mystified, or ecstatic, or deferential, or irritated. Each take a shot at guessing what mood is being conveyed, and thus identifying exactly what voice control is about. It can be both an interesting and an amusing exercise! The sentence is totally neutral so the voice has to say it all!

Bar meals are served from 7 pm and the chef's speciality tonight will be lasagne.

--- *Activity 3.2* ---------------

There is another way of looking at the importance of how we say things. Many statements have two levels of meaning. The first is the basic information being communicated by the words, the second is that which tells us something about the speaker's attitudes and feelings, but is not necessarily about the tone of voice, because it is also dependent upon which words are used to convey the information. So there are messages and **metamessages**.

Metamessages are often a form of attack, but an attack that is covert – something being implied rather than being said directly – so they can be a source of much interpersonal conflict. How do we then encode or interpret verbal and non-verbal cues accurately so we are not in danger of reading too much into what someone says – or not realizing that someone may get the wrong idea about what we are saying.

The metamessage is communicated through **tone** and **pitch** in the voice, but also through what are known as **verbal modifiers**. A simple example is 'Just a minute'. Say that out loud to a fellow student, first with the emphasis on 'just' and then with the emphasis on 'minute'. Ask him or her what these emphases say about your **emotional** state, as opposed to the message which is on the surface a simple request. The answer is likely to be that you are feeling impatient or annoyed with the listener. Some of that emotional meaning comes from the use of verbal modifiers, words which add a particular nuance to a phrase or sentence, when they are emphasized.

Examples of these are 'only', 'naturally', 'still', and 'supposedly'. Listen for others, when you hear someone talk in a disapproving or sarcastic manner. And think about them, when you make statements which could be misinterpreted because of their use and the **pitch** of voice attached to them. For instance, try interpreting the following statements at the deeper rather than the surface level. What metamessage is coming over? Again, use a friend, put the emphasis on the word in italics, and check with him or her what is seen to be the real message. The words in *italic* are the words to be emphasized, but also note the type of words used.

- 'It's *only* a fly, sir.'
- '*Naturally*, you'll want the best wine.'
- 'I was *merely* trying to organize your shifts more sensibly.'
- 'I'm *sure* you tried your best with that difficult guest.'
- 'Are you *still* trying to set up the Banqueting Suite?'
- '*Now* what can I do for you, madam?"

Now imagine these sentences spoken without the emphasis. The same words, a quite different mood or attitude coming through.

Finally, try the same thing with the following sentence, but repeat it four times, putting the emphasis on each word in turn (apart from 'to'), and see the number of metamessages, and extra information, which can be conveyed by one short piece of basic information.

This book belongs to Mary.

Thoughts on Activity 3.2

Of course you will realize that these statements, emphasized in that way, must be decoded in the light of other factors, such as context, facial expression, the relationship between transmitter and receiver. Here we are deliberately exaggerating the possibility of negative interpretations, in order to show how a communication may break down. 'I hear what you say' in itself has two levels of meaning, hasn't it?

- 'It's *only* a fly, sir.' A response to a situation which has spun off more jokes than most others. Metamessage – 'Well, it could be a lot worse . . .' (you might like to finish the joke for yourself!)

- '*Naturally* you'll want the best wine.' Metamessage – 'you are such a wine snob.' Or 'Don't you just love throwing your money about.'
- 'I was *merely* trying to organize your shifts sensibly.' Metamessage – 'Why are you being so unreasonable – I was trying to help.'
- 'I'm *sure* you tried your best with that difficult customer.' Metamessage – 'I'm pretty sure you *didn't* try your best!'
- 'Are you *still* trying to set up the Banqueting Suite?' Metamessage – 'There's no way you should be here just now.'
- '*Now* what do you want?' Metamessage – 'You really are trying my patience – you ask for too much.'

And what about Mary and the book? Again, it is quite surprising to see just how much these four simple words can convey.

- '*That* book (as opposed to any other book) belongs to Mary.'
- 'That *book* (as opposed to that pen, or notepad) belongs to Mary.'
- 'That book *belongs* to (as opposed to having been borrowed) by Mary.'
- 'That book belongs to *Mary*' (as opposed to John or Peter).

See how easily that basic simple statement could be open to misinterpretation. The final point to make about metamessages is that, if they are not to be a source of conflict, then they have to be recognized for what they are. This means that (a) you have to repeat the message in your own mind, and try to identify where the pitch, or a verbal modifier, has suggested some sort of attack, and (b) you then say to the transmitter what you think the message was, and whether it does reflect genuine feelings.

'Are you working late shift *again* tonight?' could mean a colleague who genuinely worried about your overworking, or that she feels you are showing her and the others up, because they then look bad for not offering to stay on. This is a communications situation in which the best form of defence may **not** be another attack!

--- *Activity 3.3* -------------------

Business or professional jargon may act as a barrier to communication, not only in the technical sense, but also in the psychological sense. That is, the operational lack of understanding may be compounded by the fact that we often do not like to admit we do not understand words or phrases we feel we ought to understand. It threatens our self-esteem or what we see to be our public image. It may be of course that you deliberately want to do that to someone, to create a barrier. But then you are using an important aspect of the communications process to achieve a communications objective, so you are in control – you are encoding your message in a manner which will achieve that objective. But beware of the excessive use of jargon – it may communicate to someone that it is you who are insecure – you are hiding behind the jargon!

One of the most common problems these days in terms of jargon is the number of professional terms which are represented by abbreviations. Indeed, there are so many now that there are dictionaries devoted solely to them! Just to show you how baffling this can easily become, 'translate' the following passage, which has been constructed entirely from abbreviations or acronyms (a pronounceable name made from a series of initial letters or parts of a group of words) which appeared over a short spell of time in one of the hospitality industry's professional journals.

The IPM and the HCIMA have been involved in discussions with regard to TQM and CBT in conjunction with the EC and the WTO. It is thought that despite the fall in the GDP of the G6 countries, future JDI's will require that all employees show this understanding. It is already built into many MBA courses and of course will be of even more importance as a consequence of the SEM. CHME had already set up a research sub-committee to investigate the possibilities of finance through the ESRC and, along with YM techniques and other aspects of HRM, particularly with the new emphasis on evaluating employees' CLIs as part of appraisal systems. These link up with the general desire to achieve BS 5750 in the industry.

Phew! How much does that lot mean to you?

Thoughts on Activity 3.3

Of course one would not throw that amount of jargon into one short paragraph. I put it together, using real abbreviations in a mock report. But the only reason I did not present a genuine example is that its writer might have objected, because there are many of them. This is your industry; how much of this was instantly apparent to you?

IPM   Institute of Personnel Management
HCIMA   Hotel, Catering and Institutional Management Association
TQM   Total Quality Management
CBT   Computer-Based Training
EC   European Community
WTO   World Travel Organisation
GDP   Gross Domestic Product
G6   six major nations involved in global economic planning
JDIs   Job Description Indices
MBA   Master of Business Administration
SEM   Single European Market
CHME   Council for Hospitality Management Education
ESRC   Economic and Social Research Council
HRM   Human Resource Management
CLI   Central Life Interest
BS5750   British Standards Quality Control for the hotel and catering industry

Of course, no one is denying that using abbreviations saves time and paper. But again the measure of their appropriateness in the communications process is **whose** time is saved, and for what purpose? To foster a sense of 'belongingness' to a particular group with shared knowledge and interests? Or to deliberately exclude from group? When communicating in business, watch that the time-saving factor does not create another barrier to communication. 'I don't know what this means, I don't have time to check what it means. I might just take a guess, but then I could get it wrong . . . the writer obviously wants to be taken for a real smart guy.'

But is he? Is this not a perfect example of a communications breakdown through lack of understanding of both the operational and human element in this transmission? Not the feedback you want.

Activity 3.4

The 'Campaign for Plain English', a pressure group which awards bouquets or brickbats to organizations depending upon how easy it is to process their written communications, has done a wonderful job of identifying bad practice and drawing attention to the virtue of business communication being as clear and concise as possible. In operational terms, brevity of language saves typing or writing time and paper, and precision in language saves time and energy in the decoding process, time and energy which would have been used to clarify ambiguities and vaguenesses. Direct and precise language, in public relations or human terms, means that frustrations are avoided, and more positive perceptions of and attitudes towards an organization are encouraged.

There are eight basic rules to consider in producing clear and concise business communications. And although these could be said to be **technical** rules, they come from the explicit recognition that those on the receiving end of your communications are human beings and thus the style, tone and register of your language must also reflect human needs if you want to get your message over successfully. People do not like to admit to a lack of understanding of something they feel they **ought** to understand; how many messages are misinterpreted or ignored on that account? The rules are as follows:

1. Eliminate unnecessary words (**soon** instead of **at your earliest convenience**).
2. Explain abbreviations and acronyms, pronounceable words made from a series of initials (**SWOT analysis**).
3. Eliminate jargon (**almost ideal** instead of **sub-optimal**).
4. Eliminate unnatural phrases (**here is** instead of **attached please find**).
5. Use smaller rather than larger words where possible (**pay** instead of **remunerate**).
6. Use active rather than passive verbs (**in May, sales increased by 10%** instead of **increases in sales of 10% were obtained in May**).

7. Check for sexist or ageist language (**senior citizen** instead of **old age pensioner**; **woman** instead of **female**).
8. Use the Readability Index, designed to identify such human factors as **how long on average can a sentence, or a paragraph be before it puts the reader off, how many complex words can be used**.

Now, select a random sample of letters, reports, articles from professional journals, etc., communicating on aspects of the hospitality industry, and try and identify examples of the above rules being broken. At this stage concentrate on rules 1 to 7. The Readability Index is discussed in Activity 3.5, so ignore it at present. Jot down how you might rewrite, with greater clarity or precision, the examples you have found. Use a good dictionary or *Roget's Thesaurus* if you need some ideas.

Thoughts on Activity 3.4

Obviously I cannot comment on how well you did this exercise, because I do not know what samples you have chosen. And sometimes it can be difficult to replace a multisyllabic (long) word with a shorter word because in doing so you might lose some shade of meaning, or the longer word has a specific business or professional meaning. I referred to *Roget's Thesaurus* as a source of help. It's a wonderful reference book which allows you to look up one word, and then see a number of words which have similar meanings, and which may be more familiar or shorter. The Thesaurus can also help you if you feel that a particular word you are thinking of using is perhaps not quite the shade of meaning you want, especially if you have, I hope, become sensitive to the connotations of the words you might use when communicating with certain individuals.

Those of you who use a word-processing package will already be familiar with the Thesaurus function key. A couple of examples will illustrate what it can do . 'Student' comes up as similar to 'apprentice', 'novice', 'pupil', 'scholar'. 'Hotel' comes up as 'hostel', 'inn', 'lodging', and 'motel'. But quite different images are thrown up by these different words.

Now test whether your editing of the reports or articles you have selected has been successful. Let someone read the originals, time how long it took, and then ask some questions which would show whether what had been read was understood and processed. Do the same with someone else with your edited efforts and compare the time and comprehension. Then discuss whether any essential information has been lost as a consequence of the editing.

Finally, discuss whether the edited version has lost any of its required tone and register as a consequence of simplifying the language. Business language need not be complex in order to impress. A good impression comes from communications which are neat, follow a conventional format, have clarity, precision, and area easily read. We will be picking up these points again about written communications when we look at report-writing in Chapter 8. But here's another short exercise for you to get you thinking about clarity and precision.

Compare the first paragraph (52 words) with the second paragraph (22 words) below. Which would you prefer to see in your in-tray at the start of a very busy day?

> In order to appraise you of the outcome of the marketing meeting held on July 15th to consider prospective methodologies for reducing the cost of the proposed winter marketing campaign, it is advocated that the proponents submit herewith a brief résumé of the strategy and procedure outlined for the cost reduction programme.

or

> Here is a summary of plans drawn up at the July 15th meeting for cutting costs on the proposed winter marketing campaign.

Activity 3.5

So what is actually meant by this 'readability' or 'fog' index, and how does it work? It establishes a relationship, based on an arithmetical calculation, between the complexity of the language used in a piece of writing and the number of years of education the reader generally requires to read it. It is a useful tool for achieving a general assessment of reading ease, which is a key factor in communicating within the hospitality industry, given the heterogeneous background of its employees, guests and customers, and number of communications networks. (Is **heterogeneity** a familiar word? If not, how much did it slow up your decoding of this message?)

There are slight variations in interpretation of the technique, but basically the Fog Index formula is as follows:

> Count 100 words. Even if you reach 100 words before the end of a sentence, carry on counting until the end. Now count the number of sentences in each 100 word block of writing, and divide the number of words by the number of sentences. This will give you an average sentence length. Underline all words which have three or more syllables (polysyllabic words) unless they are easily understood words like people or place names, or are simple compound words like housekeeper or undermanager. Words which are of essential use for a particular industry or profession and thus cannot easily be replaced should not be counted, like the 'hospitality' industry. Now add up the 'big' words, but don't count these exceptions. Finally, divide the total number of words into the total of polysyllabic words and multiply by 100. Add that figure and average sentence length, and multiply the total by 4.

Try this formula on the following example, taken from an exceptionally good academic study of social skills training, *The Analysis of Social Skill* (Singleton, Spurgeon and Stammers (eds), 1980).

> The empirical paradigm for the identification of skills involves systematic observation, recording, categorization and analysis of appropriate

professional–client interaction to identify skills and groupings of skills. The relative importance of these skills and, after training, the relationship to desired professional outcomes is to be determined by observation, and where possible, quasi or full-blown experiment, with associated instrumentation and statistical analysis. This traditionally scientific paradigm might be assumed to be necessary for the conditioning paradigms for skill acquisition; highly desirable in the cybernetic paradigm; useful but insufficient in the experiential paradigm; and at best a necessary evil in the teleological paradigm.

You just might need a calculator!

Thoughts on Activity 3.5

These are the words I would have picked out.

BIG WORDS

empirical paradigm identification systematic
categorization analysis interaction quasi
instrumentation statistical analysis conditioning
acquisition cybernetic experiential teleological

Total number of words = 104; 3 sentences; average 33 words to a sentence; 14% big words.

$$33 + 14 = 47 \times .4 = \text{Fog Index of approximately 18}$$

Check your findings against this table:

Table 3.1

	Readability Index	Reading level	Typical reading material
Extremely difficult	25	Postgraduate Graduate	Professional, academic journals
Difficult	19	Final year undergraduate	Quality press
	13	First year undergraduate	Quality press
Ideal range of competence	12	18-year-old school leaver	Quality hobbies and interest magazines
Easy range	13 8 6	14 year old 11 year old 7 year old	Tabloid press

Thus reading level required of that paragraph = that of a graduate. Of course, it does not necessarily mean that the piece of writing tested in this way is grammatical, or intelligible, or conveys exactly the tone and register, in the sense of its emotional or psychological content, that you wish it to. But it is an additional method of checking that the chances of your message being decoded as you intended it to be are as high as possible.

Above is a prime example of language only accessible to the academics who use it regularly. The author, or transmitter, has encoded his message in complex concepts in order to transmit the subtleties of his ideas to the receiver. And the receiver's reading level had to be fairly high for him/her to decode. Of the 'big' words, only three (**cybernetic**, **paradigm** and **teleological**) had a particularly specialist significance; the rest were words which might be considered to be part of any graduate's vocabulary. But not quite the language you might use to convey the same idea to your staff in the 'house magazine!'

Now try out the formula out on some extracts from, say, your text-books, notes given you by tutors, reports you are supposed to read, and then use it to assess the 'readability' of your own best business writing. Is there a nice match between these and your supposed reading level (13 to 19) in the Fog Index? The Fog Index is one way in which you can assess the quality of your written documentation. Without even carrying out the arithmetical exercise, you can intuitively use it to judge how well you are likely to communicate with a particular group.

Oh yes, what was it the author was saying? Basically, that one can identify social skills through use of a well-established scientific procedure; however, having done that, this information is more useful in some methods of training compared with others. But that is a precis; not the detail of what the author was saying. Words can be easy to read, but the information contained therein not very intelligible or helpful to the reader. The right balance can only be achieved if you are constantly aware of the context and the needs of the receivers.

─────────────────────────────── *Activity 3.6* ───────────────────────────────

You may or may not be convinced by the argument I outlined to you in Chapter 3 that language is the major force in constructing what we perceive as 'reality' in society. But at least you should be prepared to test it. The wilder eccentricities of the 'politically correct' language movement should not cloud the basic importance of the message that language can and does to some extent both create and reflect values, attitudes and beliefs, upon which people may act. You would find it very interesting to look at research undertaken by Linda Hicks (Hicks, 1980) which showed the importance of the language used by hotel managers in their assumptions of women recruited to the hospitality industry. The language clearly reflected the strong anti-female hotel management thinking.

Now can you work out what might be considered to be the more acceptable, less emotive, less judgemental versions of the following words or phrases? It may surprise you that they could be seen to be unacceptable in the first place, but try anyway. Looking for alternative words or phrases should improve your command of language, as well as encouraging you to be more sensitive to the connotations of words for others.

elderly; deaf; maiden name; Christian name; affliction; failure (as in an exam); crippled; poor; bald; manpower; black; stupid; waiter.

Thoughts on Activity 3.6

To repeat, no doubt you have wondered why many of these words are seen as 'politically incorrect' in the first place. This is because they have been interpreted as reflecting an insulting or unflattering view of someone, or some inequality in the distribution of power. The use of the term 'political' in this context arises from the fact that politics is generally about the study of power, who has it, or had it, why, and what they do with it.

So the use of racist language often reflects a belief which was held by society in the days of slavery and colonial exploitation, which is perpetuated through certain ethnic groups being seen as inferior, or 'second-class'. Objections to the use of sexist language are put up for the same reason. It makes manifest a social attitude which sees women as inferior, or submissive, in a male-dominated society. The use of such language is also **indexical**. It indicates something about the user's views and values, which, because they are being articulated publicly by certain individuals or groups with influence, can reinforce their respectability and continuation, however little they might bear to reality.

Thus the communications process is more than a mere mirror of society, and if we can change the language, we may be able to change the thoughts! However for our purposes, it is not grand-scale social engineering we are about, but rather raising your awareness of language which might act as a barrier to communication in your professional life. Just think about it – do those of your guests who represent what will soon be around one-quarter of the population really want to be labelled as 'elderly', with all the connotations thereof of being incapable of thought and deed without help?

1. **Elderly**: you may choose from 'chronologically gifted' or 'experientially enhanced'. The Americans talk about 'grey power'!
2. **Deaf**: aurally challenged, aurally inconvenienced
3. **Maiden name or Christian name**: birth family name ('first name' would not have a meaning in certain cultures; they do not have their 'first' name first)
4. **Affliction**: condition
5. **Failure**: incompletely successful person, individual with temporarily unmet objectives
6. **Crippled**: differently abled, physically challenged

7. **Poor**: financially disadvantaged, economically exploited
8. **Bald**: follicularly challenged, differentially hirsute
9. **Manpower**: human resources
10. **Red Indian**: first American, native American
11. **Black**: Afro-Caribbean, African-American
12. **Stupid**: having special educational needs
13. **Waiter (waitress)**: waitron

Finally, it was reported a few months ago that a certain English local authority was seriously considering abolishing the title 'manager' from among its employees, because the term reeked of sexism. It implied a male, because there is also a word 'manageress', and thus its use in job descriptions or specifications could be seen as discriminatory. The word 'officer' was considered to be more politically correct.

If you think that is carrying things too far, just try a little experiment. Ask as many people as you can be bothered to suggest a name for the 'general manager' of a hotel in a role-playing exercise you are writing up. I think you will find that the names suggested will virtually all be men's names. And in future when you see the word 'manageress' used, try to assess the perceived status of the position to which it applies. Is it the, or one of the, top jobs in the organization? Or is at a subordinate position to that of the individual with overall responsibility? The answers to these questions should clearly illustrate this 'social' association between words, ideas and attitudes.

FURTHER READING

Coutts, M. and Maher, C. (1980) *Writing Plain English*, Plain English Campaign, Whaley Bridge, Stockport.

Open University (1991) *Plain English*, Open University Press, Milton Keynes.

These books both lay special emphasis on the clarity and quality of the written and spoken word in business, where time and money are paramount considerations. They dispel the myth that long words and complex sentences are a sign of intelligence and competence.

Hicks, L. (1990) 'Excluded women: how can this happen in the hotel world?', *The Service Industry Journal*, April, 348–63: although only an article this is exceptionally interesting and useful because it illustrates so clearly the social aspects of language through the connection between language and power. It is of even greater value because the context and research is within the hospitality industry itself.

The role of non-verbal language $\boxed{4}$

When you speak to a man, look at his eyes; when he speaks to you, look at his mouth. (Benjamin Franklin)

Question 4: What about 'non-verbal' communication? What is it, what is its significance in the communications process? Why is it so important a component of our interpersonal skills?

Snapshot

Colin, the Head Chef, put his head round the door of the bar, where Floella, the Food and Beverages Manager was discussing the redecoration of the bar with Duncan, the new barman.

Colin: 'This looks real cosy. What an impact the new couches and tables make.'

Floella: 'Do you think so? Duncan and I were wondering if we had tried to make it too cosy, and people wouldn't want to be as near one another as this .'

Duncan: 'I think perhaps we are worrying unnecessarily – after all, we want to create quite a different atmosphere from the main lounge, where people can sit and drink, without being cheek by jowl.'

Colin: 'I agree. If people want to have a drink while discussing business, then the main lounge is just right, with its more formal layout and furniture. But I know where I'd bring my girlfriend – fighting your way to the bar is part of the fun!'

Floella: (silence)

Duncan: 'I can see you're not so sure about that, are you, Floella?'

Are Colin and Duncan right? Or is Floella? Why is it that in certain situations we are not too bothered about being crushed up against someone, and in others it makes us very uneasy? Why is our perception of physical contact so selective, causing us to read so many different meanings into it, depending upon the circumstances?

The above scenario illustrates this psychological response we have to the physical space we have, how we need to control it, and where we draw boundaries with regard to how others should use it. In other words, although it may initially seem strange to think of it as a facet of

non-verbal communication, space, and how it is used, can be a very powerful tool in the communications process. Although it has always been recognized by architects and designers that our physical environment can influence our mental activities and social interactions, in the main the emphasis has generally been on purely aesthetic considerations, and our responses to these.

However, our response to the built environment is also of very great interest to the social psychologists, because that response, or **spatial behaviour**, is of such significance in the communications process. Floella was right to question the furniture arrangements in the newly decorated bar, and Colin and Duncan's responses illustrate the importance of recognizing how the physical environment can interact with the humans who inhabit it.

Let's start by looking at the whole concept of **non-verbal communication**. I'm sure you know the term, although perhaps associate it mainly with facial expression and what we call 'body language'. In fact one of the reasons it's such an interesting study is that there are a number of ways in which we communicate non-verbally, and the cues which are employed are not always as obvious or as easily decoded as an expression on the face.

The scientific study of non-verbal communication, which is of relatively recent origin, initially concentrated on body motion, but as studies of the communications process in general developed, it was recognized that there are other equally important components in the process, that there is a whole range of human actions and behaviours, other than the spoken word, which have a communicative function. The more insight we have into these components or elements, the greater control we have over the process, and the achieving of desired outcomes.

In a typical dyadic (one-to-one) encounter, only about one third of the social meaning of a situation is conveyed by the spoken word, while two-thirds is conveyed by the non-verbal components. And, perhaps even more importantly, the research suggests that if we are at all uncertain about someone's feelings, we rely on the cues given by the non-verbal communication to establish certainty in our minds. 'It's not what you say – it's the way that you say it.' And it is not unreasonable to assume that these findings are also appropriate to communications contexts where more than two people are involved, and to contexts varying in formality.

Non-verbal communication has a number of important functions. It can replace speech, enhance speech, help regulate the verbal communications process, define or reinforce social relationships and patterns of behaviour. Let's think of a few brief examples before we try systematically to look at the elements in depth.

The Restaurant Manager approaches you, looks you in the eye and smiles at you as you enter the dining room (and of course you know he is the Restaurant Manager because of his appearance, a form of non-verbal communication, as it is an encoded message transmitting his role, status and expertise). He gestures with his hand to call a waiter to show you to your seat, after asking if you have any preference as to where you would like to sit. And where you sit, or are directed to sit, can in itself convey status and prestige, because your 'placing in space' has a social significance beyond that of the purely geographical.

Indeed there is some evidence that women on their own in restaurants are 'parked' in what are considered to be the less prestigious areas because they are not considered to be big spenders, or powerful people. I hope you would not treat me like that if I visited your establishment! But back to our scenario. The waiter conveys by the sound of his voice that he is pleased to see a valued customer again. He pulls out your chair for you, and unfolds your napkin, spreading it neatly on your lap, and then hands you the menu. He then . . . need I say more? You could write the dialogue from now on – and in this context the dialogue is not about the spoken word, but these other non-verbal elements in this particular communications process which, if used effectively, emphasize the concept of service and the meaning of professionalism in this particular social situation.

Here we can see the concepts of tone and register can apply equally in both verbal and non-verbal communication. The **tone** of one's voice can connote meaning (deference, anger, fear, affection) beyond, or in addition to, the actual words being used. Thus the tone of voice is a non-verbal cue, just as we noted in the previous chapter that the tone of a particular word, a verbal communication, may connote meaning beyond the dictionary definition.

The waiter and the restaurant manager think about **register** in their body language – the acting out of their role through a bow, hand signals, pulling out a chair, opening a napkin. A particular gesture, a shrug of the shoulder, may be said to be an inappropriate **non-verbal register** for such an occasion if you expect as part of the service to be directed to a chair. The shoulder shrug says non-verbally, 'Please yourself, I couldn't care less.'

When I was at school, one of my teachers, whose subject matter bored me and whom I personally disliked, accused me of 'dumb insolence'. I had certainly transmitted a message, non-verbally, albeit one which I had not intended to! A nice example of Goffman's concept of **leakage** in action – the label attached to those messages we may give off unintentionally, unless we are sufficiently socially skilled to control them.

Keynotes
1. Non-verbal communication refers to a range of human actions and behaviour, other than the spoken word, which have a communicative function.

> 2. Just as in verbal communication, non-verbal communication is coded and interpreted differently in different social and cultural contexts.
> 3. Research suggests that if there is a contradiction between a perceived verbal communication and a perceived non-verbal communication, the latter is considered to be the more reliable cue.

Non-verbal communication cues can be classified under eight general categories. Let's start with those are implicit in the above snapshot.

1. **Touch**   Our very first experience of social interaction as an infant is being touched. Despite its being essential for satisfactory human relationships and for our mental stability, there are many studies which reveal that touch and touching, in terms of consciously or unconsciously communicating emotions, is surrounded by a vast range of social norms and taboos as to what is seen as acceptable and unacceptable. We only need to think about the cultural and personal norms surrounding the distinction between social, parent/sibling and sexual touching to recognize that.

In our context we are interested in understanding touch within the communications process as a method of control, and as an aspect of a number of rituals, such as how we greet people, how we encourage them, how we show concern and show understanding. Two very simple examples are that of patting an employee on the back to signify appreciation of a job well done, or putting our arm around a colleague's shoulder to show sympathy or to comfort. A third, equally common example, is that of shaking hands with someone on meeting him. Except that if we are French or Italian, or from a Hispanic culture, we are much more likely to opt for kissing him on both cheeks. A gesture which would be looked at askance, because of possible misconstruction, in the UK.

Despite the most basic and innate human need for physical contact, we are well aware that when we are communicating through touch, we have to be absolutely clear about the effects of social conditioning and the power of cultural norms. The escort might guide the lady to their table by holding her elbow – it is very unlikely the waiter would do that.

And if we think of the example above in which you might put your arm around someone to comfort them, the male comforting a female colleague in this way is more likely to be the case than vice versa, because the woman who touches may find her actions misconstrued. Although, having said that, in today's climate, a male colleague may be just as inhibited. Which just goes to show the power of the psychological message communicated through touch.

2. **Proximity and spatial behaviour**   In the snapshot, reference was made to people being 'cheek to jowl'. That expression reflects the feeling that as individuals we all have a **personal bubble**, the psychological, as opposed to the physical space, with which we feel most comfortable, again dependent upon the particular social situation or social interaction in which we are involved. The personal bubble or space we claim around us could be said to be a socially constructed concept of **privacy** – and woe betide those who invade that privacy without our permission!

A 'crowded restaurant' may be labelled as such because the tables are perceived to be too close together, rather than that they are all occupied. We all have this 'bubble', and although it describes something which is not visible or tangible, but is 'all in the mind', it can actually be measured in the physical sense, although the distances are determined by social norms, which vary from culture to culture. In Western societies, the radius of the bubble is roughly as follows:

- **intimate** – direct contact to around 50 cm, appropriate for emotional relationships;
- **personal** – 50 cm–1.5 m, the closeness of friends; it is interesting to note here that distance more or less reflects the distance implied in the phrase 'keeping someone at arm's length', describing a relationship in which you do not want to communicate too much;
- **social** – 1.5–4 m, business, impersonal social interactions;
- **public** – 4 m or more, for public events.

Spatial claims and spatial expectations are important to be aware of because they transmit or reinforce information about us, or allow us to perceive and interpret information about others – status, power, ownership, personal, social and professional relationships between people. For instance, people of unequal status tend to keep a greater distance from one another than those of equal status. Have you noticed how the seats in a lecture theatre always fill up first from the back, as far away from the lecturer as possible? Even the angle at which we communicate may create or reflect the nature and tone of a communications process.

In Parliament, the seating in the House of Commons reflects a power relationship based on the two-party system, in that the Government sit on one side confronting the Opposition on the other – and if you 'cross the floor' literally, you are also crossing it mentally, ideologically.

An extension of the concept of the personal bubble is that of **territoriality** – the desire to feel that certain spaces 'belong' to us, that we have control over them. Students leave their bags or jackets on seats in the library or cafeteria. Football supporters have their particular part of the ground. Top management demand a room of their own in order to enhance their status. Having a room of one's own is symbolic as well as spatial significance, part of being recognized as a private individual as well as a part of a family. And if we have to share a room as a student, we soon find ways of marking out our personal territory. The 'head of the table' or being at the 'top table' as a physical positioning also shows a social positioning relative to the others seated.

An understanding of spatial behaviour allows us to manipulate physical surroundings so that we can control both the amount and the quality of any social interaction. For instance, a conference room, a restaurant, a bar, can be physically arranged to encourage or discourage the exchange of ideas, the mixing of strangers, the socializing of friends.

3. **Body movement and gestures or kinesics** You may have seen Richard Attenborough's film, *Chaplin*, the life of one of the world's greatest actors. Charlie Chaplin's career mainly spanned the period of silent movies, and he was considered supreme among actors of the time on account of his ability to portray atmosphere, ideas, humour, the whole spectrum of human emotions, through his consummate skills in non-verbal communication. He did have the support of 'mood' music and a very few lines of dialogue in the form of subtitles, but his great talent was to be able to use the appropriate non-verbal cues which his audiences could then decode and thus identify with the character he was playing, despite the lack of the spoken word.

You may also have heard of, or even seen, the contemporary internationally famous artiste, Marcel Marceau, who is spectacularly successful in the field of mime. He does not require a costume, a prop or a piece of music, but can convey a myriad of actions and emotions and situations, such is his mastery of body movement and gesture.

Chaplin and Marceau used their body language mainly to replace speech, what we call **gestural autonomous** movements. Body language can also be used to complement speech, in which case we talk about **illustrators**. I am sure you have seen portrayals of stereotypical Frenchmen or Italians who furiously wave their hands about in order to punctuate what they are saying, to signify a mood or emotion.

A famous former mayor of New York, Fiorella LaGuardia, delivered his political speeches in three different languages – English, Italian and Yiddish. He supposedly had mastered the appropriate gestures for each language so perfectly that people could tell from newsreels the language in which he was speaking even if the sound was turned down. In contrast, the Japanese are socialized into giving away far less through facial expression, body movement and gesture than do Westerners, thus offering us far fewer gestural autonomous movements and illustrators to help the communications process along. It is thus not surprising that 'inscrutable' is the clichéd adjective often attached to those of Chinese or Japanese culture.

There is no question that the less physically flamboyant the person you are communicating with, the greater the social skill required to perceive messages coming through body language and other non-verbal cues. But equally important is how well you yourself can use body movement and gesture to reinforce or emphasize what you say.

Supplementing a talk with good use of your hands, for instance, has been shown through research to be of paramount importance in maintaining listeners' interest, conveying enthusiasm, and encouraging understanding.

Communication through body movement also involves **body posture** and **positioning**. Again there are interesting social norms and social factors to be seen at work here. We stand up when someone important comes into a room, we invite someone to sit down to put them at their ease, we lean forward to encourage communication, our shoulders 'droop' when we are sad, we sit bolt upright to show attentiveness, we put our hands on our hips to show dominance. If we want to increase materially the impact of a persuasive communication, one way of doing it is through body posture and movement, for example through presenting oneself in a more upright sitting position and increasing head-nodding.

4. **Appearance** However much we are counselled about 'never judging by appearances', all the evidence from our behaviour is to the contrary. We **do** – and it is perhaps just as well on many occasions! Because if we didn't use appearance to come to some initial judgement about someone's sex, age, social and economic status, culture, personality or occupation when social contact is first made, then what a lot of time and talk we would need to establish sufficient information to get through the early stages of the communications process!

That is why 'uniforms' are employed. They give an instant message which will condition our expectations of the communications process in some way, how it will be conducted, what its tone and register will be. The status and authority of the Restaurant Manager. The hotel staff's uniform creates an image, or message, of efficiency, group identity or the general atmosphere or ambience of the hotel or restaurant which the management wish to put over. But Moira, the Personnel Manager, was quite right to worry about judging candidates on the basis of their appearance at interview. We can all 'manipulate' our hair, face, body shape, through makeup, clothes, accessories, in order to make them serve a communication function.

Moira will be well aware of very interesting findings which reveal that in a selection interview, a candidate may be selected within the first four minutes, because interviewers are so strongly affected by physical cues. Yet these can have little or no correlation with the abilities and qualities being sought. If you were interviewed for your place as a student, do you remember how you looked, what you wore? Is that what you are wearing now? Is that what you wear regularly? You know you 'dressed for the occasion', we know that you were 'dressing for the occasion', you knew that we knew, we knew that you knew that we knew, etc.

But both sides played the social skills game. You communicated that you were an appropriate candidate for a hospitality management course, we perceived that to be the case because of your appearance (and of course all the other aspects of non-verbal communications which we have identified above which suggest you were appropriately socially skilled for such a 'people-centred' profession) and thus the manipulation was successful – feedback being that you were given a place on the course! Why then do we take part in and respond to this manipulation? You might like to think back to concepts like **socialization** and **social** role which we discussed in Chapters 1 and 2 in order to answer that question.

5. **Voice**   The total package of what might be called the 'vocal quality' or tone of voice. Talking which is perceived to be 'too fast' or 'too slow', 'too high-pitched', or to have an aggressive quality, or to be 'too loud', is interpreted to be inappropriate to the social interaction, or to give off certain cues which may either enhance or contradict the actual words used by the transmitter. The study of the messages given off by the voice itself, rather than the words produced by the voice, is called **paralinguistics**.

A voice could be described as 'sexy' because it has a certain pitch or tone which appears to convey something about the speaker's general personality and potential behaviour! Margaret Thatcher, our first female Prime Minister, took voice production lessons because the pitch and quality of her voice was reputed to have lost her votes. It had been interpreted by some as patronizing, and with too high a pitch, which then suggested petulance and peevishness with her listeners. And there is some evidence to suggest that women suffer rather more than men from being 'defined' as particular types of people on account of the quality of their voice.

Lady Thatcher's voice also appeared to give off another message to her listeners, the cue of her accent. As we have noted in Chapter 3 accent can lead us to perceive someone to have a whole cluster of attitudes, beliefs and values which makes him or her 'one of us' or 'not one of us!' Lady Thatcher's accent appeared to place her in a class category which was perceived to distance her from the average Briton, the inference being that she therefore was lacking in understanding of the ordinary person's problems.

But accent can also be a unifying factor. The receptionist responding to a stranger's request for accommodation might indeed find that an initial rapport with a prospective guest is established because they share a particular accent. Do not be confused between what accents tell us about people and what the quality of a voice communicates about them. We need to control the quality of our voice or our rate of speech in order to communicate authority, understanding, patience, whether it be in Geordie, Brummie, or West Country.

6. **Facial expression**   Given the thousands of spoken languages and dialects which have existed or do exist, it is fascinating to note that the key emotions exhibited by the tilt of an eyebrow, the position of an eyelid, the furrowing of a brow or the movement of our lips, appear to

give off the same cues in all societies past and present. A smile is a smile is a smile! And indeed we need only the barest of outlines of these key facial physical characteristics to decode the message. The whole tenor of a conversation can be judged by observing and analysing the facial expressions of the participants.

After the spoken word, facial expression is the next most important form of communication. But that's part of the problem! Studies show that we find it much easier to control what we say than control the expression on our face. It is very, very easy to 'read', or misread, the slightest raising of an eyebrow, or the downturn of a mouth, which is not surprising when we know that the face alone can produce something like 250 000 **different** expressions.

The highly socially skilled person is adept at perceiving and interpreting the more controlled and more subtle movements of the facial muscles and thus recognizing before others than someone is just about to 'lose his cool' or is actually very nervous in an interview – the biting of the lip, or the twitch of the mouth. Being aware of these signs, we can more easily rethink the communications process in order to contain conflict, or put the interviewee at her ease.

7. **Eye contact** 'If looks could kill!'; 'Don't stare at people – it's rude!'; 'Look at me when I'm talking to you!' My namesake's famous smile is famous rather more because of what her eyes are supposed to be transmitting rather than her lips. Remember the saying, 'The eyes are the mirror of the soul'? Eye contact, or the lack of it, is a very powerful medium in the communications process, owing that power to its use in terms of monitoring feedback, and encouraging or discouraging the process.

We look at someone to encourage them to speak; we look away to discourage them. We look at someone to show positive emotions; we look away from someone to show negative emotions. We use eye contact to communicate that we are listening intently – or the lack of eye contact to communicate that we are bored. We use eye contact to signify authority and status relationships – in any communications process if we try to 'stare someone out', it is invariably the one of greater authority who wins. (An experiment I repeat annually is to come in to a lecture theatre of chattering students and just look at them intently. It's amazing how threatening they find that; they soon stop chattering!)

Various studies show that uncontrollable eye contact with others induces severe stress – which is why, when we are in a lift with others, we all tend to raise our eyes to watch the floor numbers flash by, rather than catch the eye of a stranger. And if we think back to the challenge to 'look at' someone, because they are 'talking to you', then the message being given by the lack of eye contact is either guilt, or disrespect. Yet in Hispanic societies the lack of eye contact would signify the opposite – the communicating of deference or respect – and in south American and Pacific Rim countries eye contact is seen as aggressive and authoritarian. Once again an awareness of cultural differences is all-important.

8. **Silence** It can be the most difficult of all social skills to interpret the 'sound of silence', as one of my favourite Simon and Garfunkel songs goes. The communications process does not break down when the transmitter or receiver – or both – are silent. Silence itself is a form of communicating. Has anyone ever said of you that you appeared to be 'in a huff' or 'very hurt'? You weren't speaking, so a message was perceived as a direct consequence of the lack of the spoken word. Just think of the phrases 'a stony silence' or a 'deathly hush'.

Silence can convey so many thoughts and emotions, but unless it is accompanied by a number of other communications symbols, like an expression on the face, or a movement of the shoulders, we may have great difficulty interpreting it. Why is it we feel extremely uneasy on some occasions when there are long spells of silence, and you are desperate for someone to say something, anything, to break that silence! Why is it so very difficult to be silent with people we do not know very well?

After thinking about all these factors, you will recognize why a 'good' telephone technique is so important in many roles and occupations. All that helpful non-verbal communication is missing when you speak over the phone. Well, perhaps not totally – think how much worse it is for some people to speak to an answering machine than a real person. Why is that the case?

To conclude, the key distinction between verbal and non-verbal communication which we have to appreciate for the purpose of discussion is as follows. When we interpret verbal cues, we hear them or read them as discrete messages, with a beginning and an end. We can stop and think about a word or phrase in a letter. We can ask someone to repeat something she has said, and specify exactly which section of speech we want repeated. But the messages given off through non-verbal communication are not so easily dissected or even identified, because they are continuous, they may overlap, and the 'whole' may be very much more than the sum of its individual parts. Each of these eight categories above could be working in conjunction to reinforce or contradict a verbal message.

Thus you may have to work overtime to interpret all the cues someone is transmitting to you in the communications process, and you may have to work overtime establishing just how much control you have over your own non-verbal communication. This is why we can learn so much by watching ourselves on film or a videotape, because although we can to some extent appreciate what our voice sounds like to other people, we cannot see what the rest of us is communicating! I never realized just how much I used my hands when talking until I saw a speeded-up videotape of a lecture I gave. I looked like a tic-tac man on Derby Day! So I then had to assess whether my hand movements enhanced what I was saying – or in fact acted as a barrier to communication because they were so distracting.

Audio and video feedback is used so often now in teaching and training situations that I am sure you are all familiar with it. And in certain respects all the activities in which you could practise your skills in non-verbal communication should be through use of audio and videotapes, which makes it a much more difficult task for me to suggest activities for this chapter than it was for other chapters. However there is one which I am sure you will enjoy.

Take time, and a notepad, with a friend or colleague, to watch three or four runs of a TV 'soap' **with the sound turned down**. Each of you jot down who you see as the 'goodies', the 'baddies', the friendly people, the aggressive people, the sexy people, the stereotypes, and why, from what you have gleaned through the non-verbal communication. Classify the cues within the categories offered above. I cannot offer suggestions for self-assessment as I have for the other activities I am presenting you with, as I do not know which particular 'soap' you will choose to watch. But you should be able to assess each other's efforts when you compare notes with your colleague.

I would be very surprised if you did not in the main identify the same cues, and in the main agree on the communication intended. Now you have a genuine academic reason for watching *EastEnders* or *Coronation Street* – good viewing!

Keynotes
1. There are eight general categories of non-verbal communication.
2. These are touch, spatial behaviour, body movements, appearance, voice, facial expression, eye contact, and silence.
3. Each of these can be equally significant in the communications process, and good interpersonal skills mean that each can be controlled and used in order to enhance verbal communication.

Activity 4.1

Non-verbal communication serves a number of important functions. Approximately 93% of the meaning in face-to-face communication comes through non-verbal cues, and we transmit, receive and decode thousands of bits of non-verbal information every day, an appreciation of these functions is of paramount importance if we want to improve our communications skills.

The functions are as follows:

1. replacing, or substituting for speech;
2. enhancing, clarifying or reinforcing speech;
3. regulating the speech process;
4. defining or reinforcing social relationships and patterns of behaviour.

Now see if you can think of a couple of examples of each of the above which you might come across in your day as a student. Jot down the non-verbal cue and then interpret it, identifying which particular function the cue is fulfilling.

Thoughts on Activity 4.1

Firstly, remind yourself of the range of actions and behaviours which comprise non-verbal communication. These are **eye contact**, **facial expression**, **body posture** and **body positioning**, **proximity** and **spatial behaviour**, **appearance**, **use of voice** and **use of silence**.

A very comprehensive list of cues to be aware of, each with its own range of interpretation, relative to the individual, the context and the culture. But the simplest examples can raise our level of awareness of the complexity of the interaction between the verbal and the non-verbal process. Here is an example I have thought about. What are the non-verbal cues telling you?

1. **Replacing speech**   You have brought me an essay, three days later than the formal submission date. You tell me that the cat knocked a cup of coffee over your first attempt, so you had to rewrite it. I **raise my eyebrows** and **tilt my head to one side**.
2. **Enhancing speech**   In conjunction with the above behaviour, I say, 'I suppose I am expected to believe that?' in a **quizzical tone** of voice, and with **very direct eye contact** which you find difficult to avoid.
3. **Regulating the verbal communications process**   You start to tell me that what you are saying is absolutely true, and you reinforce that by **drawing a cross with your forefinger** over your throat. I respond with complete **silence**. Your voice trails away . . .
4. **Defining or reinforcing social relationships and patterns of behaviour**   I **stand up** and **move round my desk** to where you are **sitting**. I look **down** at you, **threateningly**. I say, 'I'll believe you this time, although thousands wouldn't.' **Pointing my finger at you**, I add, 'Now get off your mark and have that essay to me by the weekend.' A **grateful smile** appears on your face and you ease yourself **humbly** out of my room – **backwards**, of course!

I am sure that you decoded my non-verbal messages very accurately! And you threw in two or three appropriate non-verbals yourself to fulfil the necessary function of keeping on my right side. Now think a bit more. The above scenario depicted an authority relationship; how might I have emphasized that relationship and further intimidated you through the non-verbal cue of **appearance**? Correct – I could have worn my long black academic gown – still used as a symbol of authority in some colleges and universities. Now have a go at constructing a script for some situation within the hospitality industry, with totally different examples of the same functions.

Activity 4.2

How about testing this idea of a '**personal bubble**' or a psychological boundary with someone you know fairly well as a friend. Try to establish just how near you can be to that person before s/he 'bursts' your personal bubble. That is, makes you feel uneasy, threatened, not physically, but mentally. Stand or sit next to him or her a few times – as near as you can bear it – without of course saying what you are about! (Obviously you have to undertake this experiment with some caution, and explain afterwards what you were testing.) Now think . . .

1. At what actual, measurable distance did you begin to feel unease? At what distance did you feel the other person begin to react, to show unease?
2. What came out of the experiment in terms of the expectations you had of each other when you invaded each other's territory? What messages were being given off?
3. What did you find to be your and your partner's 'size' of bubble, given the relationship between you? Why were the bubbles that measurable size – what does it suggest about the relationship?

Thoughts on Activity 4.2

This experiment should have shown you what, roughly, is your 'effective communication distance'. That is, the distance at which you would normally talk to another whom you know fairly well. But in this experiment, there will have been a number of human factors at work which will have affected that physical measurement, reinforcing the concept of personal space being a social and psychological construct.

If your partner had been very close to you emotionally – a girlfriend or a brother – then that distance would have only been measured in centimetres. In this case, you were asked to choose merely a friend. So you probably found that a metre was roughly the level of measurement, particularly if the person was of the opposite sex. Indeed, sexual harassment can be construed in certain situations to be about an invasion of personal space, even if no physical contact has been made. And generally in western culture a man moving into a woman's space is read as far more threatening than a woman moving into a man's space.

So your findings would have to be interpreted in the light of the sexes of the two people involved. Your findings may draw out other social factors. In this experiment, it is unlikely that **status** was a factor – but what sort of reaction would you have expected had you moved round your tutor's or the manager's desk to stand beside her instead of facing her across the desk?

It may also be that **culture** would have been a factor. In certain societ ies, for example, Latin or Middle Eastern, standing very close to a relative stranger, far closer than we would be happy with in our culture, is not seen as an invasion of space, but Westerners often find it very difficult to cope mentally with this physical proximity. The concept of personal space, our need to feel we are surrounded by a psychological bubble or 'buffer', whose dimensions **we** determine, can be seen in evidence in our homes, our workplace, our leisure activities, in all our relationships with other human beings.

What is perceived to be a 'crowded' restaurant or bar by one person may be perceived by another to be 'half empty'. The physical distances between individuals is the same, but the psychological impact on the two individuals is totally different. The importance of these findings will not escape you if you are planning the seating arrangements in a restaurant, or the numbers you can cope with in a bar.

--- *Activity 4.3* ---

Here's a very simple test of your understanding of how our position in space can affect the quality and direction of our social interaction. Have a look at the following seating arrangements.

Position of participants (Fig. 4.1):
The four types of interaction these seating positions suggest are as fol-lows:

1. confrontation
2. co-action, or similar action
3. co-operation
4. conversation

Allocate the appropriate description to each seating plan. Now give two examples, from your own experience, of the type of **situation** each might be reflecting.

Thoughts on Activity 4.3

Generally two people, if they have freedom to choose, have a strong tendency to take up certain predictable spatial positions, which are dependent upon the type of interaction. This suggests that they find it easier to carry on the communications process if certain spatial arrange-ments exist. So this is a test of your application of that proposition. The answers are as follows:

• Table 1 shows **co-operation or sharing**. You and another student working on a joint project, or you and the Rooms Manager working out the staff rota for the next month.

- Table 2 shows **co-action** or doing something **similar**. You and another student working independently in the Library, or you and the Financial Manager studying the monthly accounts, but for quite different reasons.
- Table 3 shows **conversation**. You trying to console a fellow student who's just received a poorer mark for an essay than he expected, or you interviewing a prospective candidate for the position of Restaurant Manager.
- Table 4 shows **confrontation**. You and another student practising your entrepreneurial skills in a game of Monopoly, or you challenging one of the bar staff about an apparent discrepancy in the takings.

You could further test these findings by an experiment of your own. Ask two of your friends to position themselves at a table, **after** you have given them an example of one of the situations you have thought of, or that I have suggested to you. Just say something like, 'You are going to be playing a game of chess', or 'You have gone for a quick beer, there's only one table with a seat, and you don't know the other person at it.' I think you will find that your friends will follow the above pattern, if you don't give them too much time to think about it, and their choice of seat is quite spontaneous.

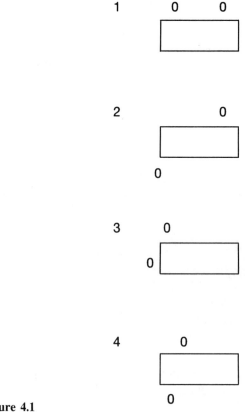

Figure 4.1

And just for a bit of extra fun, think about a table in the Coffee Bar with six empty seats . . .

Figure 4.2

Where would you choose to sit in order to divert other people from occupying the table? Test your hypothesis, or guess, if you can. This little exercise should also illustrate the concept of **territoriality**, space that people stake out as their own. The favourite chair, the favourite corner of the bar, which can apply to both individuals and groups, and which helps give them **identity**. (Remember we referred to the home team's end in the football stadium?) You can now use this understanding both to create and to manipulate personal space, including the awareness that the **angle** at which one person interacts with another affects the communications pattern. These are very important non-verbal factors in the communications process.

Activity 4.4

The manner in which we try to control and use our **space** can communicate attitudes, needs, motives, our status and role-perception, our objective in a communications process. The next time you are in any of these situations, consciously look for cues which will tell you something of the above feelings of others in the situation, and think about the functions of these spatial behaviours.

1. In a lift, observe the non-verbal behaviour, and particularly the eye contact, as the lift fills up with people.
2. Observe the pattern in which a lecture theatre or a restaurant's seats are filled up.
3. Mentally measure the physical distance between people as they queue up at a cash dispenser – or the reception desk.
4. Look at the layout of the furniture in the office of any manager you know or have worked with. What does it tell you about his or her status, personality, management style? Does the physical setting in any way reflect these factors?
5. How might you reorganize the seating in a lounge bar in a manner which you think would **discourage** communication?

Thoughts on Activity 4.4

I would be very surprised if you did not make the following observations, if you are of roughly the same Western European culture as I am.

1. The lift. If it fills up with strangers, it is more than likely that first of all, the four corners would fill up first ('keeping our distance') and then when all space was filled up, everyone would look at the floor numbers flashing past, rather than establish eye contact with a stranger! Doing that might start a communications process which was not desired.

2. Yes, you always sit as far back as possible from the lecturer! And if the lecturer is in a group listening to another lecturer, s/he probably does exactly as you – so the behaviour is not entirely a consequence of an authority relationship! It is probably more to do with a 'group solidarity' or of not wanting to appear to be a threat to the speaker, through invading his or her personal space in a highly formal setting. As far as the restaurant is concerned, say there are ten tables, each with four chairs, and ten people come in, each unknown to the others.

    So guess what? Each individual takes a separate table. A few place a bag, or a coat, or a parcel, on the seat beside them – thus marking out their personal 'bubble' or territory, a coded message that a stranger may sit opposite them, but not next to them, if there is an option! You might like to test this observation further by sitting down beside someone on a park bench, when there are other empty benches available. That someone is likely to move on fairly quickly. After all, what might you be communicating if you deliberately chose to sit next to a stranger, when there are alternatives?

3. I am sure you will have seen long queues forming outside a cash dispenser in a busy street on busy Saturday mornings. However limited the space, the person actually withdrawing money can be guaranteed at least a metre of space between him or her and the next person in the queue. It is not just a matter of hiding your PIN number. We consider withdrawing money from the bank to be a 'private' act, even if no conversation takes place and there is no other human being involved. And the psychological privacy is reflected in 'personal bubbles'.

    At the Reception Desk, the same thing happens, even if it is a busy checking-in time. An individual or a couple will be given the 'privacy' of filling in the necessary documentation, of getting their room key, because they would expect that privacy in their own home when it came to documenting personal details.

4. How near can you sit to the manager? Does the furniture arrangement allow you to lean over his or her shoulder, perch on the desk? At what angle or angles are any seats other than the seat at the desk? Do they suggest the manager expects communications to be confrontational or conversational? Is furniture in the room placed to 'give off' an air of authority or status, or to add a physical barrier to any psychological barrier? (The lecturer communicating from behind a lectern may be using that physical object to protect him psychologically from the baleful glare of a hundred students!)

5. Finally, think about the conventional arrangement of a lounge bar. Low tables, comfy chairs, arranged in circles or semi-circles, scattered around the room, in a fairly casual manner, likely to accommodate no more than eight in a group, and often segregated from the next group

by a large plant, a pillar, an extra coffee table, or other 'room divider'.

I am sure that your plan to disrupt the communications process envisages exactly the opposite of that arrangement! No tables (nowhere to put drinks, so people will not linger). Chairs designed so that we have to sit upright (people even **looking** uncomfortable and ill at ease can cause a barrier to communication). Groups of tables and chairs lined against the wall, with the central space free (so customers look like 'wallflowers' at a disco.) No physical objects separating groups. Everybody, but **everybody**, able to see everyone else, thus inhibiting intimate conversations.

Even if one cannot be heard, all the facial expressions and body language are there to tell others what is going on. It is surprising just how much we determine the outcome of a communications process through the manipulation of physical space and material objects. Or how much of an impact the relationship between the physical and the psychological actually has on us. Working close to someone to the extent that person appears to be constantly 'breathing down one's neck' is stressful because of the mental ' over-crowding' rather than any physiological effect.

Now ask two or three fellow students or friends to tackle these tasks. It is highly likely that they will come up with similar findings. And where they do not, then try to work out why the experiment's findings were different. What might have been the social or psychological factors that affected them?

--- *Activity 4.5* ---

I suggested that you had a go at interpreting the storyline of a TV 'soap opera' entirely through your reading of the cues given through non-verbal communication such as facial expression and body language. As an even simpler 'dry run' at this sort of exercise, you might like to test yourself through identifying the moods, attitudes or feelings suggested by the little drawings in Fig. 4.3. Firstly, some faces, and secondly, some figures. In both cases, you are given the minimal information, but I am sure that you will get enough to make, at least, intelligent guesses!

Thoughts on Activity 4.5

This little exercise emphasizes just how minimal **are** the cues we use to identify someone's mood and feelings. We can do this because our shared culture means we broadly share the use and the meaning of the cues, and thus come to conclusions based on these shared assumptions – that a drooping of a shoulder means a feeling of unhappiness or rejection, that a raising of an eyebrow means surprise or a suspension of belief. Other cultures may use different techniques or symbols, or the members of a particular culture may be socialized into giving less away through such facial messages or body language, for example, the Chinese or Japanese, as we have noted. So what are the messages given by these representations?

First the faces . . .

1. indifference, even boredom
2. happiness
3. sullen – or perhaps sad
4. off-colour, or tired
5. very distressed
6. questioning

and now the body language . . .

7. puzzled, perplexed
8. determined, resolute
9. excited, enthusiastic
10. shy, timid
11. welcoming, greeting
12. affected, conceited

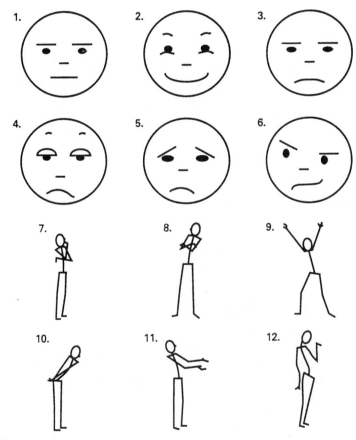

Figure 4.3

You have probably got most, if not all, of these right. But one or two may have been a bit ambiguous. Without other cues, verbal or non-verbal, you could not be absolutely sure, and determining whether someone is either sullen or unhappy, either just puzzled or in fact insecure, could be very important in the continuation of a communications process. So despite what I have said about the relative ease of decoding minimal cues, we still have to be wary about 'jumping to conclusions'.

And equally significant, this exercise complements that of Activity 3.1, in that it shows the importance of using the voice as effectively as possible in situations where there are few or no visual messages of the above sort being transmitted. Finally, these non-verbal cues in the communications process are socialized into us over our whole experience of living, so we tend to lapse into them without thinking, as if they were 'natural'. Which means that we may be totally unaware that we are giving off a non-verbal message which we do not want to transmit.

For example, a bored expression on the face when listening to a member of staff pontificating in a meeting, or body language which suggests an aggressive or unsympathetic reaction to a guest making a complaint, even if it is possibly justified. So once again, recognizing the complexity of the communications process, we are more able to control it.

_____ *Activity 4.6* _____

We have already reflected very briefly on the cues that we pick up from someone's appearance, in the sense of clothes, makeup, hair style, jewellery. Appearance is of tremendous importance in determining the context and pattern of the communications process, because we interpret so much about someone through his or her appearance, and then communicate accordingly. And not only do we interpret a great deal about the person, we also know that what someone wears can both be a consequence of that person's social role and context and a cause of that person's social behaviour. Or as Napoleon said, 'A man becomes the creature of his uniform.'

Let's therefore investigate these propositions in terms of their usefulness to hospitality managers. What information might we get about someone from his or her appearance? What specific items of 'adornment' offer us cues? The cues might be classified as follows:

1. age bracket;
2. sex and gender;
3. social class or socio-economic group;
4. status in society;
5. occupation;
6. ethnic or cultural origins;
7. personality or identity, individual or social;
8. religious, political or moral values.

Now take each one of these categories, and think of an example or two of them 'in action', deliberately constructed to give off a message, or interpreted in a particular way which would then be a factor in your communication with that individual or group.

Thoughts on Activity 4.6

You probably had no difficulty coming up with examples to illustrate these propositions. At the most general level, you might have thought of the corporate image of a hotel group or catering company being enhanced by a staff uniform. Plus the fact that the more attractive the uniform, the happier the staff will feel, and thus the more motivated. The psychological comfort we get out of feeling 'well-dressed' is partially on account of our being seen to express ourself and our identity through our clothing, so if there has to be a uniform, then let it be as flattering as possible.

It is not just for the fun of it that stewards and stewardesses on airlines have outfits which may be 'uniform', but are not quite seen as 'uniforms', because they are designed by top international fashion designers. And I'm sure if you were choosing a uniform for your waiting or housekeeping staff, you would consciously or unconsciously have a view as to what was appropriate to their average age.

If it were a very young team, then no doubt you would feel the choice of style and colour might be rather more flexible than if there were some more mature members in the team – you would not want any perception from guests that you had 'mutton dressed as lamb'. And I suspect, given the general conservativeness of the hospitality industry, that **all** staff uniforms clearly define the sex of the wearer. However fashionable the trouser suit might be, I have yet to see a female hotel employee in one, whatever her level in the organization! (Although some housekeeping departments are now giving chambermaids uniforms with trousers, certain themed restaurants such as T.G.I Friday have trousers and waistcoats for both male and female waiting staff.) But you will be well aware of the gay and lesbian community's use of clothing to 'flag' their sexuality.

Occupation and status can be seen clearly defined in the tail coat and striped trousers of the restaurant or front of house manager, and the checked trousers and tall hat of the chefs. If we note that two of the guests in the restaurant are wearing turbans, we assume that they will not be wanting the chef's speciality that night if it is 'Pork Escalopes'.

And there are other clothing cues as to religion which you will be able to identify, which will also identify distinctive eating habits. If the two guests are wearing the kilt, we might assume that with their after-dinner coffee a nice malt whisky might be worth offering, rather than a Napoleon brandy or an ouzo. If a couple arrive dressed in highly formal dinner jacket and evening dress, then the waiter assumes that they wish highly formal service – in fact see the whole occasion as a highly formal one, and thus this will colour their expectations of how they should be treated. Additionally, they will have different expectations of the gentleman who is wearing the tail coat and striped trousers, than they will have of the gentleman at the front door in the somewhat military uniform.

And why that military uniform in the first place? Because it appears to encourage a certain pride in a job which in itself might be seen as essentially low-status. You probably also thought of the example of many up-market hotels and restaurants who have a 'dress policy' for guests. No denims, no open-necked shirts, jackets for the men, dressing for dinner – meaning rather more than merely covering one's body! Guests who wished to imbibe the atmosphere of a prestigious establishment along with the food have to comply, whatever their financial standing. Why? Society and culture had defined what was appropriate clothing for that sort of establishment, which was nothing to do with what might be seen to be a more important factor, the reality of whether the guest could pay or not.

In Mars and Nicod's book, *The World of Waiters*, to which I have already referred, there is a section where they discuss how waiters classify customers as they come into a restaurant, in order that they know what to expect from the customer, what s/he expects from them, and how best they should maintain goodwill. Where there are any doubts about the interaction process, waiters appear to use as conclusive proof, the form of dress. It may be a rough and ready guide, but it 'helps place people on the social map' and 'clarifies the nature and purpose of the diner'. So as usual, Shakespeare seemed to have got there long before the social psychologists, when he wrote, 'Apparel oft proclaims the man!'

FURTHER READING

Argyle, M. (1975) *Bodily Communication*, Methuen, London: the seminal book on body language. Despite its highly academic approach, the background research and examples referred to are immediately accessible – you do not need to be a social psychologist to appreciate them.

Morris, D. (1977) *Manwatching*, Cape, London: 'pop' psychology this time, and with a politically incorrect title, but nonetheless a very interesting introduction to most aspects of non-verbal communication.

Sommer, R. (1969) *Personal Space*, Prentice-Hall, New York: another seminal book, which, despite its date of publication, is still probably the best in the field for our purposes. The concentration here is on spatial behaviour relative to the built environment, but the psychological concepts are the same as those referred to in the chapter.

Interpersonal skills and conflict-resolution 5

The soft word that turneth away wrath. (Old Testament)

Question 5: Is it as easy to talk one's way out of trouble, as it appears to be to talk one's way into trouble? What's the 'soft word that turneth away wrath?' What is the language of conflict-resolution?

> ### Snapshot
> Marie: 'I thought I'd take the two guys from the interior decorator's to that new French bistro just as a change to entertaining in the hotel restaurant, but it was a big mistake. Talk about making a drama out of a crisis!'
>
> Campbell: 'That surprises me. I like that place, the staff are so professional and customer-friendly.'
>
> Marie: 'It's not the staff – I agree with you – they couldn't be more professional. The glass of house wine we ordered was pretty unpalatable, probably because the bottle had been sitting around open for too long, so our very obliging and understanding waiter replaced it. But on our way out, the manager confronted me with the challenge "I understand you didn't like the wine" in a tone which suggested I was obliged to, and when I said "no" , he literally snarled, "What do you expect for £1.30?"'
>
> Campbell: 'Well, I would certainly at least have expected something drinkable, if not memorable. And given the probable mark-up on the bottle, it wasn't a cheap glass of wine anyway, so it was an unnecessary as well as a rude comment.'

The potential for conflict arises during the communications process when two people or a group of people have a disagreement over a fact, an idea, an objective, or a value. But because conflict is generally perceived to be negative, we are inclined to shy away from arguing, being emotional, or showing disagreement. So sometimes we agree too easily – and then lose the advantage that conflict can bring. That is the avoidance of bad decisions and the bringing out of alternative ideas and decisions. This may require that we have to **assert** a position, make a statement, even if we think it might initially cause some unease.

The sources of conflict within organizations are many, but the human element is always there somewhere, and it is worth taking a minute to reflect just how often conflict in organizations with which you are familiar has come about either because of poor communications and interpersonal skills or has not been resolved effectively for the same reason. Let's look initially at this concept of **assertiveness** and its role in avoiding or dealing with conflict.

There is a school of thought which argues that women should go on 'assertiveness training' courses, because the female socialization process is such that women find it very difficult to 'stand up for themselves', to be able to complain without sounding as if they are 'whining', to give orders without sounding 'authoritarian', to argue their case without sounding 'domineering', or to take criticism without bursting into tears! Whether you agree or not that is the case, you will certainly recognize that these are obvious examples of what appears to be the communications process breaking down.

In other words, either in transmission or in reception, the message is interpreted as negative, and unlikely to encourage a continuation of the process, as a consequence of what has been given off by the tone and register of the communication. Now the problem may be a matter of **male** perception, that our mainly male business and professional world tend, because of their male socialization, to label women as 'the gentle sex'.

Women have to a great extent been socialized into subscribing to that role, and thus it is can be difficult initially to adopt the more formal tone and register of business and professional communication, and thus to be assertive. And the woman who bursts into tears when she is angry or frustrated with a business colleague is reflecting the norms of society which does not allow her the freedom to show her feelings through other forms of communication. The tears are in place of a few choice curses!

But is assertiveness training something that is peculiarly required by women? The ability to be assertive, to be able to state openly and clearly your feelings, point of view, objectives, in situations of potential conflict and communications breakdowns, and to stand by what you honestly feel and think, without being perceived as aggressive, is an interpersonal skill which may be required even more by men, because of **their** socialization process, which in our culture generally encourages that behaviour. And in our snapshot above, the male restaurant manager appeared not to be able to defend his wine or his reputation without being aggressive.

This was in fact a real incident. The snapshot was constructed almost verbatim from a letter that was in a national Sunday newspaper some months ago. Here indeed was assertiveness – a British customer who dared to complain about the wine in a restaurant – responded to in a manner which certainly discouraged the communications process, and lost three, possibly four customers to the restaurant. How unnecessary – even if the wine were undrinkable, and the manager knew it! Incidentally, you might like to muse as to whether the manager in the snapshot would have responded in such an aggressive way to an assertive male customer!

Assertiveness skills are useful in any communications process in which there is likely to be a conflict of ideas, power, objectives, even personalities. For example, in leading and motivating, giving and receiving feedback, taking an active part in meetings, or negotiating. And as ever the narrow boundary between what is success or failure in these areas may depend far more upon the tone and register of the language used, not upon the facts, issues, or goals in the communications process; we could 'eat our words' when what seemed to be a simple straightforward and even appropriate statement or comment has escalated into unnecessary conflict.

So a clear appreciation of what is considered to be assertive behaviour – a very positive way of controlling situations through the communications process – is yet another facet of interpersonal skills, another way of thinking about 'it's not what I say, it's the way that I say it'. Let's see what this means in practice.

Initially we could try to classify styles of communicating and types of behaviour (always remembering that non-verbal communication contributes to the overall tone and register). Firstly, there is the **aggressive** communication, which threatens, and which is likely to create barriers to the process because of fear, resentment or anger. The receiver backs off, or comes back equally aggressively. Both parties have lost control of the situation. Then there is the **passive** communication. The transmitter backs off, opts out of continuing a debate, or apologizes for the sake of peace.

Thirdly, there is perhaps the most difficult to deal with, because it may not be so obvious, and that is the **manipulative** communication, cunning, the achieving of one's goals 'through the back door', without being open and honest, appearing to be submissive but in fact aggressive by its nature in a different way. Finally there is the **assertive** communication, in which the transmitter recognizes that s/he has a right to an honestly held view, a right to be heard, and a right to have that view considered by others.

Now how would **you** have handled Marie if you were the restaurant manager in the above situation? Passive – 'Yes, I agree, madam, it's obviously the fault of our suppliers, it's nothing to do with us.' Manipulative – 'Well, of course, madam, perhaps you're not very well acquainted with the style of our house wine. I've not had any complaints before, our customers generally seem very happy with it.' Or assertive – 'I'm sorry you do not like it. It is usually quite popular, although obviously wine is a very personal taste. Can I offer you another comparable wine instead?'

I'm sure that you can think of a number of ways you could have asserted (a) you are generally happy about your house wine and (b) you know enough about wines as a professional to be able to make a proposal which will encourage the customer to come back, which, hopefully, she does, because her views have been treated with respect, even if you personally did not agree with them.

> ### Keynotes
> 1. Conflict arises during the communications process when two people or a group of people have a potential disagreement over an idea, objective, or value.
> 2. 'Assertiveness' is the label for behaviour, verbal and non-verbal, which implies personal confidence and control of the communications process, without the creation of conflict arising at the expense of either the transmitter or the receiver.
> 3. Alternative styles of behaviour, which lead to loss of control and produce negative results, can be labelled as 'passive', 'manipulative' and 'aggressive'.

So practising how to be assertive, what sort of language, style, tone, register, is required to deal with simple disagreements, will go some way towards not being perceived as 'whining' (manipulative) or 'domineering' (aggressive.) At this stage you might like to test your understanding by deciding how you would label 'bursting into tears'. Is that manipulative, aggressive, or passive behaviour? I am sure you will say, 'It depends upon how it is interpreted by the person on the receiving end – whether he or she is frightened by it, suspicious of it or contemptuous of it.'

However it is important to remember that all conflict is not simply a matter of a communications breakdown, or of poor social skills. If we are involved in conflict, we are necessarily involved in communicating, but the conflict itself does not necessarily come from poor communications. Indeed conflict may be based on genuine intellectual disagreement between two people or within a group. If you are involved in a disagreement as to the conclusions to be drawn from certain data collated by, say, marketing research specialists, then the disagreement or conflict may result in much better information change or decision-making.

It's the **management** of the conflict, the ability to keep disagreement out of the realm of personalities, attitudes, values, as opposed to disagreements over facts, which requires the sophisticated communications skills. This is not nearly as easy at it seems, because we live in a world in which very often there does not appear to be any objective 'reality' or intellectual impartiality, and each side in a conflict perceives his or her 'reality' to be the correct version.

Think about the following case study of interpersonal conflict over a restaurant meal, again a real situation, which featured in perhaps a rather unusual channel for such debate, the letters page of a national

newspaper during June 1993. It builds on elements of what was interpreted by one party as being assertive, and by the other as aggressive
behaviour, and it illustrates how that behaviour eventually resulted in
real conflict.

The correspondence took place between Michael Winner, one of
Britain's most famous film producer/directors, and the Head Chef
of one of Britain's most prestigious gourmet restaurants. It was the
consequence of Michael Winner writing fairly light-hearted articles
evaluating the food and service at a number of English restaurants,
ranging from the highly famed to the relatively unknown. The correspondence centred around a conflict as to whether Mr Winner had
received both the food and the service he thought he was entitled to
from this prestigious establishment, given what he had paid for his
meal. A conflict which I am sure you will recognize does happen every
so often in restaurants!

The correspondence gave the facts as seen by both parties. There
appeared to be a conflict over the size of the table Mr Winner was
given. There appeared to be a conflict as to whether that table was too
close to other guests. There appeared to be a conflict as to whether he
had to wait too long for his meal. There appeared to be a conflict as
whether the food was any good when it did arrive. This is a simple and
yet very good example, at the **interpersonal** level (we will be coming
back to conflict at the **organizational** level in a later chapter) which can
be used to illustrate beautifully for us the dynamics of a conflict situation, the sequence of events. The correspondence did not reveal in so
many words the outcome of the conflict – except that we can be fairly
sure Mr Winner will not be visiting this restaurant again – and probably would not be welcome if he did!

There are usually a number of verbal and non-verbal cues which
suggest to us when an 'argument' is about to become a 'conflict'. The
shift from what is seen as assertive language to that which is interpreted as aggressive is often quite obvious. But it was not necessarily
so in this case, where the 'surface' causes of the conflict seemed to be
about the organization and administration within the restaurant, and
the quality of the food. Now one could certainly argue quite amicably
about the quality of a meal, because that can be a very personal judgement. But in this case, it is unlikely that a meal costing £120 (for two,
I would hastily add!) would not by most standards be very, very good,
given that the restaurant in question had two Michelin stars.

So what **was** the conflict about? Was it about facts or emotions? Was
it about interpretations of specific 'events' – things seen, heard, tasted
– or about personalities, attitudes, status? Was it about values and
ideals (in this case the 'ideal' food and service, the concept of value for
money.) Probably none of you know Mr Winner, or the Head Chef in
question. But to understand what that conflict was about, we can draw
upon our general bank of understanding human behaviour in the communications process. I don't **know** what the conflict was about – but

let's review these human elements which could play a part. **Not** matters of fact, but perhaps matters of status, role-perception, self-esteem.

Can this conflict be analysed and explained through these concepts? Could it have been resolved by having an understanding of these human elements, and handled in a manner which asserted the authority and professional skills of the Head Chef, but contained the incipient aggressiveness when a customer is not seen to be 'always right'? At what stage did it become a conflict? And how might it be resolved? Does someone have to concede defeat, lose face – a result which most of us would take to rather unkindly? If that is the case, then that is not a 'recipe' for a continuation of the communications process.

So it is important to establish the stages of another 'recipe', in this case the recipe for conflict. That recipe is a dynamic process, with a sequence of steps or stages. Recognition of the 'ingredients' and how and when they interact allows the outcome to be controlled, just as knowing how and when the interaction of egg and olive oil emulsifies into a smooth mayonnaise – or curdles into a grainy mess!

Firstly, we have to be aware of a basic ingredient in certain communications process, that of the **latent** stage, when conditions exist which are potential irritators. Power differences, role pressures, competition for scarce resources (which may be physical, material or human – say, a claim on limited space in an office, or on someone's time or attention). In the situation above, the conditions were that the customer believed he was entitled to certain standards of food and service, and was well-known and vociferous about it, the restaurateur had a highly successful reputation in that area to uphold, and there was pressure on space in the restaurant.

Secondly, there is the **perceived** stage, the **recognition** that a conflict does exist. The customer is perceived by the restaurateur to be making unnecessary or arbitrary demands – a table when the restaurant was already fully booked, and a table of a certain size.

Thirdly, there is the **felt** stage. The conflict has become **personalized**; both parties are beginning to articulate their feelings, to show awareness that there is now tension. Mr Winner states that ... the Head Chef responds that ...

Fourthly, there is the **manifest stage**. There is a public, observable argument taking place, initially in the restaurant, then in the columns of a national newspaper, and one which draws in other observers of the argument, which further perceptions of what appeared to have happened. This is the stage when the conflict must be resolved, or some positive value be drawn from it if effective communications is to continue. ('Will Mr Winner ever go back to the restaurant, whatever its gourmet reputation? Will the Head Chef ever want him to, whatever Mr Winner's bank balance?)

Finally, the **aftermath**, which describes the resulting relationship between the parties in the conflict. That was the dynamic, or sequence, of events. But was the conflict resolved – or merely suppressed? Resolution? Mr Winner tries the restaurant again, having been placated by

Respect.

the Head Chef, who presents his point of view, in a manner which is assertive, not passive, so his self-esteem and credibility is not at risk, while Mr Winner accepts the position in a manner which allows him to assert his point of view without losing his self-esteem and credibility. Suppression? Mr Winner does not visit the restaurant ever again, advises his friends, and readers, not to – and the Head Chef continues to prepare and present his food in the manner to which he has always been accustomed, ignoring the complaints as merely a sign of a customer with an aggressive nature.

That example of a conflict situation also illustrates the 'two-faced' nature of conflict. As I pointed out initially, conflict can be healthy, it can lead to improved ideas, new approaches, a surfacing and resolution of problems. Should one start from the premise that the customer is always right – in which case there is no latent stage or cause? And did the conflict result in the Head Chef reconsidering his booking practices, his menus, his recipes, thus preventing possible future conflicts? Or was the aftermath actually a suppression of the conflict – neither party prepared to concede, opposing perceptions reinforced, self-esteem challenged, ignored? What do you think?

Keynotes

1. A conflict generally goes through a number of identifiable stages.
2. In order to manage conflict a first step is to recognize these stages.
3. They are as follows:

Stage 1	Latent conflict
Stage 2	Perceived
Stage 3	Felt
Stage 4	Manifest
Stage 5	Aftermath

We have thought about how conflict can arise from merely an ill-chosen word or phrase through a combination of verbal and non-verbal factors, and a pattern or stages of development. Can we now work out how to deal with it, to make it 'work' for us? For example, what interpersonal skills help us deal with complaints without either party 'losing face'. 'Shoving it under the carpet' or suppressing it is not good for business.

As stated previously, we in the UK are very bad at complaining – unlike our American or Continental European equivalents (yes, that is another cultural difference in our behaviour – we do not appear to have the interpersonal skills to complain, or receive a complaint, without 'creating a scene'). So if we get bad food or service in an hotel, or restaurant, we 'vote with our feet'. We just do not go back – and the management then never learn what they are doing wrong.

Yet research (Gilbert, 1989) shows that very little is spent on buying advertising by most hotels outside the major hotel groups, as so much custom is overtly designed to come from the generation of repeat business. Which of course supports one approach to removing latent conflict – encouraging customers – or indeed staff – to complain, and rewarding them for it! And in addition, what is spread by 'word of mouth' advertising may be the only manner in which 'brand difference', the distinction between one hotel or restaurant and another, is identified. Indeed, you might like to undertake a little survey among hoteliers you know; ask them how many would share the views of one country house hotel-owner who believed that one should 'earn one's custom, rather than buy it'.

Interestingly in this context, the final letter in the Winner correspondence came from an 'outside' but self-interested observer, the chairman of the company which owned the restaurant, who remarked that the more publicity the restaurant got through Mr Winner's statements, the 'more customers are, as a direct consequence, visiting and enjoying the restaurant'. So who **were** the winners in this conflict!

Let's get back to thinking how we might go about using our communications skills to resolve conflict at this interpersonal level. There are a number of possible ways in which we can manage conflict. Of course, you can do a 'Marco Pierre White' and throw a tantrum, or a frying pan! Or, as he also has done, refuse the offending customer entry on another occasion. Now, that's a recipe for disaster! (Unless of course we feel that being on the receiving end of a Marco Pierre White tantrum does something positive for our image or self-esteem – which for some people it might. That certainly tells us something important about the irrationality, and thus unpredictability, of human behaviour!) So let's look at the less dramatic techniques which are available to us.

Firstly we have to establish our overall goal or **strategy** – are we making an omelette or a soufflé? Or if we keep to the scenario above, do we care if this customer comes back? Might we gain more in the long run, if we concede the customer **must** be right, and offer him another £120 meal free to compensate for what he perceived to be bad food and service, in the hope that he will renew his custom, honour being satisfied ('honour' of course being about self-esteem) In other words, do we want the outcome to be a **win/win** situation (honour on **both** sides being satisfied).

Or are we prepared to accept a **win/lose** situation (I have retained my self-esteem, maintained my stance on what good food and service is about, even if I have lost a high-paying customer). The strategy we decide upon with determine the style and tone of the communications process.

Obviously what we want to achieve is the **win/win** situation, which may require considerable interpersonal skills on occasions! Having to clarify exactly what the problem is, and therefore the appropriate strategy means working back to the stages of **latent** and **perceived** conflict. But it is often difficult for one person to avoid a **lose/lose** situation, or to change a **win/lose** situation into a **win/win** situation on his or her own – both parties need to be involved. And that means sharing exactly what you are disagreeing about, trying to see the situation from the other person's point of view, and then getting involved in a **transaction** (remember that word from Chapter 1?) in order to come to a real solution, not merely a surface agreement.

You don't want the conflict **aftermath** to be that of a problem being pushed under the carpet, to re-emerge on another occasion or in another context. Was Michael Winner right about the cramped conditions in the restaurant? Did the Head Chef in question achieve a **win/win** situation through his correspondence with Mr Winner? He was certainly publicly prepared to emphasize his own standards; could that have brought him increased custom? Was there anything in it for Mr Winner, perhaps getting better service as a result in other restaurants?

Compare two approaches.

One starts with the statement 'I understand why you are upset. I think I probably would be too, in the circumstances. Can we [note 'we', not 'I' – this implies to the listener an openness to negotiating, rather than stating, what the problem is] identify exactly what you would see the problem to be?'

The other starts with the statement 'Anyone can see that . . .' or 'If you really knew what you were talking about . . .' an approach that was apparent in our opening snapshot.

So what are the guidelines for the language of **conflict-resolution**? Again, we want to draw on some general methods, just as we might consult a recipe book which suggests 300 ways of serving eggs. There could be said to be several methods, which may be used individually, or in combination.

We have made reference above to **force**, in the physical sense, in fact, the use of a frying pan. No, I am not suggesting Marco Pierre White should deal with recalcitrant customers, or staff, for that matter, by hitting them over the head with a frying pan! Although I must say I would find him rather frightening even if he were only waving it around! Of course, you can use 'force', as a manager. You certainly can resolve a conflict by threatening a member of staff, by harshly reminding them that you are the boss, and what you say, goes.

Is that a **win/win**, or a **win/lose** situation? Or is it in fact ultimately a **lose/lose** strategy? We will be returning to this debate in another context when we discuss **leadership** in the next section, so keep it on the 'back burner' at the moment. But let's assume for the present discussion that physical force is not an option, and threats generally cannot be other than a lose/lose strategy, for obvious reasons.

One alternative is complete **withdrawal**. Avoid the person, ignore the cause of the conflict, hope it will 'go away'. Sometimes we do this because we are not capable of being assertive enough to handle the situation. Back to the observation about the British finding it very difficult to complain about bad food or bad service! But now you know what being 'assertive' is all about – so you won't withdraw!

Another similar tactic is often labelled as **smoothing** or **placating**. Try that tactic with a colleague or fellow student – what I call the 'there, there' approach. Better still, get a colleague to try it with you. Does it resolve the conflict? Or does it just sound patronizing? Or does it perhaps offer a verbal cue to an opponent – that one is frightened or insecure as to their position? And it's often linked up with a non-verbal cue – a tone of voice, or a facial expression or some body language that suggests a backing down.

If you think about the message being given off in a negotiating situation, then you will realize that there may be occasions where appearing to be placatory for the sake of the communication process continuing, then you will see its inappropriateness in that context. The 'soft word that turneth away wrath' may be merely another form of **withdrawal**. Then there is **compromise** – reaching a solution in which you both win something – but not everything. Is that about the best of both worlds, or the worst of all worlds? You will perhaps be better able to judge the answer to this when we look again at negotiating skills in formal meetings in Chapter 8.

Finally, what about the **problem-solving** approach? You may of course argue that all the previous approaches are about solving the problem – just solving it in different ways! So perhaps another food analogy would help. When we add salt to our soup, it is one way of tackling the problem of the soup not being properly flavoured. But in fact, we may exacerbate the problem, as it was not salt the soup needed, but instead a good rich basic stock. The soup is now too salty, and the real problem is still there, although we might find the soup initially more palatable.

So the problem-solving approach requires us to face up to the real issue, confront it, and discuss it with your opponent. This means that you **level** with each other, that you are able to present, you can assert your own emotions, attitudes, beliefs, values, perceptions, as well as listening and attending to the other person's emotions, attitudes, beliefs, values, perceptions. The issue at the heart of the conflict is then seen not only as an establishing of some agreement as to the **facts** of the situation, but also the **feelings** which it arouses in both of you, and the **context** within which the conflict arose.

In the Winner conflict, was the food in the restaurant **really** bad, the service **really** poor? To repeat, we don't know. But could Mr Winner have identified a latent cause of conflict when he wrote what he thought to be a fairly frivolous but provocative article? Could the Head Chef have responded differently once the conflict had reached the manifest stage? Could each have faced up to the **real** problem, which caused the breakdown in communications, that of both parties perceiving it as a personal threat to their status and self-esteem?

To conclude, another school of thought, in quite a different discipline from that of social psychology and sociolinguistics, would argue that conflict is endemic in the human condition. If we do start from that base line, then management has a responsibility to anticipate its latency in any human interaction, not through cynicism, but through recognition of the reality. Organizational studies reveal that even in the best-run and happiest of organizations, the interests and goals of the individuals within it may conflict with the interests and goals of the organization, and we will be making reference to these findings in the following chapters on leadership and group dynamics.

You may already have had many debates within your business and financial studies on the conflict between offering that which the guest or customer considers to be the best of service in the hospitality industry, and the maximization of profit. 'Boil-in-the-bag' meals, computerized reception desks, automatic drinks vending machines in corridors, are just a few examples which get my students stirred up. And it is very easy to appreciate that the statement '**the customer is always right**' is indeed a perpetual latent recipe for conflict!

Keynotes

1. There are two possible positive strategies for conflict-management. These are a win/win strategy, and a win/lose strategy.
2. The third outcome of conflict-management is a lose/lose result, which may be the outcome of having no strategy at all.
3. Methods for reducing conflict include force, withdrawal, smoothing, compromise, problem-solving and levelling.

Activity 5.1

When did you last disagree with someone? Within the last few days, hours, perhaps minutes? It would be a strange, and probably very boring world, if we were all in agreement all the time! It is not always that a disagreement or argument looks like ending in real conflict, but there may be many occasions on which you feel it is going to, although you most sincerely hope not. So being able to 'manage' an argument to ensure that it does not slide into conflict is a very useful social skill.

We want to be able to continue the communications process – to 'agree to disagree' – so that we can get on with the people with whom we work, even after significant disputes. And this is even more important if we are working in a team, or the setting is very formal. For instance in a committee, where disputes are recorded – and emotions may be! Obviously it helps enormously if you appreciate what **type** of disagreement, or conflict, you are involved in, in order that you can work out ways of dealing with it. So think of your last disagreement, or row, with a fellow student, or friend, or relation.

- Was it a dispute about **facts**? 'What is . . .?' 'What does . . . mean?'
- Or was it about **people**? Someone throwing his weight about? Someone ignoring a social 'norm'? Or just someone you didn't like and so couldn't bear to agree with?
- Or was it far more fundamental – over **basic values** – someone's religious, moral, or political views?

Jot down your answers to these questions, recognizing of course that you may not be able to separate out one specific factor, but that there is an overlap, and your disagreement actually involved two, or all three of these factors. If so, try and establish which caused the initial breakdown, and then try and evaluate which you found the most difficult to deal with – either from your own viewpoint or that of your 'opponent'. Then, dependent upon the identification of the problem, how might the conflict be resolved?

Thoughts on Activity 5.1

What sort of things did you jot down? 'I had a disagreement with a colleague about whether we should have had red and white or blue and white flowers delivered for the banquet this evening.' 'I understood she was to come on shift at 10 pm, and we fell out when I complained that she was half an hour late.'

A conflict over facts?   What order had gone into the florists? Whether you had been told there was a change of mind some time between your agreeing on blue flowers and someone deciding there should be red flowers? What time you expected the head receptionist to take over, and when she actually arrived?

Resolution?   Check the florist's invoice. Ask why the change. Point out that you had not been told there was a very good reason for the change (it was St Valentine's Day) which you would certainly have supported, had you known. Check the staff rota. The head receptionist had been given an extra half hour off because she was at a special family function, and the manager had forgotten to let you know. You respond positively by accepting his apologies, and negotiate an extra half hour time off for yourself on another occasion.

A conflict over personalities and attitudes?   'He refuses to tell me anything, because he hopes he'll get the credit for a good idea.' 'She just takes advantage of her position, and I don't see why I should stand for it. And it shows that the manager doesn't care about us minions.'

Resolution? 'Why don't you tell me know when you've have a good idea like that – I can tell the others and you'll get even more credit.' 'I appreciate your reason for being later, but perhaps you could point out to the boss that I was a bit put out by him forgetting to tell me – I wasn't quite sure what was happening.'

Or did you think the conflicts were about **fundamental views and values**? 'He has no feeling for the need to communicate with staff.' 'Basically he is not interested in "human-relations" management techniques.'

Resolution? Think – is there one? Isn't this a bit about arguing over religion, or politics? Aren't these disagreements about someone's view of the nature of people – about their needs and wants? Is this a situation where we just have to 'agree to disagree' – and it's stress management we are talking about, perhaps?

The above shows us the importance of understanding **exactly** what a conflict is about. Because unless we understand what it is about in the first place, we cannot think our way through to the appropriate communications skills we need to resolve it – or to live with it!

Activity 5.2

The following exercises will not only test your perception of the tone of the statements made, but also, because you are going to be reading what I perceive the reponses to mean, bring home to you that you and I could genuinely differ considerably in our perceptions! Which is part of the problem. Did your mum or dad ever say to you, 'Don't speak to me like that!' and you wondered what 'that' meant? Such is the nature of these exercises – and of perception.

A. Each of the following statements can be categorized as either (a) **aggressive**, (b) **manipulative**, or (c) **passive**. Identify which each one is, and re-phrase it in an **assertive** manner.

1. 'Just because I'm a new member of staff doesn't mean to say I've not got some worthwhile views.'
2. 'OK, so the dessert collapsing tonight was a disaster. What's happened to your sense of humour?'
3. 'The date set for that finance meeting clashes with another meeting for me, but I suppose I should go along with it if everyone else is happy.'

B. Now, how might you criticize a member of staff for an incorrect procedure without shattering their self-esteem but while maintaining your superior role?

C. What about valid and invalid criticism – can you respond assertively, as opposed to aggressively, to that? You have (validly) been accused of forgetting to attend an important business meeting. And you have (invalidly) been accused of having a poor attitude towards your work?

D. Finally, how do you say 'no' to (a) your boss, who wants you to work overtime at short notice and (b) a guest, who is insisting on calling the general manager to deal with an issue which can easily be dealt with at your level?

Thoughts on Activity 5.2

A. This is how I would perceive the tone of these statements. Of course you will recognize that the tone of the statements, in terms of the **words** used, would be complemented by the tone of the **voice**. A great deal depends upon what you know of the transmitter, as the same statement made by different individuals in differing contexts could be interpreted in different ways. So all I am doing here is giving an **example** of a statement which could be labelled in one of these three ways. This should encourage you to 'tune in' to statements which might be interpreted in similarly negative ways, and help clarify the distinction between responses which are negative and responses which are positive, or **assertive** – taking a stance, making a point, in a manner which will not be a barrier to further communication.

1. An **aggressive** statement, likely to invoke an aggressive response, which may set the mood for the ensuing communications process. However this is a good example of the possibility of other interpretations or another category for the same statement. A coquettish tone of voice for statement 1 could indicate that it is in the **manipulative** category, rather than the aggressive category, although that would also be considered a negative way of communicating.

Assertive: 'I know that I have not been with the organization very long, but I have already some idea of what is going on, so I would certainly be prepared to offer my view of the situation.'

2. A **manipulative** statement, making the receiver feel as if s/he is failing in some way, rather than who or what caused the problem referred to. Manipulating emotions rather than dealing with facts, a form of controlling in an insidious way.

Assertive: 'I agree that the dessert collapsing was a disaster. Let's just make sure it doesn't happen again, and no doubt one day we will laugh about it when we look back.'

3. A **passive** statement. The individual concerned is obviously unhappy about a proposal, lets him/herself become a 'victim', will not or cannot

make a constructive response. Again the mood being set for the occasion is likely not to be the most positive if there is an unwilling participant.

Assertive: 'I actually have another meeting at that time, which I would be unhappy to miss. But I will give my apologies if the time is the most suitable for everyone else.'

Now let's look at Exercises B and C. It is never easy to give or to respond to criticism as our natural tendency to become defensive becomes a communications barrier. So the trick is to avoid being aggressive towards the **individual** but assertive about the **behaviour**. Not 'that was a very thoughtless way you handled that situation'; rather 'that sort of situation might have been handled better had you tried . . .'

Exercise C suggests two situations in which you have to **respond** to criticism, again being assertive rather than aggressive. The objective of the communications process is that you retain your control and personal dignity while giving the appropriate **operational** response – meaning that, whether the criticism is valid or invalid, you are entitled to be heard and responded to as a human being with feelings and needs as well as a member of an organization which depends upon you to fulfil certain functions.

These might be your responses:

1. **The valid criticism**   You own up and offer a positive solution. 'Yes, I did forget the meeting, and there is really no excuse for that. However I shall make extra sure I get filled in on all the details and any decisions which affect my responsibilities as soon as I can.'
2. **The invalid criticism**   You do not reject it initially, but prompt for more specific information. 'I'm sorry you feel I've got the wrong attitude to my work. I wonder why you think that. What exactly is bothering you?'

C. Finally, how to say 'no'. The technique here is to make sure that you are rejecting the request, not the person. Say exactly what you want to say at the outset ('No') and be polite but firm (the tone of voice is a key cue here). For example, to the boss, 'No, I'm afraid I can't tonight. I already have a previous commitment. But I'm quite happy to do an extra shift next week.' And to the guest who is insisting on speaking to the general manager. 'The general manager is not available this afternoon, madam. But I know that I can deal with your problem, so let's discuss it right away.'

Remember, assertive behaviour is about saying what you mean and meaning what you say, without being arrogant or selfish or insensitive or disinterested in others' needs or rights. And interpersonal skills are not about being nice, self-effacing, apologetic, always seeking approval in defence of our own needs or rights. Individuals who see the communications process as about the latter usually end up being described as 'nice' or 'pleasant' or 'unassuming'. Fine. But these are not generally the sort of people who become role models, leaders.

Self-assertion is basically about believing in ourselves, with all our strengths and weaknesses, and having the confidence to convey this belief to others. We will be looking at these characteristics again in Chapters 5 and 6 when we look at conflict-resolution and leadership skills. So don't lose sight of these relatively simple communications techniques.

Activity 5.3

Your first understanding of the importance of committee work could be while you are a student, where you have to think about the role and skills of the student who represents your interests on a committee within the college or university. And just as in many other committees, the human elements of self-esteem, role and status may intervene in the formal communications process and provide a recipe for conflict. Think about the following scenario.

You are the student representative on the Departmental Course Committee, which is chaired by the Head of the Department, and comprises, in addition to you, all members of staff who teach on your Hospitality Management course. Your role is as follows:

1. To represent the views of your fellow students as individuals, as a group or as the whole class. These 'views' can be ideas, problems, requests for information and/or explanation, proposals for improvements, your evaluation of the content, presentation and administration of the course as a whole.
2. To give your fellow students, as a class, feedback on whatever the Course Committee's deliberations are, whatever decisions are made and why, and the consequences of these decisions for you all, individually or collectively.

To do your job as representative properly, you must be fully briefed as to what you are to say. You must also be aware of how you are going to represent your fellow students, of the **desired** outcomes of your being part of the Committee, and of the **possible** outcomes, given the role, function and membership of the Committee.

Thus in advance you must establish:

1. What items you have to put forward and why?
2. What sort of approach (the 'encoding' process) you think should be taken on these items?
3. Which of these may cause conflict and why?
4. How much conflict can be 'negotiated away' – how can a WIN/WIN situation be established?

What strategies should you be discussing with your fellow students, given what you know of this formal communications mechanism (the operational requirements of the organization) and of the informal (or human needs) aspects which have to be taken into account? That is, the personalities,

goals, motives, needs, of those involved. Just as you would want to prepare for a demonstration of nouvelle cuisine by having all the ingredients
required for your recipe to hand before you launch on the demonstration,
so you have a number of 'ingredients' to be thought about before you
launch into such a meeting. So what's your recipe for success in this
scenario?

Thoughts on Activity 5.3

Of course, I can only guess at the sort of items you might want to put
forward, but my experience on such a committee suggests that worries
about the amount of assessment and the relevance of some of the content of the course are fairly regular subjects! So let's use these two issues
as the basis of our discussion.

At the outset, the **desired** outcome for the students is likely to be that
the amount of assessment is cut, and the course content you think is irrelevant
is replaced by material which you think is relevant. However, the **possible**
outcomes are that either nothing changes or any change is minimal, but
clarification has been given as to why things are the way they are. So as
student representative you know you will probably not achieve what your
'constituency' wants. The conditions exist for conflict; it is **latent**.

Is the conflict likely to be over facts? Or values? Or the human elements
in the situation – power needs, self-esteem needs, role and status? What
is the likelihood that you can negotiate a win/win outcome for your fellow
students? You are armed with the facts; the number of assessments, the
pacing of the assessments throughout the year, the specific content of the
syllabuses which are causing the disquiet.

But you know that in challenging these administrative or operational
factors you are also questioning the Course Committee's ability to do its
job (organize the course) and individuals' ability to do their job (decide
what is appropriate for you to be taught).

Furthermore, a prestigious committee like this will not want to see a
student overturn its decisions – even though you are all theoretically equal
on the committee, it can be very difficult to overcome the reality of the
status differences, and any challenge to these. And that factor could be in
addition to another human element. The need to justify one's existence,
the importance of one's subject matter, the necessity for a tutor in a
particular area. So you know that the facts may not be the issue when the
debate takes place.

What then is to be your strategy? Well, the win/win outcome demands
that you gain some concession, but not at the expense of the opposition.
You cannot withdraw from the conflict, hoping that it will 'go away'. Your
fellow students won't let it! You can't just say to them, 'There, there, that's
what being a student is all about.'

You must plan to 'level' with your colleague on the committee, discuss
the students' feelings about the issues, persuade them that there is a
problem, a problem of perception, if not of fact. But you must also be
sensitive to the tutors' feelings; you have to think how you might phrase your

language so that their status or self-esteem is not threatened, perhaps by working out a solution which appears to come from them, rather than you. And equally you have to be aware of your rights in the context.

You are entitled to assert the viewpoint you are representing because of your role and status on the Committee. This may be difficult in the face of such power, but being an effective committee member is just as much an interpersonal skill as an operational skill. If your general strategy is successful, then you will be able to go back to your fellow students at least with the committee now having the remit to look at the issues in detail with a view to making improvements for the coming year.

You have had the students' views minuted, got the problems on the agenda. No one has 'lost face', because you have encoded your arguments in the appropriate language for the audience and the context. Of course, it may be that you have managed to cut the assessments by half, and had one-quarter of the syllabus changed. But is that likely to be a win/win situation? It depends on how you went about winning your case, the tactics you used to influence your fellow members.

Activity 5.4

There are a number of ways in which we can influence or persuade people, and thus avoid conflict. However the tactics we could use may be limited by the power we have, the information we have, nature and characteristics of the person we are trying to influence, and the context in which we are trying to influence them, and our own credibility. The context of the last activity illustrates that. So it pays to have some sort of checklist, in order to assess what tactics are open to you, and thus how you might work through the communications process in order to find the least stressful and least time-consuming way of gaining support for your argument. Have a look at this checklist.

POSSIBLE TACTICS

1. **Rational debate**   The use of facts, evidence, logical argument to support a request or change of attitude.
2. **Persistence**   Attempts to gain support through repetition or exaggeration – hearing a message over and over again does encourage people to have a more positive attitude towards it (although hearing it more than four times has been shown by research to be counter-productive!)
3. **Insistence**   Demands for compliance through threats or use of formal authority.
4. **Exchange tactics**   Bartering what you can offer, be it financial or status, rewards, the giving of a favour, or asking for the return of a favour previously given.

Now, assess the interaction between (a) your powers, (b) the sort of person you are trying to influence and (c) the context, in this scenario, using the checklist to clarify your ideas. There is a debate between you, the General Manager, your Financial Director and your Personnel Manager, as to whether you can afford another assistant manager. It is three to one against your view that it is essential to have one, because of increased business. Jot down what might go through your mind in terms of each of the above tactics.

Thoughts on Activity 5.4

You are well-prepared for your meeting with your three colleagues. You have a main goal (another assistant manager right away) and a contingency goal, the minimum you would accept (a promise that if the circumstances are the same in three months' time, then another assistant manager will be taken on). But what are your tactics if you have been wrong in your assumptions or objections are raised which you did not anticipate?

You find out that one of the stumbling blocks is that the Personnel Manager is holding out for a graduate with several years experience in a big hotel group, which the Financial Director knows cannot be obtained within the salary range the organization could offer in the foreseeable future. Or the General Manager's view is that increased business can be coped with by greater productivity by the present staff, including longer hours for the same wages.

How then do you handle the discussion, what communications techniques do you now use in the on-going debate to emphasize the benefits of your proposal? To help you work this out, check back on what you have learned about questioning and listening skills, verbal and non-verbal behaviour generally, and the distinction between assertive and aggressive statements.

Obviously there are occasions on which, whatever your tactics, you will fail to persuade. It may be, just may be, that the person you are trying to influence is so obstinate that no argument would prevail! But at least by evaluating the tactics you could use, you are better prepared for the influencing exercise. This activity reflects a very simple part of your planning. In this context, two of the group are equal in status to you, and one superior. Thus arguably at the outset you have not the formal authority to insist, which might suggest that option 3 is out. But is it?

The fact that there is a debate at all suggests that the General Manager is open to persuasion. And remember that power can be about far more than formal authority. It may be that the real decision-maker in this group is **not** the general manager (an aspect of power we will be looking at in Chapter 7). So you have to direct your influencing skills accordingly, while remembering that that the general manager's **apparent** power base is not challenged. You have to keep reminding yourself of the human element as well as the operational element in this communications process.

Facts and figures, formal distribution of power and decision-making, may not be what the debate will be about. You will only achieve your objective if you understand the needs of those whom you are trying to influence. Let's assess what they are likely to be.

Firstly, let's think of the **rational approach**, **Tactic 1**. Which aspects of your argument might meet their needs, be beneficial to them, and which aspects might threaten in some way? For example, if your facts and figures are too divorced from those of the Financial Director, then her status and self-esteem is at risk.

If your argument is accepted, will the General Manager see it could be to his credit? How do your opponents make decisions? Do they need time to think about things, or do they rely on intuition? Are they interested at the outset in the debate, or do you have to start off with a fairly dramatic statement in order to catch their attention – in which case some fairly spectacular point at the very outset will allow you to take the high ground and control the discussion. Will your facts and figures need to be modified in order to respond to objections, or can you argue that the pros outweigh the cons?

What about **Tactic 2 – persistence**? Can you reiterate your message a number of times in a number of different ways? Pointing out the benefit to each individual (increased business is good financially, but it is looks like good planning on the part of the General Manager and the Financial Director, and for the Personnel Manager, another member of staff to share the burden of the management team). Pointing out the consequences of not adding to the team, of not taking up an opportunity to further expand the organization.

And **Tactic 3 – insistence**. You do not have the formal authority to achieve your demands. But are there any 'threats' you might make, like suggesting that you cannot continue to work efficiently without some support? Or suggesting that the rest of the staff will see it as a 'vote of no confidence' in the organization's future if expansion is denied? The first 'threat' could be seen to be an operational threat; the second a human needs threat. But remember, threats are effective only if you can carry them out. Which takes us back to the question of your credibility. Do they believe you?

Finally **Tactic 4 – exchange tactics**. What might you barter, what 'favours' might you give, in order to win your point? More productive efforts on your side? More time to put together your ideas on long-term strategies to increase business, to cut costs? A promise to re-assess and reorganize your own workload in order to make the best use of a new colleague?

Whatever you have thought about, in terms of your goal in this influencing exercise, you have to establish quite clearly **before** you go into such a meeting that (a) you are clear about your objective, and (b) you are clear about your tactics.

--- *Activity 5.5* ---------------

We have noted that there are three possible outcomes of a negotiation aimed at avoiding or resolving conflict. These are **win/win**, **win/lose**, **lose/lose**. In each of the following circumstances, suggest how the parties concerned might use their interpersonal skills to achieve a **win/win** result.

1. You and your friends are debating where to go on Saturday night. Some fancy going to see an up-and-coming group at the local disco, some a visit to the new multiscreen cinema.
2. The Head Housekeeper is trying to placate an angry guest because his room was not cleaned before 11 am.
3. The Domestic Services Manager of a hospital is debating a pay deal with the big public sector UNISON.

Now any negotiation goes through a number of stages. To achieve a win/win result, each stage has to be recognized and 'worked at'.

Stage 1   Preparation

Stage 2   Establishing the climate

Stage 3   The process itself – involving interactions between bidding, exploring needs and coinage (bargaining strengths and weaknesses)

Stage 4   Clinching the agreement

Avoid concentrating too much on using **facts** to win your case; facts don't speak for themselves in social interaction!

Thoughts on Activity 5.5

If we go back to the very first chapter in the book, you will remember that we defined interpersonal skills as about communicating in a 'mutually beneficial manner to a mutually beneficial conclusion'. We also used phrases like 'social stroking'. Now it just may be that the facts can settle a debate or conflict of the types described in this activity. But the previous activity has already shown that facts are interpreted in contexts and within human needs, emotions and values.

So I am sure that you would probably consider it a lose/lose situation if the Head Housekeeper's response to the angry guest was to point out that he should have realized that the chambermaids cleaned the rooms in a certain rotation, and that it was always the case that the last floor to be done was where he had his room. The disgruntled guest goes off, swearing never to return – not a lot of social stroking there! What type of social stroking might lead to a win/win situation in the context of the above definition?

STAGE 1   PREPARATION

What are the facts, who is most likely to dispute them, how and why? One of the facts in the dispute over what to do on Saturday night might be a comparison of costs and who can afford what. The same dispute over available money is quite likely to be a fact in the UNISON discussion. But whereas the amount of money available within your group of friends is not likely to be other than a practical issue, as far as the union is concerned, money not only represents a particular face value, it also represents power and status in relation to other groups of workers. And the hotel guest may see his problem only about **value** for **money**.

What will be the initial mood of those involved? The friends? Probably quite happy because one way or another both 'sides' will get what they want eventually. The guest – angry! The union – suspicious! So tactics have to be thought out in the light of these circumstances. Which then leads us to the next stage.

STAGE 2   ESTABLISHING THE CLIMATE

'Let's have a quick beer, and work out what chances there are of seeing the group another time, and whether the film is on for a long spell'.

'I understand your reaction, Mr Anderson. Would you like to join me for a cup of coffee while I explain why this has happened.'

'I appreciate that your members want the best possible settlement, as I am sure you will appreciate that we have certain constraints on what we can offer, so let's sit down and see where we can both meet our objectives.'

STAGE 3   THE PROCESS ITSELF

'I'm prepared to wait till next week to see the film, if you can definitely establish that the group is only here this weekend.'

'If you would prefer your room cleaned first every morning, Mr Anderson, I think I can arrange that.'

'I know the last thing I want is disruptive industrial action, and the last thing you want is for your members to lose wages, so let's keep these points in mind.'

(Making bids, exploring needs, and recognizing bargaining strengths and weaknesses.)

STAGE 4   CLINCHING THE AGREEMENT

I probably don't need to suggest the dialogue for you now. The important human factor here is that each party in the negotiation believes it has come off best, has won – the mutually beneficial conclusion to the communications process – but allows the other to think that it has won – the social stroking involved in the process!

Activity 5.6

We have noted that conflict often escalates unexpectedly and unnecessarily. This can happen for a number of reasons. An example we have already noted is that one or other of the parties involved says or does nothing (responds passively) in the hope that the conflict 'will go away' of its own accord. But without resolution, the conflict becomes **latent**, with the potential to recur, even if it takes another form. This is particularly so if the conflict is about attitudes or values – although even objective facts can sometimes be very unwelcome in human terms! Follow through this example of conflict escalating through the stages we identified in Chapter 5.

Catriona and Ishbel share the running of a wholefood restaurant with three other people. Catriona has been working there for eighteen months and feels she thoroughly knows the ropes, whereas Ishbel has only been around for a couple of months. Catriona has never really felt Ishbel was committed to the restaurant's 'co-operative' 'back to nature' concept, but there had not been much choice among the applicants for the position, although Ishbel did not know that she was only the best of rather a poor lot. She and Catriona have never really hit it off together. Ishbel in fact is rather afraid of Catriona, and is very unhappy about working alone with her.

One evening they are clearing up prior to closing after a very busy session. Catriona asks Ishbel to help her re-arrange a number of jars of dry goods and trays of fresh vegetables in the larder – a task which although it will lead to more convenience, is not a priority. Ishbel asks her to wait a minute as she is occupied with checking receipts. A shouting match follows, which is overheard by Donald, the other worker on duty that evening, and which ends with a pile of crockery being knocked to the floor and shattering to smithereens, and the two women almost coming to blows. Donald has followed the escalation of this conflict, and has observed the following incidents:

- At the outset, Catriona makes it quite clear to the others that she is unhappy about Ishbel.
- Donald suspects, because of her attitude towards him, that Ishbel has overheard a conversation, about a week after she has started work, between him and Catriona, during which she has complained about Ishbel's appointment.
- After another two weeks, Catriona complains to Donald that Ishbel is hopeless at taking decisions or accepting responsibility, and has to be told what to do all the time. This has not been Donald's experience, but he does not say so to Catriona.
- A week later Ishbel forgets to give Catriona a message that a meat order will be three hours late. Catriona is furious when Ishbel finally remembers.
- A few days later, Catriona discovers that an order for their speciality breads which had been put aside for another customer has been sold. Ishbel publicly admits responsibility but does not apologize.

- Catriona begins to criticize Ishbel's work in front of customers.
- Donald comes in at the end of a conversation between Ishbel and another worker, Scott. Ishbel is talking about looking for another job which pays better. Donald wonders if Ishbel is thinking of leaving because of the friction between her and Catriona, or if Catriona was right and Ishbel was never really committed to the co-operative concept.
- Ishbel fails to turn up for work one day when she is working alone with Catriona.
- Three days later, the row between them takes place.

Now think:

1. At which points can you identify the stages in the conflict?
2. At what stage(s) could Donald have intervened, and in what way – what might he have said and done?
3. Why did he **not** intervene? What do you think prevented him?

Thoughts on Activity 5.6

One might say at the outset that the latent conflict here lay in the organization itself, a 'co-operative' without a clear command or managerial structure, which could be one reason why Donald did not intervene. In other words, the operational needs of the organization and its members were not taken care of. But I am sure you are aware of the fact that it is often very difficult to separate operational needs of organizations from human needs.

Organizations need leaders generally because people need leaders – and the reason people need leaders we will be looking at in the next chapter. So Donald's lack of intervention could have been because he lacked, or did not employ, the appropriate leadership skills. However the main point of this exercise is to trace the development of the conflict, which certainly appears to have happened because every party in it hoped it would 'go away' of its own accord.

1. **THE LATENT STAGE**: THE POTENTIAL

- the experienced worker, Catriona, and the new girl, Ishbel;
- the feeling that one party, Ishbel, was not committed to the organization's values;
- the uneven power relationship – fear and unease on behalf of Ishbel rather than respect for Catriona's experience;
- the inferior quality of Ishbel – not accepting responsibility, making mistakes.

2. **THE PERCEIVED STAGE**: THE ACTUAL, OR 'TRIGGER'

A conflict over organizational priorities, which was the culmination of a series of latent stages which were 'swept under the carpet', for example,

Ishbel's work being publicly criticized, a mistake with two food orders, Ishbel failing to turn up for work.

3. **THE FELT STAGE**: THE PROTAGONISTS OPENLY SHOW HOSTILITY

- They shout at one another.
- Crockery is broken.
- Physical violence appears to be threatened.

4. **THE MANIFEST STAGE**: OTHERS BECOME INVOLVED

- Donald overhears what is happening.
- An outside party becomes involved, in itself likely to harden attitudes and make for more difficulty in resolution.

5. **THE AFTERMATH**: WHAT DO YOU THINK?

- Will the row have cleared the air?
- Will Ishbel now certainly leave?
- How will working relationships within the organization be affected by the manifest hostility?

Now when and how might Donald have intervened? Well, it would seem to make sense that he should have intervened at stage 1, as soon as he realized the potential for conflict was there. He might have discussed with Catriona her unease about Ishbel in order to establish what exactly the problem was. Was it one of attitudes or abilities? Perhaps he could have encouraged Catriona to **level** with Ishbel – spell out her initial worries about Ishbel's commitment, always remembering that it is **behaviour** that is important. Ishbel could be a competent worker without necessarily believing in the 'back to nature' concept.

Or perhaps Donald could have tackled Ishbel – suggested a compromise if the two girls just did not get on, because we can't make people like one another. For example, ensuring that they worked different shifts. Or would such a compromise merely be keeping the real conflict at the latent stage? Donald equally might have tried to placate the two girls either individually or together – the 'there, there' approach. That might have worked – sometimes an open recognition that a problem exists is sufficient for it to be coped with. The value of this approach is seen by management when they set up staff/management consultative committees – no powers, but at least grievances can be aired, and the recognition that they exist is a 'smoothing' communication!

But Donald did not intervene. Why? I did suggest at the beginning that it could have been because he felt that he had 'no right' to do so; he was not in control. Of course, he may have been too frightened to intervene – or couldn't care less – or would have been quite happy to see Ishbel leave.

But none of these attitudes or feelings was likely to further organizational goals. The **facts** and the **context** demanded an appropriate resolution of the conflict.

Perhaps Donald should have recognized that he did have rights, the right to assert himself if a situation demanded that he did so. In other words, to make **his** point of view known to the others. In other words, Donald had a perfect right to say at the outset that while he could understand the two girls's points of view, the overall atmosphere in the restaurant was suffering because of the situation, and therefore it was well worth seeing if some resolution of the problem could come about soon. He did not need the formal authority to lead the discussion; he had that right to lead through being a human being.

But if we do reflect on the initial point about an organization without a formal leader, when I have presented this scenario to my students, there has generally been a number who say that the problem would never arisen had there been a formal 'leader' or manager. How many ways do you think the problem could have been handled?

FURTHER READING

Casse, P. (1992) *The One Hour negotiator*, Butterworth-Heinemann, Oxford.

Fowler, A. (1990) *Negotiating Skills and Strategies*, Institute of Personnel Management, London.

Two books which speak for themselves! They are both very straightforward and thus are good 'confidence-raising' books, appropriate for all types and levels of negotiating.

McCann, D. (1989) *How to Influence Others at Work*, Heinemann Professional, Oxford: a more general book for background reading, looking at both the formal and the informal circumstances in which we might want to influence others in the work situation.

The science – and art – of leadership

6

There are men who, by their sympathetic attractions, carry nations with them, and lead the activities of the human race. (Ralph Waldo Emerson)

Question 6: Is leadership all about charisma – qualities and talents only a few are privileged to have been born with? Or is it a particular package of social skills which we can employ when necessary? Can we learn to be good leaders?

Snapshot
Two of the chefs in the Lewis Island Hotel are discussing a potentially dangerous chip pan fire in the kitchen that day.

Ian: 'That was really quite frightening today, wasn't it? These mock "safety at work" exercises are all very well, but when something like that happens, then your mind just goes a blank.'

Murdoch: 'Yes, and what's more, it was not Colin who came to the rescue but Jenny. I know that she's considered to be a bit of a "non-person" among us lot, she's so quiet and mousy, but she fairly swung into action there – even had the Restaurant Manager jumping!'

Ian: 'Probably because she seemed so sure of what she was doing, while we were all looking at each other in panic and working out which particular extinguisher was the right one.'

An essay question I regularly set is:

All managers are leaders, but not all leaders are managers. Discuss.

I do not know where the quotation came from originally – maybe I made it up myself – but it does encapsulate the discussion in this chapter. Most, if not all of you, will hopefully be moving up in your chosen careers into positions of responsibility. You will thus have power and control over some or even all areas of your work, and over other people.

That power will be vested in you officially, through your job specification and the formal structure of the organization. You will have to 'lead', in the sense of making decisions and asking others to implement them. And those you manage, by virtue of their role and position in the organization, will have to do what you tell them. If some official line of command did not exist in formal organizations, then they would find far greater difficulty in achieving their goals.

Of course, no one is suggesting that the staff of a 25 bedroom hotel are 'led' in the same manner as the troops in the Falklands War, or that decisions in either of these examples are made in the same manner as they might be by the workers in a wholefood co-operative. But whatever the organizational context, there will be a method of control, a formal leader or group decision-making process, a 'manager' or 'management' is required in order to co-ordinate the efforts of individual members of the organization towards organizational goals.

But when we analyse what we actually mean by the concept of **leadership**, we usually find ourselves thinking about a **human** quality, or pattern of behaviour, or set of attributes, which may or may not be associated with the person who has the **formal** position of a manager. And these attributes or behaviours do not necessarily come with the position and title; although people tend to respond to the expectations others have of them, it does not mean that they have the capabilities to respond appropriately.

However the nub of the question I set above is that an individual may have the formal power to tell someone what to do, even if he does not want to. But to get that person to do it willingly, to believe in the purpose of the action, to put his best effort into the action, even if he does not necessarily see something in it for himself – that's what good leadership is all about! The ability to motivate people is a major factor when discussing someone's leadership skills. There are many examples in our history of heroic acts undertaken without question, because leaders were trusted, were inspirational, and thus were followed for reasons beyond that of their formal authority, or technical knowledge.

Try thinking about the issue in another, far more familiar context. If you were at an old-fashioned, very traditional school like i was, the organization would have rewarded the best-behaved pupils, those who consistently conformed to organizational rules and norms, by making them class monitors or prefects. They were then to offer the rest of us leadership, to be a good influence, a role-model for us.

But in fact, the real influencers may have been the deviants, who did not subscribe to formal rules and norms, and who often were in trouble because they were castigated for their ability to lead others astray. They could very easily get us to break the formal rules of the organization, even although we knew it was wrong and we would get into trouble. The organization considered them a bad influence – but I am sure you will realize that they could be only be that if they were very good leaders!

That should get you thinking about what **leadership** actually means. And you do not need to think about leaders at the national or international level, in the historic or contemporary context of big business, religion, politics, or military ventures. You can start with your own social group, your friends, your fellow students, establish those who have the most influence in the group, and then begin to work out for yourself why? Because the purpose of our investigation is to identify those leadership qualities and behaviours in order that you can be even better managers.

'I do not want to be just a manager – I want to be a leader. At the very least, it will make life much easier for me, and if it helps create a stimulating work climate for those I am managing, then organizational goals will more easily be achieved.' The exercise of influence over others at work is a fundamental interpersonal process in organizations.

Keynotes
1. Being a 'leader' can be about a formal operational position, or about an informal social relationship with a group.
2. Leaders by definition are those who can make others perform tasks without being coerced through force or formal authority.
3. Managers by virtue of their formal position are supposed to be leaders. The real leader(s) in a formal organization may not be managers, because others may in fact be able to exert more influence.

There are a number of academic theories which attempt to explain the phenomenon and process of leadership. While it is necessary for us to have some appreciation of the debate as to whether leaders are 'born' or 'made', in order to isolate the factors in which we are most interested, for our purpose it does not really matter whether there is or is not such a thing as a born leader.

We are interested not so much in the origins of those properties of leadership as in those interpersonal **processes** in which leaders are involved and which they employ to influence others, and which are external to and separate from the use of pure formal authority or coercion. Although they might be used in conjunction with formal lines of command, they might also be used in opposition to them, and informal influence may win over formal power and status, to the detriment of organizational goals.

Therefore in this chapter we will concentrate on trying to identify the general interpersonal processes, and have a look at the specific **tactics** appropriate to specific **situations**. But there is a great deal of food for thought or meat in this debate, and we are really only able to extract the essence and get the flavour of it!

Perhaps one way to do that is to think again about acting and roles. Let's take a very famous Shakespearean play, *Henry V*. History tells us that King Henry V was a great leader. Shakespeare, who obviously could not have met Henry V unless he had a time machine, wrote the play, *Henry V*, in which the words and the actions given the actor who played Henry had to symbolize to the audience those qualities and attributes which enabled him to lead 6000 English soldiers to overwhelming victory against 25 000 French soldiers at the battle of Agincourt in the year AD 1415. And Shakespeare, in constructing the language he put into Henry's mouth, obviously understood what leadership was about, long before we academics got interested in the concept.

Numerous actors have played that role – and those who have been the most successful have been those who through all the processes of communicating, verbal and non-verbal, thoroughly put over to critics and audiences the power and influence which Henry must have had to ensure his success as a leader. In other words, the character they portrayed was **believable**. You could imagine being one of Henry's followers if he behaved as the actor portrayed him.

Now whether Laurence Olivier or Kenneth Branagh, two great performers in this role, were actually **born** leaders, we do not know. But they certainly **acted** as if they were! Which directs us to its importance in the context of this book, as I have no doubt you have already realized. Shakespeare is considered to be one of the world's greatest **communicators**, precisely because he was so brilliant at creating characters through language, at creating roles which were entirely credible.

Let's look, albeit it briefly, at the theoretical background, so that we can more easily tease out what is useful to us in terms of interpersonal skills. The ancient Greeks were the first to think analytically about leadership. They did believe that leaders were born, not made. The word **charisma** is a Greek word, meaning a divinely bestowed gift or talent, which was subsequently used to describe someone who has enormous capability for influencing large numbers of people. This came from having unique characteristics or **traits** which were innate, happened as the result of a genetic luck of the draw, and which emerged when a situation required a great leader.

We have already discussed this belief in innate qualities when we were thinking about the concept of personality back in Chapter 1. But this belief was challenged when Western society became much more democratic during the nineteenth century. 'Leaders' had to be found for the military, the civil service and the new businesses and industries, as it was now considered unjust that people should inherit positions of power purely because of their birth and breeding. Indeed, it was a series of military disasters arising from poor leadership from within the ranks of the 'landed gentry' which hurried the process along, as the army tried to find new ways of identifying great leaders, instead of military commanders automatically gaining their position through their 'blue blood' rather than their military competence.

However it soon became apparent that there was a flaw in the theory that leaders had certain unique and innate qualities which could be easily identified. Analyses of men who were great leaders (and it nearly always was men until recently – which in itself is going to become an important part of our understanding of the appropriate social skills) certainly revealed a number of qualities or traits they appeared to have in common, or qualities they had more of than non-leaders. But as I am sure you will have already worked out, that does not tell us where these traits came from, or why they were there in the first place.

Despite a number of studies, there seems to be no universal 'core' cluster of traits which differentiates effective from non-effective leaders, although there did appear to be a few traits which turned up fairly regularly. And, surprise, surprise! Among the most frequent is a very high level of communications skills – the ability to communicate ideas, enthusiasm, trust, empathy, faith in a goal and the ability of the group to achieve it. (There is a nice new 'buzz' word which encompasses these qualities which we will pick up again later. That is **visioning** (see page 124).)

To return to our objective. Can it be as simple as that? Because if it is, then we can **all** be leaders, although some of us may become better leaders than others. If it is just about our communications and inter-personal skills, as we already know, these skills can be learned or enhanced. Well, you will not be surprised to learn that it isn't quite so simple, and this is why we have to have a quick look at other theories or approaches to the study of leadership.

If leadership is not about something we **are**, just as having a 'nice' personality is not about something we **are**, but about something we actually do, we can quite easily identify what effective leaders are doing, if we analyse their behaviours in conjunction with others. For example, are they particularly good at encoding their messages in the appropriate tone and register in order that their followers can decode them correctly and respond accordingly? Yes, that does appear to be the case – but now do you remember exactly what we mean by **register**?

We are talking about the use of exactly the right language for the context or situation, taking into account any formal rules which may structure that language, and the informal, or social and human element which is also involved. And that brings us very nicely with the other approach to the study of leadership, which links up behaviours, or

styles of leadership, with **situational** factors. This approach argues that good leadership is certainly about a pattern or style of behaviour which will influence people, but just as importantly, will reflect the **needs** of the situation – the **goal** to be achieved – in conjunction with the needs of those being led.

Style theories and situational theories of leadership offer us two strategies for understanding what good leadership is about. The style can be **autocratic** (the leader dictates without consultation), democratic (followers are involved in the decision-making), or even **laissez-faire** (there is no 'leader' as such; the group just gets on with it.) Or if we approach it from the aspect of group needs and group goals, the social context, the situation can demand that the leadership is **task-orientated** ('Cut the cackle and let's go for it, lads!') or **maintenance-orientated** ('We're all in this together; let's see how we can best support each other.')

To illustrate the situational factor, further there appears to be no consistent relationship between task-orientated leadership behaviour, maintenance-orientated leadership behaviour, and group effectiveness. One person can be more effective in some situations and another person in other situations. What sort of leadership skills did Jenny show in our opening snapshot? Why were they effective? Would you use the same skills communicating with a number of your staff who have just been made redundant, do not know what to do with themselves, and are looking to you to offer them new ideas, new goals? This should help identify the relationship between the general organizational concept of leadership and the specific communications concept of register.

Keynotes

1. Leadership can be studied through analysing behaviours labelled as such in interpersonal processes and tactics.
2. Charisma or trait theories of leadership suggest effective leaders are those born with the appropriate characteristics; style and situational theories suggest that effective leaders arise as a consequence of employing the appropriate styles and techniques for a given goal or context.
3. Styles can be labelled as 'autocratic', 'democratic' or 'laissez-faire'; leadership styles and techniques can be labelled as 'task-orientated' or 'maintenance/human needs orientated.'

So this brief scene-setting analysis can be summarized by stating that **good leaders are those who can persuade, through the most appropriate manner and style, others to follow them because they show a concern for the task, the people and the situation**. Which supports of course the earlier contention that good leadership is basically about good communications skills. However you will have recognized that although these theories makes you think about leadership **role-perception** and **behaviours**, for our purposes we need to carry that thinking into how this is applied through our communications and interpersonal skills. So it is useful to sit back for a moment and think about some of the characteristic skills and behaviours which have been associated with effective leaders.

The following fairly universal characteristics have been identified. Self-confidence, awareness of others' feelings and needs, persistence, a sense of responsibility, articulacy, supportiveness, initiative, enthusiasm, ability to inspire trust – to name but a few! (Leaders also appear to be taller than is the norm – but even that genuinely genetic tendency can be socially manipulated through the way we dress, or our posture!) Try to judge for yourself whether these characteristics **are** traits, or innate qualities, or more rightly could be described as **behaviours**. Think about 'self-confidence'.

We **are** generally inclined to want and to accept leadership from someone who appears self-confident in a specific situation. But note the use of the word 'appears'. How do you know someone has self-confidence? Can we see it in the same way as we see someone has blue eyes? Have we not already recognized that believing someone is self-confident comes from our reading of a number of cues, verbal and non-verbal? Like a 'confident tone of voice', strong, unwavering. A 'confident use of language', no hesitancy. A 'confident body posture', leaning forward, standing up.

If effective leaders are seen to be self-confident, then there is nothing so far which suggests that that **appearance** cannot be developed. The next time you are listening to a speaker whom you would label as **lacking** in confidence, look for the cues which tell you why you have come to that conclusion, whether they are to do with the spoken word, and its sound, or body language, then work out how you would advise that person in order that he or she could disguise the nervousness.

Or think about another example of what could be called 'self-confidence'. The soldier who wins an award for bravery under enemy fire, through inspiring his colleagues to undertake what seems a hopeless task. The media have reported on a number of occasions that such a soldier, describing his actions, has said that he was actually 'sh**-scared', but that was not the message which came over to the group. In other words, the cues the group decoded in such contexts were certainly **not** the innate responses or behaviour which 'Nature' intended us to indulge in, in times of personal threat or risk – which is to run away as fast as possible from the situation, unless we were absolutely positive of winning!

The message which was coming over was that of supreme confidence in winning, whatever the odds. Or much less dramatically, the manager who leads a team through a new marketing plan based on a very high-risk strategy. So the manager describes his new plan not as a high-risk strategy, which sounds defeatist, casts doubts, but as an 'aggressive new marketing campaign', with all the intonation of success!

If leadership is about the ability to influence others, then there are a number of situations in management in which you could be involved which are about influencing and persuasion, although you might not have so readily identified them as to do with leadership skills and qualities, for instance, in negotiating, in situations in which it may be necessary to adopt a high-risk strategy.

The skills required by the effective negotiator include the skill of presenting oneself, through control of verbal and non-verbal cues, in a manner which suggests to the opposition that you are sure you are going to win – and conversely not presenting through **leakage**, through cues which you do not intend, that you think you are on very weak ground. (Just think why the expression 'the poker face' came about.)

There have been a number of studies which claim to identify the key techniques which successful negotiators use, and there is an obvious connection between leading successfully in a negotiation and conflict-resolution, which we looked at in Chapter 5, although the examples were rather more about conflict at the interpersonal level, rather than the formal situation.

If we start from the assumption of successful leadership and control in the negotiating process, the ensuring that 'the other side' do what you want them to, then it is not surprising that we see these same skills and abilities delivering the goods as we do in the more obvious leadership situations. For example, good negotiators keep control, lead from the front by asking more questions than the opposition, with the consequence that the opposition have less time to think, the leader has more time, and asking questions is seen as being pro-active rather than reactive.

Good negotiators also spend time summarizing and clarifying, so that the stages in reaching the objectives of the process are precisely identified, thus reflecting the persistence and single-mindedness of the good leader. And good negotiators show absolute confidence in their arguments; they do not dilute them or open them up to becoming a wider target to be attacked by offering too many, nor do they reveal weaknesses in their arguments, so that they can exude confidence and vision with regard to their proposal or stance. Keeping control of the negotiation process is also about 'leading from the front'.

A final illustration from the general points made above is that effective leaders are usually 'highly articulate'. Meaning that they have no problem finding the right words in the right tone and register in order to achieve the purpose of the communications process in which they are involved. It is highly improbable that anyone would believe that coherence and fluency in language could be innate, and much of what you read in chapters 1, 2 and 3 is also of relevance here.

Being highly articulate is something we can work at, just as we can work at enhancing our skills in any area. In this context it is very interesting to note that contemporary evidence suggests women are far better at communicating verbally than men, because to a great extent the socialization process entails that women are expected to be more expressive and supportive through verbal communications skills.

Nowhere is it suggested that women are 'naturally' more articulate than men. Thus women generally bring a 'high relationship-' or maintenance-orientated approach to managing and leading, which includes a willingness to listen, to seek participation, a wish for disclosure and a greater concern about maintaining good interpersonal relationships. In fact, a new model of management now has been argued which uses the words 'masculine' and 'feminine' to label the particular styles and techniques, and these labels are accorded totally independent of the genetic and physiological characteristics which determines one's sex.

It has been argued that in today's business and professional world, with flat management, and reduction of hierarchies, team work – as opposed to boss–subordinate relationships – and the general democratization of power within organizations, suggests that the 'feminine' style of management may be far more appropriate. If this is the case, study the communications and social skills of your most articulate and best-liked female fellow students – you could learn something very useful! Because if you look back at that list of leadership characteristics, does it not suggest to you that if any one single characteristic could be labelled as the most significant or important, then it has to be good communications skills?

To sum up, to be accepted as an effective leader, you must direct your general skills of perception and self-presentation, and specific use of verbal and non-verbal language , so that those who are leading have the belief, get the message, that you are competent, in control, see yourself as part of the group and sharing its needs, interests and goals, and that you will do all that is required to achieve that goal. One of the world's most effective leaders for some considerable time (and we do not need in any way to support what he did and why, to have that view) was Adolf Hitler, who led the German people out of the Depression of the 1930s, and for a while looked like fulfilling all the military, political and economic ambitions of the German people.

Hitler was not a particularly physically prepossessing person, nor was he very well educated, and he certainly did not come from a background which you could have argued endowed him with any natural or social advantages which would enhance his leadership performance. But he did demonstrate what appear to be the core traits or qualities involved in leadership, and he did use all the understanding of the psychology of communication, and indeed, the psychology of the available communications technology at the time, to create in the German people a belief in their goals, and a positive desire to achieve them.

Despite our initial discussion, it is interesting to note that the idea of **charismatic** leadership has almost come full circle. Very recent studies seem to suggest that perhaps there is something in this idea of innate qualities, and talk about **visionary** leaders. It may indeed be that, as we can all learn to drive a car, but some of us will learn more quickly to drive, or to drive better because we have some physiological advantage over others, so, it is argued, certain qualities of visionary leaders may come through their genes.

Visionary leaders emerge and become accepted because they help their followers to make sense of an environment or situation or task or goal that is confusing and hard to understand. This is because they appear to have an **intuitive** ability to interpret, to predict, to assess more effectively than most. And 'intuitive' does suggest 'innate', or 'instinctive'. Because that allows them to reduce uncertainties, and help in making choices, they can then more easily co-ordinate individual efforts towards a common sense of purpose. But again does this not bring us back to communications and interpersonal skills? Even with that inspired understanding, they still have to **impart** their vision to their followers.

We are going to think about leadership skills in action through the activities, but don't get too locked in to the debate as to what is 'nature' and what is 'nurture'. That really is a purely academic debate for us. What is important is that if there is such a distinction, then we are trying to work out in very practical terms how best to nurture nature!

Keynotes
The abilities of visionary leaders are as follows:
1. Their **perception** of a confusing environment is more accurate than that of the people around them.
2. They are very **articulate** in verbalizing their perception.
3. They show a very strong **belief** about what should be done and provide the **drive** to do it.
4. They show a very strong **empathy** with their potential followers, and an understanding of their needs, hopes and fears.
5. They show **resolution** to succeed, through showing determination, enthusiasm, courage, and refusal to quit.

Activity 6.1

Last year a very interesting article about leadership appeared in a Sunday newspaper. It reported that the British Army was having to restructure its officer training at Sandhurst Military Academy because the new generation of officer cadets were a 'different breed' from previous generations. Here are some of the reasons why restructuring was thought to be necessary.

1. There no longer appeared to be a natural talent for leadership.
2. The modern generation lacked automatic respect for hierarchies, and were less self-reliant, because they lacked experience of the outdoor life.

3. Recruits had to struggle to express their ideas clearly and were less capable of leading groups in practical exercises.
4. They had less self-discipline and were less prepared to stand out from their peers.
5. They were more likely, when asked to lead a group in a practical exercise, to turn to colleagues and ask if anyone had any ideas.
6. They had very little initiative and were lacking in oral and written communicative skills.

The article went on to report that some recruits seemed to have very 'strange' views on leadership. For instance, Hitler was identified as a great leader even although he failed in his objectives. It was stated that the Sandhurst training was now 'stronger on leadership', and that the first trainees to go through the new regime had completed a revamped course designed to engender leadership by giving them more responsibility for organizing sports, lectures and their own fitness programmes. The causes of the deficiencies as identified by Sandhurst were as follows:

1. Schools now place less emphasis on discipline, self-reliance, prefects and competitive sports.
2. Schools have become more caring institutions, with more adult supervision and support, and thus it is harder for pupils to experience leadership and responsibility.

However the article also put over an opposing point of view. Some academics felt that Sandhurst was looking for an 'outdated authoritarian leader instead of someone who manages by consensus', that the 'aggressive extravert' is no longer an appropriate role model for the late twentieth century. What does this article tell us about what is seen to be the nature of leadership? What does it tell us about the problems of finding leaders, and the possible solutions? How does this analysis fit in with your own views and experience? What do you think about there being an 'appropriate role model for the late twentieth century?'

Thoughts on Activity 6.1

I chose this article for us to discuss because it quite clearly illustrates all the interesting 'common sense' questions and views which exist about the nature of leadership, the difficulties of 'unpacking' the abilities and skills which leaders seem or need to have, and how they are acquired. Thus it is a good starting point for the activities for this chapter, particularly as the first theoretical studies on leadership were undertaken with a view to producing effective military leaders. So I hope you managed to pick up the following cues as to the thinking behind the observations being made.

1. The assumption that there is a 'natural' talent for leadership – something some people are born with.
2. That hierarchies (systems arranged in graded orders of superiority) should command 'automatic' respect, as happened in the past, by their very nature.

3. That 'outdoor life' encourages qualities of self-reliance (considered to be a leadership requirement).
4. Being articulate, both in the spoken and the written word, was a key leadership skill for group management.
5. The modern officer cadet tended towards having a democratic rather than an autocratic style of leadership rather than take the initiative him/herself. (As it happens, the article inferred that the cadets were all male; given that a percentage would have been female, it would have been interesting to know if the same findings applied to them as a group.)
6. There were contradiction as to the reasons for these 'problems'. On the one hand, it appears to be suggested that 'nature' no longer produced leaders; on the other hand that it was all to do with the socialization process, not qualities some one is born with. Modern education discouraged leadership skills, because the nicer and more 'caring' we are about each other, the less we are likely to produce leaders.

There are a number of different issues here on which to reflect, and which should test your understanding of the theories of leadership discussed in this chapter. You might like to start by thinking about the context.

- Are the skills of leadership required in a military organization the same as the skills required in the sort of organizations in which you will be functioning?
- How much do the skills relate to the goals to be achieved?
- Can an organization like the army work effectively through consensus or democratic management?
- Before officer academies were established to train officers for the forces, where did the skills of the world's great military leaders of history come from?
- Can one talk about an 'appropriate role model for the late twentieth century' or are leadership skills and abilities timeless?
- What sort of leader would you like to have in the circumstances you might find yourself in if you were in the army?
- Is it possible to reconcile authoritarian, aggressive leadership with a caring and 'involving' attitude towards your subordinates?
- Is leadership only about achieving objectives?

Sufficient 'meaty' questions to keep you going for a long time! And hopefully you can now consider these questions and relate your thoughts to your future role as a manager and leader.

--- *Activity 6.2* ---

No one would deny that communication and motivation are management functions. But they are quite different functions from, say, planning and organizing. The former are concerned with the **social interactions** between individuals and groups. And, as Rabbie Burns said, 'the best-laid plans . . . gang aft agley' (often go very wrong) if they are not communicated effectively, and those involved do not feel motivated to carry them out.

So what do we expect leaders to do, once a goal or plan has been established for a group? Why is it often insufficient to merely make a plan known, through a formal communication mechanism or system? What is it that distinguishes the **leader** from the mere **manager**?

Basically, it is the distinction between **formal** authority ('Do this because I tell you to, and I have formal sanctions I can apply if you don't') and **social** authority ('I will do this because I want to, not because you've made me.') What then are these functions that we expect of our leaders? If we can identify these, then we can look at the communications and interpersonal skills which are required to carry out these functions.

To undertake this activity, think of one or two individuals you know or know of whom you would consider to be very good at leading, or influencing people, getting them to do things willingly. They can be alive or dead, famous or just known to a few; the influence they have does not necessarily have to be for the good, and they do not need to have had a formal position of authority. But in your mind you see them as leaders. Given the objective or goal having been established, what functions did they, or might they have performed, in their role as leaders?

Thoughts on Activity 6.2

The following list of leadership functions is not exhaustive. You might have an even longer list, or a list which includes functions I have not identified. One of the reasons why the list is interesting is because you do not need to be a formal 'manager' to carry out these functions. This is why contemporary leadership studies strongly suggest that teams may be more effective at achieving organizational goals, and that 'flat' management structures, rather than hierarchical or 'line' management structures make far more operational sense.

After you have compared this list with your own, and thought about it in conjunction with the qualities or capabilities of the leaders you have identified, why not think about it in connection with the fellow students with whom you are most friendly or familiar, and see how these functions match up with their patterns of behaviour in social interaction. Who's good at what?

FUNCTIONS

1. establishing and communicating goals;
2. clarifying and solving problems for others;
3. offering information, advice and specialist knowledge;
4. overseeing performance and giving feedback;
5. providing social and emotional support;
6. identifying, organizing and controlling resources;
7. dispensing rewards and punishments;
8. being the 'front' person for the group and where the 'buck' is seen to stop;

9. being decision-maker on the group's behalf;
10. being the referee or peace-maker in controversy or dissension.

It is possible that you could identify eight different 'leaders' carrying out eight different functions, or playing eight different roles, in a group of eight students.

───────────────────────── **Activity 6.3** ─────────────────────────

The actual behaviour we label as 'leadership' behaviour may take a number of different forms, and be identified through different cues in different contexts. Here are three scenarios, each outlining how two people described leadership in action.

Scenario 1

Two domestic cleaners are discussing their new supervisor over their teabreak.

Donna: 'Debbie's turning out to be a much better supervisor than I ever thought she would.'

Della: 'Why do you say that?'

Donna: 'Well, I wasn't at all sure about it when she was promoted last year, but she's making a really good job of it. She's very approachable and adaptable, and she is obviously quite happy to let us get on with things if we seem to know what we are about and are prepared to get on with it.'

Della: 'I agree – but she certainly doesn't let you get away with things – she's in there fast, wanting to know why, if anything is not going according to plan.'

Donna: 'Yes, that's true, but she doesn't overdo it. I feel she leaves me in peace to do things the way I see best, yet when I couldn't quite get the hang of that new floor polisher, she was right there to help sort out the technicalities.'

Della: 'Same with me – I've generally been left to get on with things, but she appreciates that I'm not all that happy with the new electronic equipment, and she's been very supportive there.'

Donna: 'Yes, it's amazing how her new position seems to have brought out her leadership talents. I never really saw her in that light before.'

Scenario 2

The Hebrides Hotel Company's Managing Director is talking to the Personnel Manager over a working lunch.

MD: 'Chloe's done a splendid job with the accommodation services division in the year since she took over.'

PM: 'Yes, they really seem to have got their act together at last, and are far more sure as to what's expected of them and how they might achieve their goals.'

MD: 'She's been very good in that she's encouraged them to be creative in thinking of new and better ways of doing things, instead of always having to work with systems brought from outside.'

PM: 'And she's got them working as a team, rather than the previous situation with all that backbiting, time-wasting rivalry between the purchasing and the design sections.'

MD: 'It's great to see the enthusiasm there now – Jim Calder, their head purchaser, was telling me that the job satisfaction is such that they often have to be chased home at night!'

PM: 'Yes, Chloe is a real whizz kid when it comes to motivating the staff. I wish we had more like her around.'

Scenario 3

Two of the staff of Trossachs Tour Operators are relaxing after lunch in the staff rest room in their smart new offices.

Maggie: 'I understand through the grapevine that Neil's finally decided he'll take early retirement. It's a great pity – I just can't imagine this place without him.'

Jeannie: 'I agree with you. There are very few people, I'm sure, who could have got us through all the problems we've had in the past two years.'

Maggie: 'When you think of that mess old Willie left us with, Neil's record is even more impressive. He was just so good at working out what were the positive aspects of the company, and what had to be changed.'

Jeannie: 'Yes – although he did tread on a few toes in the process, in order to get these changes through. But it was all worth it in the end.' Maggie: 'But that's what was so good about him – he realized that you can't make an omelette without breaking eggs, and he was not afraid of making decisions if he believed he was right. And the example he set by sorting out top management strengthened his hand relative to implementing other new ideas.'

Jeannie: 'Too right. He really turned the company round – we would have collapsed without his leadership.'

Although these three individuals are at quite different levels in their organizations, Debbie, Chloe, and Neil are seen to be 'leading'. And the speakers have identified them as leaders as a consequence of their behaviour, which in fact is very different in each case. What are these differences? Which theory or theories of leadership best explain their individual success?

Thoughts on Activity 6.3

One way you might have analysed these behaviours was to think of them as about **style** and **role**. Whether it is about style or role seems to be related to the size of the organization and the task in hand. This scenario could in fact be a good illustration of what is referred to as **Contingency Theory**.

Debbie is most interested in enhancing the capabilities of her colleagues in relation to their present job or task. She obviously sees her particular behaviour or **style** as appropriate for the immediate circumstances and environment – how to get things done efficiently and properly.

Chloe concentrates her behaviour on interpreting the **role** she has in the organization – to create a team, to produce new ideas, to work towards clear goals.

And Neil appears to have combined the two – the **style** he saw as appropriate (leading 'from the front', making unpopular decisions when necessary, authoritative) and the **role** (working towards the long-term, encouraging people to adapt so that their and the organization's full potential could be achieved).

I'm sure you will have recognized, however, that Neil's leadership behaviour would not necessarily be attached to a formal role within an organization. He appears to have been accepted as a leader because he has 'made sense' of an environment that has been difficult to understand, the process referred to in the chapter as **visioning**. With reference to the theoretical debate, and your interpretation of these three scenarios, you might like to meditate on the interaction and balance between personal qualities and learned abilities.

Activity 6.4

The chart in Fig. 6.1 is how one academic interested in leadership behaviour saw it as a range of behaviours which were the consequence of particular leadership styles.

Imagine that you are in charge of a luxurious but not very profitable leisure complex attached to a large city centre hotel which is part of a national chain attracting business travellers and tourists equally. Head Office have notified you that you have to change your pricing policy and to open up the facilities to the locals in order to increase income. You have your doubts about this directive for a number of reasons, but 'orders is orders'.

Very briefly, jot down the words you might use to communicate the order to staff (assume here you would be using the spoken word) if you had to write a 'script' to reflect each manager's view as to how he or she should use his/her authority. Remember how style, tone and register (Chapter 3) in language communicate attitudes and beliefs.

Thoughts on Activity 6.4

Perhaps you found it difficult in this exercise to divorce yourself from phrasing your statements in the manner in which you yourself would make them, or not to think about whether one style of leadership was behaviour

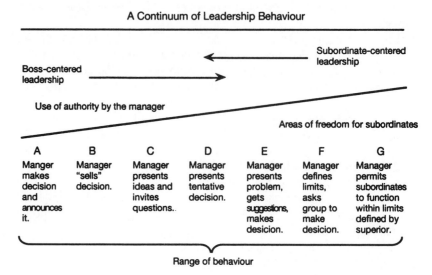

Figure 6.1 A continuum of leadership behaviour (Source: Tannenbaum, R. and Schmidt, W. (1973) How to choose a leadership pattern, *Harvard Business Review*, May–June.

was more appropriate than another in this context. But we are not really interested in the style of leadership or use of authority here.

We are much more interested in assessing how and why certain ways of communicating are the consequence of the style, such as how we can tune in to the interaction between the style and communications process; and how we can use that understanding either to achieve our personal communications objectives or to understand the clues given through the communications process about someone else's attitudes and beliefs – in this case, as to how leadership and authority should be exercised.

These are my 'scripts' – your words and phrases may be quite different, but give off the same message. After all, Shakespeare's style was quite different from Oscar Wilde's, although they both wrote comedies.

Manager A: 'This is just to let you all know that as from next week, I will be advertising in the local press that the facilities of our leisure complex are now open to non-residents, with charges which will compete more than favourably with the local authority's charges for their swimming pool complex.'

Manager B: 'This is just to let you all know that as from next week I intend advertising in the local press that the facilities of our Leisure Complex will be open to non-residents. After careful analysis, I believe our charges will compete effectively with those of the local authority's complex, and thus the increased custom will make our complex more viable and safeguard all our jobs.'

Manager C: 'Head Office wants me to find ways of increasing revenue from our Leisure Complex. I am proposing that we open it to non-residents, and offer the facilities at charges less than that of the local authority for their facility. This seems to me to be a viable proposition, but I would be interested to hear if anyone can come up with something else.'

Manager D: 'I have been discussing with Head Office how we might increase the revenue from the Leisure Complex. We have provisionally agreed that opening it to non-residents at very competitive charges is a strong option. However if any of you thinks that there is an argument for modifying this plan, it is, as yet, not "set in tablets of stone".'

Manager E: 'Our problem, as Head Office see it, is that we do not make enough profit from the Leisure Complex. I invited you all to make suggestions for improvement, and I was pleased to hear so many imaginative ideas. However you seemed to be in two minds over one proposal – that we open the Complex to non-residents. This was because some of you appeared to feel that doing so might take away some of the exclusivity and privacy for our own guests and it could also lead to overcrowding. I appreciate the worries, and I accept that these results might come about, but as it seems to me the benefits will outweigh the disadvantages, I have decided to go ahead with the proposal that we do open our doors to the locals.'

Manager F: 'The situation is this. There are a number of possible options and ideas as to how we might bring in greater profits, some more feasible than others. However we are to a great extent limited by the fact that Head Office seem to want this to be a general policy for the Group, so it seems to me that what we have to decide is how many of you are prepared to support for our Complex.'

Manager G: 'The bottom line is this. We have to find some way of making the Leisure Complex more profitable. As we all have to live with and work as a team to successfully implement the decision we make, it seems the best way forward is for you lot to work out a strategy which you all agree with and which brings in the lolly.'

Only a score or so of words in each case. But they tell us the power relationship between individuals and groups. Our communications skills can informally reinforce or undermine a formal power relationship like that of management and staff. The language we use not only communicates pure information; it also communicates status, role-perception and role-performance.

Activity 6.5

Leadership is basically about motivating people to do things you want them to do **willingly**. And motivation is the mental process through which individuals choose desired outcomes and then go for them through the appropriate behaviour. So the good leader tries to identify a desired outcome, or personal goal, for his/her followers which will also achieve a desired outcome in terms of organizational goals. But motives, which come from human needs, are often very complex, can vary enormously from individual to individual, and of course cannot be **seen**.

So once again we have to turn to theories, or 'guesses', as to what will motivate people, so once again our interpersonal skills come into play. Assessing the appropriate channels and codes through which to communicate with your colleagues has already involved you in thinking more carefully about human needs as opposed to organizational needs, so thinking about how you might communicate to motivate someone to work harder or get more job satisfaction should not present much of a problem.

You will no doubt have come across a number of theories or models of motivation in your studies on organizational behaviour, but here I want you to think about one with which I am sure you are familiar. That's Maslow's famous 'Hierarchy of Needs'. Just to remind you, here is the diagrammatic manner in which it is usually presented in textbooks.

Self-actualization is not a concept coined by Maslow, but one which he used to label what he saw as our desire for self-fulfilment, to reach the limit of our potential, whatever that might be. You will find in some textbooks that there are another two needs identified by Maslow, which he considered to be essential prerequisites of all the above, so they are not necessarily always referred to.

These are: the need for social conditions which encourage free expression, justice and honesty, and the need to know and understand, the curiosity and experimenting needs. You would want to take them into consideration as underpinning the above, even if they are difficult to place within the hierarchy. Now if we are arguing that leadership is a social skill, which involves the understanding of and responding to our staff's needs, then any model which helps that understanding is of value to us.

There have been criticisms of Maslow's model, which I am sure you are aware of, but at least it gives us a starting point for thought. So let's apply the above model in terms of the communications process. You are a hospitality manager, and you recognize the need for a good formal communication system within your organization.

But you also recognize that merely putting out memos, pinning up notices, or calling official meetings, may in fact be barriers to communication, because your staff perceive such operational methods of communicating to be impersonal, cold, distancing, not taking into account pressures on their time, their feelings as to what participation in the organization should be about, or even their ability to process information presented in a formal way. So think how you might communicate with members of your staff when you take into account the human needs element.

Let's imagine that you have seven members of staff, each of whom you believe can be motivated to take on board, get involved in, respond to your communications, if they see the content going towards satisfying one of the above needs. What do you feel could be the most appropriate way of involving them in the organization's communications system and thus improving not only the system but also the working spirit of the group?

For simplicity's sake, assume three of those seven are your immediate subordinates, part of your management team, and the other four are at supervisory level or lower. And again for the sake of simplicity, let's link each individual (A, B, C etc.) with only one need, although you know that each may have several of these needs, or different ones at different times and in different contexts.

Thoughts on Activity 6.5

Employee A, a young waiter, desperately needs every penny he has. He is a student, with a lot of financial worries. He gets brought in as casual labour only when there are big functions. The communication he wants is not exhortations in oral or written form to work harder, to achieve targets, to be proud of working for the organization. He also does not have time to read or listen. His **physiological** need (**level 1**) is what drives him, so the communication which recognizes these factors, and is linked to some aspect of his wages or 'perks' to which he is entitled will be instantly received and interpreted. He will be a good medium for passing on such information to prospective staff!

Employee B, is a full-time commis chef. He works in what could be a dangerous environment, and is very concerned about that aspect of his working conditions. He has strong **safety** needs (**level 2**). He is therefore the best person to involve in communicating to the staff new healthy and safety regulations, because he will be the happiest to help pass them on to his colleagues.

Employee C, the Head Receptionist, is an extremely sociable young lady, a strong believer in the 'human relations' school of management, and thus likes to communicate the idea of the staff being 'one big happy family' (**level 3**). She is just the person to tap for ideas about encouraging open communications in the organization, for example, likely to be very happy to edit the organization's house magazine.

Employee D, presently one of the Housekeeping staff, believes that the house magazine is the best way to communicate with staff, because it can be used to pass on the sort of information which makes staff feel good, responds to their **esteem** needs (**level 4**), like photographs, praise for particular tasks well done, sharing of good ideas to improve service or productivity. He and C would work well together, with him acting as the information-seeker.

Employee E, the Food and Beverages Manager, is a highly imaginative person. She likes to see her skills with words not just applied to her style of running the restaurant and banqueting suite, but also in creating and implementing new ideas and themes for food preparation and presentation. Given this **self-actualizing** challenge, she and the Head Chef work well together as a team, and could be given the task of stimulating the rest in the group to contribute further ideas.

We are left with Employee F, the Financial Director, and Employee G, the Assistant Manager. I have not spelt out the possibilities there so that you can use your imagination, actualize your potential! What would you build into the communications system, formal or informal, which would satisfy F's needs for freedom of inquiry and expression, and G's needs for knowledge and understanding, and thus motivate them to work harder?

Thus the formal communications systems within organizations can be enhanced by using them both as a means to an end (more effective information flow) and as an end in themselves (a way of positively motivating staff by satisfying their human needs through their involvement in the formal system).

Activity 6.6

'Leading' can be seen to take another form, in an important aspect of a manager's job. That is leading in negotiations, always being on the winning side. We have already looked at negotiation in the context of interpersonal disagreement or conflict. Let's shift now to the more formal aspects of negotiation, say, in the context of industrial relations, or a big renovation contract. How do clever negotiators get their own way, always manage to lead in the negotiations process? What interpersonal skills do they employ? We have briefly identified a number of key behaviours; now is the time to expand upon them, and look at what they mean in practice.

1. Have prepared, and be prepared, to ask lots of questions. This allows you to control the agenda, limits the other side because it demands re-action, thus limiting pro-action. And it can be a substitute for, or post-ponement of disagreement.
2. Summarize regularly. This ensures that misunderstandings, genuine or otherwise, do not arise, and each stage of the negotiation process is identified.
3. Develop a good negotiating style. For example, 'gift-wrap' what you want so that it does not seem like a challenge, an 'or else'. The 'social stroking' approach discussed in Chapter 1 results in the other party

feeling socially pressured into responding in a conciliatory manner, not taking a stance for its own sake. For example, instead of just stating baldly what you want, saying something like 'If it is at all possible, I would like to have . . .'

4. Avoid being unnecessarily provocative, making comments which could be perceived as attacking the person, rather than the facts, or crediting you with better or 'purer' motives than the other side.

5. Try not to let the temperature escalate. The ability to contain the negotiation at a level which avoids the desire in the other party for confrontation on the basis that the 'best form of defence is attack'.

6. Show confidence in your proposals, and if you do have to concede anything, show firmness in your final stance. You are not giving in, but again leading from the front by putting up alternative ways to achieve your vision!

Now imagine you are negotiating the timescale for a programme of renovation for the Function Suite with the representative of an interior design consultancy. Draft out some dialogue which would reveal a **poor** negotiator, and then the dialogue for a **good** negotiator.

Thoughts on Activity 6.

The scenario: the negotiation has been going on for some time, the manager is desperate to have the consultancy's ideas implemented, but is very uneasy about the proposed length of time required for the renovation programme. The interior designers seem adamant the job cannot be done more quickly without a loss of quality.

Do your scripts look anything like mine? Is it easy to identify from the language and the tone of each negotiator as reported which was the failure and which was the success?

A. THE FAILURE – 'HE COULD NOT NEGOTIATE HIS WAY OUT OF A PAPER BAG!'

Think back to the general guidelines as to how to lead, keep control of the process . . .

1. 'There seems to be no way round this. We dare not have the Function Suite out of commission for so long. I can't believe you need this amount of time.'

2. 'Whereabouts have we got to? What was that last point? It's not clear to me how what you are saying fits in with my proposal.'

3. 'What extra costs are likely to be incurred doing it like that? And why can't you see you way to getting some temporary staff to help out?'

4. 'I have my guests to think about – I don't want them disrupted unnecessarily. It seems, despite the fact that you are offering a service, you don't have much understanding of what the word means.'

5. 'It's all very well you getting annoyed at our inability to reach some sort of solution. I've got better things to do than waste hours over this, when the solution seems to obvious.'
6. 'Oh, well, I suppose at the end of the day I have no alternative, even if the outcome of our discussion is not in line with what I think should be done.'

B. THE SUCCESS: 'SHE COULD CHARM THE BIRDS DOWN FROM THE TREES!'

1. 'Can you clarify the following points for me? Are you putting all your staff on to this job? Is there a possibility that you might get temporary staff in order to meet the deadline? In fact, is there any way I could deploy some of my staff to help out? What exactly would we lose in terms of a quality product if we did simplify some of the finishes?'
2. 'So we are agreed that it could help with the timescale if I lent you two of my housekeeping staff. And that you will consider alternatives to some of the more complex features.'
3. 'Of course, I do appreciate the time involved in such a re-think, but perhaps at the end of the day, time will actually be saved, and both my staff and yours will benefit. I'm sure you will think it worth a try?'
4. 'This would be a difficult exercise to undertake, whoever did it. And of course, it's understandable you feel your professional credibility is at stake.'
5. 'The important thing at this stage is not to let our emotions get in the way. I know I find it difficult to keep cool when we have such time and financial pressures on us.'
6. 'Right, then. That may have seemed a very long drawn out discussion, but it was worth it, because I believe we shall get an even better result out of the exercise, because of the proposed reorganization of the timetable. I'm glad that at the end of the day, our Function Suite is still going to be the best in the town!'

'**Pacing**' a negotiation in this way, sign-posting that you have not been out-manoeuvred, or hastily had to agree to something you did not want, requires you to be in control of the **tone** and **register** of the discussion, to determine and lead the overall mood. Using the appropriate communication styles results in a **win/win** situation – or at least the other side not feeling they have lost!

You might like now to have a shot at this exercise with a fellow student, using an industrial relations scenario – remembering that trade union officials often have a professional training in negotiating skills!

FURTHER READING

Adair, J. (1984) *The Skills of Leadership*, Gower, Aldershot: a major writer on leadership in organizations. Strong theoretical background, but with clearly spelt out practical applications.

Keegan, B. M. (1983) 'Leadership in the hospitality industry', in Casse, E. and Reuland, R. (eds), *The Management of Hospitality*, Pergamon, Oxford.

Worsfold, P. (1989) 'Leadership and managerial effectiveness in the hospitality industry', *Proceeedings of the International Association of Hotel Management Schools' Symposium*, Leeds.

Two short but very interesting articles which discuss the relationship between leadership as an abstract concept and those leadership skills seen to be required by the hospitality industry. Useful for comparing theory and practice.

Informal group management $\boxed{7}$

A good deal of confusion could be avoided if we refrained from setting before the group what can be the aim of only the individual? (T.S. Eliot)

Question 7: Does working with groups require special skills – or are groups no more than a number of individuals? How can we improve our interpersonal skills in order to use work groups effectively and to build teams?

Snapshot
Isla: 'That was quite a risk Gordon took, when he decided to try out this idea of a sort of "adventure weekend" for the management team, especially with their different professional backgrounds and positions in the company.'

Bruce: 'Yes, and he even included the two newcomers. It must have been quite a shock for the guy who came up from working in one of London's luxury hotels to have to rough it with the new Head Receptionist.'

Isla: 'But it seemed to have worked – he must be a real bully, that same Gordon, to get them do some of the things they had to do, even if such courses are the "flavour of the month" in management training these days.'

Bruce: 'Perhaps there's more to Gordon as a boss than meets the eye. He certainly was able to weld that lot into a team.'

Let's imagine that you have overall responsibility for launching a new 'theme' restaurant. You have already seen to it that the name and the decor of the restaurant reflects the image you wish it to have. That's a form of non-verbal communication which we have already thought about, and you are quite pleased with the total concept and the specific name – The Buon Appetito – because your restaurant is planned along the lines of an Italian *trattoria*. The staff have all been selected and are in position, and you are enthusiastic about your new role and very pleased with your team.

What 'team'? No, that's not a silly question, or a misprint. You have at this point a number of individuals, about whom you have a considerable amount of information as to their skills and abilities, and you have some impression at least as to their characters and personalities, which you have constructed from your perception of their behaviour during interviews and the inferences you have drawn from that. For instance, the Head Chef does appear to be a bit temperamental.

(What has told you that? His tone of voice? His body language? Remember, enhancing your own social skills depends partly on your consciously trying to identify the **observable** behaviours which lead you to determine someone's mood or temperament. But is your new Chef **really** temperamental – or is he acting out a role – he thinks perhaps the Marco Pierre White image would fit in well with the Italian theme? Just a small reminder of what we're about in this book.)

Let's return to the idea of the 'team'. I want you to think of 'groups' and 'teams' as having rather more interesting and important qualities and characteristics than the common-sense view which would suggest that all we are talking about is a number of individuals as a collective unit, or a number of people on one side of a sporting contest. Eleven people at a bus stop are certainly not a 'team'. Indeed, we would not think of them even as a 'group', unless certain factors existed. One factor could be that if the anticipated bus does not turn up, the individuals may start sharing their irritation or worry with each other. For that period of time, they have a mutual need or desire to communicate through a mutual understanding of a problem, and it is this common need which gives them at least a temporary **group identity**.

But eleven people, dressed in the same outfits, each with a role to play, each with particular and shared talents and abilities, and a common goal, are likely to be perceived as a 'team', whether they are playing a game of hockey or performing as the restaurant staff. Even then they may not in fact **act** as a team. In order to do that, certain socio-psychological dynamics need to operate. These may come from the individuals themselves, or from whoever is **leading** them.

That person may not even be one of the team; s/he could be a 'non-playing' captain, or the general manager. But unless the captain or manager understands the socio-psychological dynamics, can manipulate them, can apply all his or her interpersonal skills to control them and use them to further the team's objectives, then the individual talents and skills may not flourish, let alone the group talents. In other words, a team is more than a group, and a group is more than the sum of its parts.

So we are looking in this chapter at those human elements which play a part in the process of bringing together your individual employees as a group and then as a team. Although it can be said that, in the formal numerical and organizational sense, a group or team has been created, individuals do not become teams in social and psychological terms until important internal mental processes take place within the members, and it is in these processes that managers need to be very much involved.

The team-building may happen within the staff at the Buon Appetito without your involvement. But that just could suggest that **real** power and influence rests within the group, or within one person in the group, who has become their **leader**. This in itself is not a bad thing, but it could result in someone other than you, the formal leader, or manager, assuming the formal and informal control functions you require to do your job properly. Unlike the Duke of Plaza Toro in Gilbert and Sullivan's operetta *The Gondoliers*, you do not want to lead your army from behind!

So how do we establish where and how one's social skills can foster the creation of a positive team spirit which furthers the organization's goals? The study of groups in an organizational context, which became part of the 'human-relations' school of management, developed from the findings that groups, independent of management directives and desires, have an internal power to create and manipulate opportunities to work either with or against management. This is partly because individuals may gain more from the rewards of being a member of a group than those which a manager could offer him or her as an individual.

These findings have obvious implications for the achievement of organizational goals. You will be fully aware from the media, and probably from your own experience, of the problems that group loyalty and good teamwork **can** present, if the group's needs and goals are diametrically opposed to those of the organization – just think of many industrial relations conflict situations! And the punishment of being labelled a 'blackleg' in an industrial dispute can far outweigh the financial reward of turning up to work when your peer group is on strike.

If we return to the point about a group being rather more than the sum of the individuals, we can more easily understand this concept when we actually observe group dynamics in action. For example, a group will indulge in behaviours in which the members, as individuals, would not necessarily subscribe to. Think of the excesses which a 'mob' may get up to, once they get into the spirit of things! We will be investigating that tendency later in the chapter when we look at the concepts of **group-think** and **risky-shift**.

So persuading a group to do something may be easier than persuading an individual, for reasons which are nothing to do with the time saved in putting over a point to six people at once, rather than to each individually. Or, of course, it may be more difficult! Communications patterns within groups of three or more people in face-to-face interaction are generally quite different from those that occur between two people, and the difference is not just a matter of numbers. And a group has a personality, feelings, needs, motives, which again, the members as individuals may not have.

Now many of those aspects of the communications process which we have already looked at with reference to individuals do also apply to groups. For example, our thinking about the concept of personality and the impact of **personality** on the framing of any communication.

But additional new factors can affect the communication between members of a group, because groups communicate through **networks**, varying patterns or chains through which communication takes place, which influence the nature and quality of relationships within groups. William Whyte, in his seminal study *Human Relations in the Restaurant Industry* (1948) showed how an order from a customer may go through a communication link involving four different people in order to get to the chef. Any distortion, or problem, in the message cannot be checked by the chef with the customer, or renegotiated in any way.

So the type of networking within groups will influence the satisfaction individuals get out of group membership, their ability to make decisions and to clarify information, and their ability or inclination to interact with new entrants to the group. We need all this understanding in order to communicate effectively within groups and to lead groups, just as we need to have an understanding of the individual in order to communicate effectively at the individual level.

Keynotes

1. The nature and characteristics of groups and teams are not merely a matter of the nature and characteristics of each of the individuals, and the concept of 'team' implies a deeper relationship than that which applies within a group.
2. Group and team identity comes from the interaction of certain socio-psychological dynamics which may develop spontaneously within the group or are manipulated by a leader.
3. Group behaviour can work both for and against management objectives; teamwork can be both a positive and a negative force in an organization.

Let's now refresh our minds as to what we mean by a 'group'. Textbooks on organizational behaviour lay heavy emphasis on the study of groups because organizations are almost always made up of groups and sub-groups, and you will no doubt have looked at or be looking at the general theoretical and conceptual debates. In this context we are not evaluating the theories as such, but trying to draw out those features and factors which link the study of groups with the communications and interpersonal skills elements, and see their applications through in the activities. But no doubt a reminder of the theoretical background will help, in order that you and I keep this particular communications process going!

Formal groups are created in order to serve the needs of the organization. They have a specific function, and their membership is clearly defined and stated, by virtue of the role played or the task performed, not the personal characteristics of any individual. The Buon Apetito needed a certain number of staff, and that number could be split formally into two sub-groups, the kitchen staff and the waiting staff, each with different but complementary group goals directed towards the organizational goals.

In a big hotel, the formal sub-groups are usually known as departments – personnel, marketing, housekeeping – each with their own specific functions, responsibilities and goals. Other formal groups within that context will arise out of the necessity to formalize, speed up, or in some way simplify the communications process. For example, regular staff meetings, or an ad hoc committee to address a particular problem or issue like staffing difficulties or the development of a new tourist facility.

These groupings have a form and purpose which exists external to and in spite of their individual members at any one time, although individual members may alter that form and purpose, for both formal (overt) or informal (covert) reasons. An example of the latter might be a formal committee which is used as a 'platform' for a member of staff to prove that she is the 'natural successor' to you in the chair! In Chapter 8 we will be concentrating on the communications aspects of formal groups; in this chapter we are more interested in investigating informal group behaviour.

Informal groups arise spontaneously, as a result of human, rather than organizational, needs, and the members relate to one another as a consequence of social and psychological factors and needs which may not or cannot be easily controlled by either individual members of the group or by management. Group dynamics in action are what make all these movies featuring aeroplanes with damaged engines, sinking ships, hijacked trains, and burning skyscrapers so exciting.

In these, a number of individuals become a group or a team, because they share a common awareness, a common perception, of a problem, and part of the drama is that they behave in ways which they would not as individuals and for reasons which they would not have had as individuals! I suggested at the beginning of the chapter that you observe the behaviour of your fellow students, friends or relations, in order to work out what being 'temperamental' actually looks like. Now you have a wonderful excuse, an academic reason, to watch 'disaster' movies in order to see the group dynamics in action!

Do informal groups perform a useful role and function within an organization? If so, what additional interpersonal skills do we require to tap their potential for positive contribution and to work effectively with them? During our investigation we will be touching regularly on **motivation** and **leadership**, both of which were referred to in more detail in Chapter 6. You may be well aware of what motivates you, or the head waiter, but would the same reward(s) motivate a group? And if groups require leaders, does anything about the group's personality or characteristics tell us about the type of leader you might require to be, or the skills you might need?

Because at the end of the day, we know that motivating and leading people is mainly about the implementation of certain interpersonal skills. These are obviously of key importance in the context of group dynamics. As the manager you can order the group to do something, but if the group dynamics are not right for you, then that formal order may not produce the result you want.

Let's now unpack the theory which helps explain our initial observations about the nature of the group, as opposed to the individual, personality. How does a group personality come about – what processes does it go through in its formation? Just as the individual is socialized through certain contexts and processes, so is the group.

What then become its characteristics, and thus the implications for its behaviour? Informal groups develop spontaneously as a consequence of individuals coming together because group membership gives them something, or enables them to achieve something which they could not so effectively achieve as individuals. So our definition of a 'group' in this context as three or more individuals who are in a **unifying** relationship because they share one or more of the following characteristics:

1. common needs (security in a new environment – your first week as a student, or in a new job);
2. common interests (swimmers join the University Swimming Club, or you, the Assistant Manager, the Personnel Manager, and one of the receptionists at your new job, discover you have a mutual interest in photography);
3. common goals (an interest in organizing an educational trip abroad with fellow students and two or three of the tutors, or a weekend outing with certain staff from personnel, marketing and the restaurant. In both cases, the boundaries of the formal groupings as designated by the organization are crossed by the informal groupings;
4. common background or culture (the sharing of age, gender, regional or ethnic origins);
5. physical proximity (you have been formally placed to work in a large open-plan office, and you find that others in that spatial setting share with you one or other of the above features).

It is not at all surprising, therefore, that in every formal organization there exist factors which permutate very easily to produce a number of informal groups. The upper limit in numbers of such groups is usually about ten. This is because the key factor is that the group members have the potential for close and frequent face-to-face social interaction.

Any formal committee, or any informal gathering of friends or fellow students, over a number of 12 or so, soon splits up into smaller sub-groups, in order that individual members can more easily take part in the communications process, and then each of these sub-groups will develop its **own** personality and work towards its own particular goal. A formal committee often splits into smaller sub-committees in order to do its job more effectively.

It is a recognition of this need, even in an informal or social grouping, that the Restaurant Manager takes into account when s/he is deciding upon the seating arrangements for a function, is it not? The spatial arrangement in itself will influence the communications process (a round table or an oblong table?) but so also will the number of covers at a table (six? eight? ten? twelve?) The larger the group, the smaller the percentage of individuals who contribute to group discussion and decision-making, and this can be divisive in terms of group needs and goals.

Of course one could argue that the 'common-sensical' explanation of that observation is that the larger the group, the proportionately less time there is for everyone to have his or her say, even if they wanted to. But in fact it's not as simple as that. Once again it's the human element or factor coming into play. People in larger groups are generally found to have a heightened fear of participation, either because they lack confidence, or they feel their status or self-esteem might be threatened if they do not perform effectively or make a fool of themselves in some way.

At the outset of this chapter you were asked to imagine that you were to manage a number of individuals whose goal was to take a new restaurant right up to the top echelons of the *Good Food Guide*. But by now you will have realized that we would not be discussing this topic if that goal was purely a matter of the technical and professional skills required to produce the best quality food in conjunction with the appropriate service.

It is essential that these individuals also develop a psychological 'bonding' – that something we call 'team spirit' – which will greatly increase the prospects of achieving organizational goals because the bonding ensures that the priority becomes the group goal rather than the individual goals. Thus the latent power of the group to achieve a goal is that much greater than that of each of the individuals within it. If we understand the nature and characteristics of the bonding process, it can then be deliberately encouraged or nurtured through appropriate interpersonal skills.

From the outset certain of your new staff may very quickly become friendly and thus work better together, because they already share one or more of these unifying characteristics. In addition their more general social or psychological needs, which we all have to some degree, may be far more important in determining social interaction, in encouraging team-building. Whatever the formal group goal, each individual member may be motivated by other, or further needs beyond that of earning a living, or making a profit for the organization.

For example, the psychological need for **security**, **affiliation** or **belongingness**, or the social need to acquire **self-esteem** or **power**.

Indeed it may be that these human **motivators** or, as they are called in some theoretical models, **satisfiers**, are actually in conflict with formal organizational goals, thus causing formal groups to fragment. So an appreciation that these needs exist, and can be extremely influential in creating team spirit and drawing out the best in people, allows you to use them to your advantage.

Affiliation or belongingness needs can be satisfied at the simplest level by trying to ensure that the members of your work groups actually like one another. These same needs, in conjunction with self-esteem needs, can be satisfied by encouraging a corporate image for an organization through words or deeds or appearance (a smart uniform) thus creating pride in one's role or company.

It would be very nice if you could pick your team to run your new restaurant on the basis of some initial psychological bonding or 'togetherness'. But that is not generally possible. Your team is far more likely to have been picked because of their individual formal and observable talents and abilities, although you might have got an inkling of that human element in that the challenge of launching a new restaurant appeared to be a factor in some of the staff's minds, despite the concomitant job insecurity.

Or perhaps you guessed that your new Head Chef, who had come from a much larger and already prestigious establishment, now preferred to be a 'big fish in a small pond', where he would have more power, and thus that was a greater motivating factor than salary! So you may have already used that psychological perception in your interviewing and selection procedures – not just gone by the formal job specifications.

Keynotes
1. Formal groups are created to serve the needs of the organization and exist independent of the individuals in them.
2. Informal groups form spontaneously when individuals find that they share common needs, goals, interests, or backgrounds. Informal groups continue to exist while these needs are met.
3. 'Bonding' within groups offers management a chance to exploit the group's talents to a much greater extent.

So how well can you interpret, or decode, the messages given you which tell you about your staff's group needs? How soon can you identify an informal group developing within your formal team? How can you use that understanding to enhance your achieving of the formal organizational goals, and to ensure that close bonding within groups does not lead to counter-productive behaviour within the organization? To repeat, groups inevitably throw up leaders, because groups need leaders to co-ordinate and direct their efforts, and your ability to be an effective leader and to motivate is more dependent upon interpersonal skills which apply that psychological understanding than upon your formal authority.

But first of all, we need to be able to identify the processes involved in the initial group formation. If you can do that, then you are more likely to be able to initiate and then manipulate the processes and the group to your advantage. Let's take one of the classic theoretical models of group formation and apply it to the individuals in your new restaurant. Figure 7.1 outlines the process in the context of your new staff getting together to achieve the formal organizational goal – to ensure the success of the Buon Appetito through offering a 'meal experience' as near as possible to that of a real Italian restaurant.

Then, in one of the activities, we'll analyse the development of an informal group who look like they will do the opposite – almost certainly disrupt the progress towards that achievement. Thus we can assess the behaviours and communications processes which are going on, and what might be your part in them, as manager – your formal role – and as leader – your psychological role. Let's hope your 'real life' experience does not reflect the negative development I have suggested as a possibility in the related activity!

I am sure I do not need to spell out to you the message we can draw from this mini-script of individuals beginning to work towards a common goal. They are more than the sum of the individuals; they are a team, performing in a way which hopefully will satisfy their external, or formal, need for money and job security and their internal, or social need for self-esteem, belongingess and achievement. They are identifying for themselves their talents and assets, an extremely important factor in motivating staff.

Now you might like to assess just how much of what they are saying to each other could have been drawn out by you, leading from the front, anticipating what would 'turn them on', how they could reinforce each other's individual technical capabilities and respond to not only their own social needs, but those of their prospective customers?

In addition, out of a group socialization process such as this (forming, storming, norming and performing) a group personality and identity will emerge, which in itself will have to be taken into account in the communications process. So although the 'receiver' of your communications may be several individuals instead of just one, this does not mean that you no longer apply the general rules of encoding and transmitting messages.

You still have to think about the **context** of the communication, which will be a factor in the **group** attitude and response to it – the group's values, beliefs, patterns of behaviour. This group have already shared ideas, allocated tasks, within this particular context. The test of your interpersonal skills will be whether you can encourage the same positive response in quite different contexts. For example, through what means can you harness this group cohesion to deal with a few weeks' very poor takings in the new restaurant?

Figure 7.1 Formal group development: forming, storming, norming and performing

Process	Description	Example
Orientation or forming	The individuals see the task and decide how they are going to interact with each other.	'Launching a new restaurant is a real challenge – let's make sure we all throw ourselves into it heart and soul.'
Definition or storming	The task is looked at in detail, its demands recognized and specific views as to response are mulled over. Conflict can arise here – over means, priorities, time scales needed to achieve the goal(s).	'We must watch our competition – we don't want to look as if we are offering the same as Pizzaland.' 'I don't think that will happen – after all, we are emphasizing that the food represents all the Italian regions, not just Naples.' 'That's a point we'll need to get over right from the start in our advertising.'
Co-ordination or norming	Information is collected about the nature of the task, alternatives analysed, differing emotional responses discussed, members' participation invited.	'Our straw poll does show the locals would appreciate real Italian food. But it will mean a bit more explanation from us with regard to the less well-known dishes – without of course appearing to patronize our customers. We could perhaps make the menu more detailed, and at least know how to pronounce the names of dishes.' 'You're not suggesting we learn Italian, are you? I was always rotten at languages.' 'No, hardly, but we could have some fun practising popular phrases on each other!'
Formalizing or performing	The implementation of and the assignment of roles in order that the group's needs are satisfied and matched with the needs of the task.	'OK, for the first night launch, let's make Maria the Head Waiter. Her grandad was Italian, so she has a smattering of the language, and she looks Italian, so she can set the atmosphere. The rest of us can then concentrate on the overall effect, and review our roles after a week or so. Don't you think it would also be a good idea to introduce the Head Chef to the diners – even if he is not called Antonio Carlucci! The kitchen brigade don't often get a look-in when compliments are flying – as we hope they will be.'

Groups, just as individuals, also adhere to **rules** and **norms** of behaviour, which arise informally and spontaneously through convention or consensus rather than being formally imposed from outside. You are already aware of the concept of a **role model**, of learning by example the rules and norms of behaviour expected of a particular social or professional role. The informal work group can be far more influential in determining work patterns and standards than that which management would wish to apply, because the social bonding, or group loyalty, ensure that the sanctions applied by the group are generally a far more powerful deterrent against deviance than any formal orders.

I am sure you well remember at school if anyone tittle-tattled to the teacher about who flicked the chewing gum at the blackboard, the punishment meted out by fellow pupils was seen as much worse than any the teacher could inflict! Or think about what happens to the acquaintance who manages regularly to avoid buying his or her round of drinks – yet there is no formal **law** stating that everyone must take a turn at buying a round. The strength of group norms has been researched in depth in industry, looking at production targets and workloads, because they generally appear to reflect what an informal group has decided should be the appropriate productivity of the organization rather than any work study specialist.

In our scenario, if the suggestion that each member of the group does not learn a few words of Italian, or show some understanding of how to pronounce the recipe names, the disdain or scorn of the rest will be far more likely to ensure compliance than a managerial diktat. This understanding has now been applied in many sectors of industry, firstly, through leaving agreement on productivity rates to group decisions on the shop-floor, and then widening its application through the creation of quality control groups.

The informal has now been formalized, and Total Quality Control groups and teams are being implemented in many sections of the service industries, including the hospitality industry, linking up nicely with the concept of **empowerment**, where every member of a team is an 'expert', and 'accountable' to the group for the group's performance. An interesting case study of this aspect of group dynamics is described in *Personnel Management*, November 1993, where it has been implemented by the Harvester restaurants, part of the Forte group.

Keynotes
1. Formal and informal groups exhibit a tendency to go through four stages in their formation. These are 'forming, storming, norming and performing'.
2. A group has a personality, attitudes, values, rules, roles and norms.
3. These group characteristics may more powerfully determine behaviour rather than any formal behaviour demanded of the group by management.

Finally, let's make sure we understand why group behaviour may be disruptive or negative, when the group personality can result in it consciously or unconsciously subverting organizational goals. In other words, like power, informal group behaviour is in itself neither good nor bad – it depends what is done with it! The general labels for those features are **group-think** and **group risky-shift**. These are the shorthand labels, or **concepts** used to describe and identify the processes within groups which lead to their behaving in ways in which the individual members would not.

These aspects of group behaviour are even more important today because the whole culture of management is moving more and more towards decisions in organizations being taken by groups rather than individuals. This has come about because of findings in the psychology of motivation, and studies in participative styles of management arising out of the contemporary Western democratic tradition, both of which have been seen to complement formal or operational methods and techniques of achieving more logical, efficient or productive organizational decisions.

Group-think refers to the tendency of individuals in groups to repress their own personal views if they hear others strongly arguing differently. These arguments may come from individuals of higher status or more power (although I hope you will now know without telling, power does not necessarily come from higher **formal** status). It is the consequence of the fact that the greater the bonding and the more cohesion the group has, the less likely dissent by individuals is voiced – the prospect of rejection by the rest of the group is too terrifying!

Thus a sense of consensus may exist which is in fact spurious. The wrong decision may be made, because it has been ill-thought out, or appropriate talent not tapped (a practical problem for the organization) or underneath resentment may simmer because certain reservations or specialist knowledge has not been voiced (a human problem.) It is therefore not surprising that contemporary research suggests that other methods of discussion, problem-solving, coming to decisions, may be more appropriate in circumstances where a formal group decision is not required.

Group risky-shift relates to other contradictory dynamics within a group which can result in the same effect. Decisions taken by a group as opposed to an individual are identified with the group, not the individual. Thus not only can group members be more easily persuaded because of group pressures into supporting hazardous or speculative decisions, risks which they would not have the courage to take themselves, but in addition these decisions cannot be associated with, or blamed on, any one member of the group, thus freeing any individual of the responsibility if things go wrong. The 'nothing to do with me, it was a committee decision!' syndrome.

So – you have been warned! As a manager and a leader, you have to be absolutely clear in your mind as to why and when you want to utilize the benefits of group cohesion. Which, as I am sure you already realize, mean that on occasions group risky-shift or group-think can be useful tendencies! However the above discussion also illustrates that on certain occasions or circumstances your interpersonal skills may be better employed handling a social interaction on a face-to-face basis, or through some other communications medium or code. And, as we have noted from the outset, the choice of the medium and code for a communication is a social skill in itself.

Activity 7.1

Research suggests that out of every six messages within organizations, five are carried by the 'grapevine' rather than through the formal organizational communications network. So it seems to make sense that we look at that method of communications within and between groups before we start on the more formal processes!

The **grapevine** is the unofficial, informal, some would say 'underground' communications channel, generally oral, but not necessarily so, which exists in an organization, in addition to, and despite the existence of, the formal communications channels. It will come into existence whenever people come together in an organization, and it is likely to extend beyond the organization. The grapevine has three basic characteristics.

1. It transmits information in every direction, and all at the same time – horizontally, vertically, diagonally, externally, ignoring any formal communications channels which exist, or connecting organizational units which have little formal connection.
2. It transmits information extremely rapidly, as it is not limited by formal policies or procedures.
3. It is highly selective in terms of who is in it.

There are several communications paths which the grapevine could take. If we take, for the sake of argument, eight people in an organization, the paths could look like those in Fig. 7.2. The diagrams illustrate the start of the process, its pattern, and where it stops. You, as a manager, can use the process to your organization's advantage if you recognize the significance of this information. So, given the characteristics of the grapevine, and the above possible patterns of information flow, how might you manipulate it? Where might it be used to complement the formal flow of information which you require? In what sort of situations might you deliberately choose to use it rather than a formal method?

Thoughts on Activity 7.1

The grapevine could be said to be a barometer of the quality of the formal communications system, as it is often a response to pressures upon that formal system, as well as existing in its own right. Let's think firstly about the implications of its characteristics. As a manager you cannot suppress the information which goes through the grapevine, nor can you control its boundaries. So where you know of its existence, question why this is the case. Is it because information does not flow freely through the formal channels, or is there too much flowing freely?

For instance, there are financial problems within the organization, but exactly where and why has not yet been established. The Financial Director has let this slip, but has then refused to discuss it with the rest of the team. Or perhaps has done the opposite – articulate his worries without appearing to give any hint they might be resolved. Too little information, or indiscriminate sharing of information, increases staff speculations. Or has the grapevine swung into action because the Financial Director is not trusted by the staff to put over information accurately, because of their previous experience of his communicating with them through the formal channels? Or is it the nature of the formal information required which presents the problem? Perhaps it concerns colleagues being paid off, or promoted.

The human need to cope with feelings of insecurity, self-esteem, role, means that we compensate for psychological unease by using rumour and gossip to fill in gaps. Management is not filling gaps in information fast enough or truthfully enough. Quite a different example of the grapevine in action is when your new staff find out about you and your organization

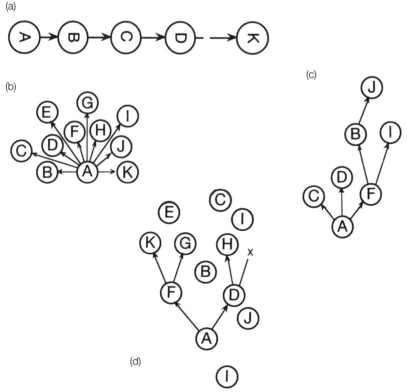

Figure 7.2

through asking 'What's it like here?' This can happen despite your offering a well-constructed and well-delivered induction programme.

Secondly, let's look at the diagrams showing the process in action. The simple chain shows A telling B something, B telling C something, and so on, until the last person to hear is H. This could happen if each individual is in a different department, or there is more than one organization involved. The chances are that the original message will be so distorted as to be meaningless when H hears it. But of course you may want that to happen – you want a gobbledegook version of your new marketing plan to reach your competitors!

The pattern which reflects a sharing of a message with everyone and anyone is not quite as simple as it looks. A may know that B, D and H will want more information than F and C and F probably won't believe it any-way, while G and E are the most likely to do something with the informa-tion. In other words, its impact on those who receive it will vary. But as far as you are concerned, it's what G and E will **do** that interests you (they are the most influential within the formal group, but you can only get to them through A).

The third pattern, which shows that only certain people might get the information and others will be denied it hints that this could be a useful technique to float a new idea in order to test the response to it. You just want a sample response in order to give you some idea as to the universal reaction, and you don't really care too much about who in fact responds or even how many. But you are likely to get some feedback as to whether it is worth floating it formally.

Finally, the last example, although it looks rather similar to the third one, reflects a certainty you can employ to your advantage. Starting with A you can be sure that the information you want passed on will go to the indi-viduals you want it to. These are well-established relationships – staff who lunch together, come into work together, socialize together.

Of course you have to be very aware of these informal groupings in the first place, and that may test your interpersonal skills of perception and interpretation to the utmost! Using the grapevine also demands that you are sure of who A is, or should be, in the first place. For example, what sort of relationship exists between you and your personal assistant, the Head Receptionist and the Head Chef, the Doorman in your establishment and the Doorman in that of one of your competitors? Are there occasions when **you** might want to be A? Is it the same A in all circumstances?

To recap, informal group behaviour, that most powerful of forces within an organization, thrives on the use of the grapevine. To understand the behaviour, you have to be aware of the grapevine and how to manipulate it to the benefit of the organization. Now I suggest you ask your fellow students for examples of the grapevine working in your department or your university. What sort of patterns are being followed? What is the effect on the participants? Do they end up with better, more accurate or fuller information than the formal system allows them?

How much misinformation comes through the grapevine? Or **dis**-information – information which a particular group has deliberately presented in a form or manner which conceals reality or aims to achieve a dubious objective? This is one of the major **dis**advantages of the grapevine, the lack of a formal record of what is communicated. The effective manager must be very well aware of the negative aspects of the grapevine, in addition to recognizing and using its existence as a useful measure of his or her managerial communications skills.

Activity 7.2

Building upon the study of grapevine networks is the study of the strengths and weaknesses of various communications patterns by the psychologist Harold Leavitt in the 1950s. He was interested to see how interpersonal communications are affected when restrictions are placed on how people have access to information. Leavitt's experiment revolved around a number of people being given a simple problem to solve, through communicating in written messages in a particular pattern with others in their group. He was interested in the occurrence of three important characteristics in the interactions. These were: the **speed** of the decisions made; the **quality** of the decisions made; and the participants' **satisfaction**.

These findings are of great interest to us, as they illustrate the significance of the interaction between the **operational** needs of organizations (quality and speed of decisions) and the **human** needs (participants' satisfaction). Thus depending upon the specific importance we attach to each characteristic, we can to some extent control the outcome of a group communications process. For instance, speed may be more important than quality on one occasion, and on another, participants' satisfaction more important than either of these.

Here then are Leavitt's **networks** (Fig. 7.3). Can you speculate what Leavitt's findings were, under these three headings, from the spatial pattern and direction of the communications as shown by the arrows?

Think about this in relation to formal or informal communications networks in your own experience – within your educational establishment, a big hotel or any other organization with which you are familiar. To what extent have you seen these findings replicated?

Thoughts on Activity 7.2

Obviously, these are rather 'artificial' networks, in that it would be very rare in real life for the communications process to be so tightly constrained. But we do recognize that the hierarchical system reflected in example **Y** is reflective of many organizations, and particularly so when there is a line of authority which to a great extent depends upon a grading of work skills from unskilled to highly skilled, as is usually the case in a hotel.

In William Whyte's famous study in 1948, *Human Relations in the Restaurant Industry*, he described a different kind of link – that of the chef in a restaurant receiving an order from a customer via a runner, a pantry worker and a waitress. The problem likely to arise here is that of distortion in the message – it can't be checked or negotiated by the chef, nor can any problems about it be discussed. Not only may link **Y** reflect an overall organization, it can also reflect communications within sub-groups in the organization. For example, within formal committees, in that all communication should be 'through the chair'.

These findings suggest that if you want to take your team along with you in a radical new business policy, your preference should be for a pattern such as that of **Concom**, which is a **de**centralized network. If you

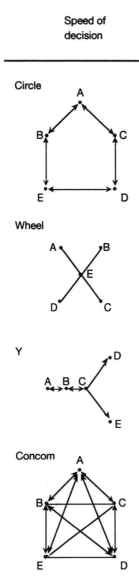

Speed of decision	Quality of decision	Satisfaction of participants

Figure 7.3

Table 7.1

	Speed of decision	Quality of decision	Satisfaction of participants
Circle	Slow in making and implementing	Poor; many errors made	High for all members
Wheel	Fast in making and implementing	Medium number of errors	Low for those on outside, high for person at centre
Y	Slow in making but fast in implementing	Medium, but dependent on how well person in junction (i.e. leader) did job	Person in junction most satisfied; others less so
Concom	Medium: bit slower than wheel	High; very few errors made	High for all members

need to identify and evaluate alternatives, discussion is most essential, so a completely connected network is the most effective. Or the Concom model could be seen to be appropriate if it were a formal (Y) board of directors having a 'one-off' meeting with a formal (Y) managerial team. (Of course Concom could also reflect the 'grapevine'!)

Or if it is an emergency decision to be made, or one in which it is critical that the content of the message is identical for all receivers – say, a new food regulation, then the **Wheel** would be the most effective. When a group is newly formed, the Wheel also comes into its own, so that a large amount of information can be communicated as rapidly as possible to the new members.

An example of the **Circle** could be a team of housemaids, where information can flow freely without having to go through a 'leader', thus all have access to the same information. The most effective network is the one in which a **fit** exists between the network, the relationship of the group members, the needs of the group members, and the nature and goal of the task. Centralized networks, such as the Y and the Wheel, are superior, in terms of accuracy and speed, for simple communications and tasks, and decentralized networks, such as Concom, are superior on complex communications and tasks.

However the **needs** element is also a factor you would want to consider. In centralized networks, if you are on the fringes of the group, you are likely to have less power than those at the centre, because they control the flow of information. So you are likely to have a lower level of satisfaction with both the process and the outcome. It is therefore not surprising that hierarchical management communications techniques are giving way to flatter decentralized systems. And it is important to note that we are not just talking about oral communications here, but also many of the forms and channels of written communication. Where do memos and notice boards fit into this thinking?

Activity 7.3

Let's look again at the process of group creation and try and identify how something could go wrong at any stage, how the human element might interfere in the process. Imagine the following characters are having a discussion which has the same objective as that scripted in the matrix in the text. Character A, B, C and D are members of the restaurant staff of a large hotel. D has an academic qualification in hospitality management, which the others appear to be jealous of, because they have had to 'learn the hard way, ' as they see it, and it does not help that he is inclined to make unnecessary reference to his studies.

The group get together to work out how they might 'put him down'. They then discuss his reactions to their efforts, and what they might do further. Eventually they are pleased at having achieved their goal. Within the matrix and guided by the concepts in the text, can you write a suitable 'script' for the three members of the group, which shows the group process developing in a manner which reinforces the negative aspects of informal group behaviour and thus lessens the chances of the formal group working together as a team in the restaurant?

Thoughts on Activity 7.3

As always there are many different scripts you could produce, so Table 7.2 is just a suggestion, just one way of showing how the formal group splinters because certain members share a need for self-esteem and a need to find some way of controlling a relationship within the group which in itself has nothing to do with the formal organizational goals.

I am sure I do not need to spell out the obvious likely consequences of such behaviour. Firstly, the formal organizational requirement that all members pull their weight to the best of their abilities may not be met, because someone with particular talents may be being ignored for 'human' reasons. Secondly, the formal organizational requirement that members of the group bond together as a team may not be met because of intra-group conflict due to attitudes, personalities and the resultant behaviours.

It is important to keep a constant eye open for the human element in any formal group situation. Appreciate the insecurity or resentment which might be latent in a group if one member of the group is likely to have a different attitude or understanding of how to achieve organizational goals. Work out where you could manipulate or step into the group formation process and manipulate it to prevent divisive situations like the above developing.

Table 7.2

Process	Description	Example
Forming	The individuals see the task and decide how they are going to interact with each other	'It's nice to be working with someone who isn't in their position through having a bit of paper – I think "hands-on" experience in this job is far more important.' 'I agree, and so does Jenny, I think. We were just saying that we'd have to find a way of dealing with Matt's know-it-all attitude, just because he's been to College.'
Storming	The task is looked at in detail, its demands recognized and specific response are mulled over. Conflict can arise here – over means, priorities, time scales needed to achieve the goal(s)	'One way we can do that is to make it clear to him at the outset the group of us are not very impressed with his manner.' 'Do you mean, actually say something to him when he gets pompous?' 'Not necessarily. We could just pointedly ignore what he says, and continue talking to one another.' 'Agreed. I don't imagine it will take long for him to get the message.'
Norming	Information is collected about the nature of the task, alternatives analysed, differing emotional responses discussed, members' participation invited	'Well, how did he react when he saw you re–arrange the tables without telling him?' 'He didn't seem to notice – is he being very stupid or very clever in doing that?' 'Perhaps one of us could casually make some comment about the new table plan and see how he reacts?' 'OK, Liz and I will have a go at him.'
Performing	The implementation of the task, and the assignment of roles in order that the group's needs are satisfied and matched with the needs of the task	'I should think that he has now got the message. I feel rather less inferior, and he's certainly not so over-confident. Our efforts should certainly have put a stop to him always acting as if he knows best.'

Activity 7.4

For this exercise I want you again to undertake some observation of your own. The objective is to try to identify those interpersonal skills which contribute positively towards groups achieving their goals. Your observations should also highlight skills which are lacking, being applied at the wrong time or for the wrong reason. You should also be able to draw out the **task** and **maintenance-orientated** behaviour and how it affects groups functioning. So make a copy of the following table.

You will see it has a list of categories of behaviours, and a number of columns at the top of which you insert the names of the members of the group you are observing. I have only created four columns, sufficient to show you the format, but you could have up to eight. (Above that number, it would be too difficult to keep an accurate record of your observations.)

Now 'sit in' on your chosen group, using your social skills to think of an acceptable reason to do so which does not give away the real objective of the exercise! Tick ✓ under the appropriate column each time a member of the group 'behaves' according to a particular category. Try also to jot down examples of the communications styles and techniques employed. When you have finished, add up the number of ✓ each member has. This will give you a rough 'profile' of the role(s) he or she has played within the group.

If possible, repeat the observation with the same group over a number of occasions, the more the better, although even doing the exercise once should be illuminating. And don't worry if you cannot record exactly what was said (or communicated through other non-verbal means, such as tone

Table 7.3

Category	Names				
	A	B	C	D	Total
PROPOSING – anything said putting forward a new idea or course of action					
BUILDING – anything said which develops or expands an idea or suggestion made by another or others					
INFORMATION–GIVING – anything said which presents facts, views or opinions, or helps clarify those of others					
SUPPORTING – anything said which states agreement with or support of other(s) in the group					
INFORMATION-SEEKING – anything said which asks for facts, ideas or opinions from others					
DISAGREEING – anything said which offers a criticism or disapproval of another person's statements					
SIDE-TRACKING – anything said which distracts from the point of issue under discussion					

of voice or body language). Just try and identify the most meaningful or key words and phrases, or behaviours, which suggest a category.

Thoughts on Activity 7.4

You should have found that even a simple piece of observation like this not only allows you to identify the particular behavioural tendencies of individuals involved in group discussion, but also can present you with a number of ideas about techniques in information-giving and drawing out, in persuasion, negotiation and conflict-resolution.

These behavioural tendencies lead individuals to play out particular social roles in any group activity, such as staff meeting. I'm sure that you, as a student, could pinpoint examples of these roles, relating to the categories of behaviour, played out by certain of your fellow students in tutorials. And the less structured the group, the more people will construct their own roles, and live up to them!

But this element of predictability does allow us to assess the likely contributions of individuals to discussion, and to work out how to manipulate these to our purposes, e.g. the diplomacy we require to ensure that disagreement is constructively presented, that its value is not ignored because it always seems to be the same person who enjoys the role of 'stirrer'. ('I don't know how many times I have shown that marketing policy is a non-starter.') Or the individual who regularly puts forward new ideas is not eventually constrained because the others get tired of 'smarty pants', and thus new ideas are stifled.

As these patterns of behaviour are identified, then it allows you as chairperson or leader to draw out when required the particular role associated with an individual, e.g. an occasion when you need the 'builder' or the 'supporter' to be dominant because group-maintenance is your main objective at a particular time. I'm sure that you will appreciate that the tendency to play certain roles allows for an element of predictability as to how individuals will behave, and that in itself enables you to have some sort of social control over the communications process, e.g. through selecting 'horses for courses' relative to a group's objectives.

Activity 7.5

Even in the most harmonious group, conflict occasionally can come about as a consequence of the way in which individual members perceive their role. Now conflict can be constructive, in that it may encourage new ideas, the rethinking of previous decisions and stances. But when conflict looks like stopping the group achieving its goal, or serving its purpose, then the leader has to contain, or avert the conflict in some way.

In formal committees, this can be relatively easy, as procedural rules (we will be looking at these in Chapter 8) can be employed to achieve this objective. At least they will solve the practical problem if, for instance, everyone wants to talk at once ('all discussion **must** be directed through the chair') although they may give the leader, or chairperson, some human problems to deal with later!

However, many working groups are not formally organized and controlled, and thus a more subtle form of communication is required to keep the group in order. This could be labelled the **content-to-process** technique. A member of the group draws attention to **how** the discussion is being conducted, the **process**, and away from what is actually being said, the **content**. Thus conflict is reduced or resolved because it focuses on the **style** of the communication as opposed to the relevance or force of an individual's views. Here are a few snapshots of individuals who can be very disruptive indeed in a group, for a variety of reasons.

These snapshots are another way of labelling or identifying the roles played by people in groups, and the exercise here is to think out how you might communicate with these individuals in a manner which does not threaten their self-esteem and create an aggressive environment by attacking them personally. What sort of language might you use to control such behaviour if you use the content-to-process approach? Let's imagine you are leading your management team (which runs a university's halls of residence) in a discussion on the implications of semesterization for the residences.

Stars: those who like to have all the attention, to hold the stage, to be in on every discussion, show they have the best ideas, the smartest answers to all problems.

Defeatists: the pessimists who always emphasize the down-side of a proposal or policy, who see so many snags, both likely and unlikely, and seem to take a delight in spelling these out.

Dominators: those who more interested in being in total control, in running things their way and at their pace, even if that is not appropriate to the task in hand.

Aggressors: those who use group discussions as a medium for settling old scores, getting in malicious or sarcastic remarks about others.

Storytellers: those who get too involved in sharing their own personal experiences, ideas, problems, and other irrelevant information with the group. They prefer to do this rather than concentrate on the job in hand.

Clowns: well aware of the purpose of the discussion, but there to show off their skills as a joke-teller, as the organization's wit.

Axe-grinders: whatever the issue being talked about, they always see it through the filter of their own pet obsession, see any problems as a consequence of their pet hate.

Jot down the 'script' of your response to these problem group members. Just to give you a clue as to what to do, here is how one might communicate in terms of process with a group in which several members insist on talking at once . . .

> I'm finding it awfully difficult keeping track of all these arguments because we're all talking at once. There seem to be some very good ideas floating about; let's see if we can share them one at a time without distraction.

Thoughts on Activity 7.5

I sincerely hope you never have a committee to handle in which the members exhibit **all** of these tendencies! But here are some suggestions as to how you might use the 'soft word' to get the discussions back on course. In other words, you are choosing not to take issue with the **content** of what is being said, but rather trying to keep to the **process** of the discussion, because the content may not be relevant, being only the reflection of individual quirks or attitudes.

1. **The star** (He has been to the United States, and has seen it all before.) 'I appreciate that your specialist knowledge of the American system, but I think we need to concentrate on the particular circumstances we are faced with here.'
2. **The defeatist** (Nothing but bad can come from such changes.) 'I understand your worries, but I would argue that the advantages outweigh the disadvantages.'
3. **The dominator** (Determined to bring the discussion to a close fast.) 'I agree that the issue will probably need to be resolved with a vote, but for that vote to be an informed one, we need to discuss the issue more thoroughly.'
4. **The aggressor** (She has been suggesting that it's all about more money for certain people.) 'The financial situation at this stage is irrelevant to the discussion, although I agree that we do have to think about the implications for staff's present responsibilities.'
5. **The storyteller** (Insists upon talking about a friend's negative experience of such a change.) 'We appreciate that the system does not appear to have worked for your friend, but unfortunately our time is limited in this meeting to discussion of what we might do.'
6. **The clown** (The whole issue is one big joke around processing students like fast food.) 'It's good to see the funny side of these things, but there are serious considerations we must not lose sight of.'
7. **The axe-grinder** (Sees the issue as one on which to attack the government of the day.) 'The reality is that we have to implement this policy, so let's work out how best to do so.'

These are just simple examples of how one might control the input of those group members who see discussion and debate as a means of satisfying their individual needs, rather than the needs of the group. And it brings us full circle back to the 'rewards' people get out of group membership. To be able to control the dynamics of any group whom you have to lead or with whom you have to work means that you have to be aware of the needs of individuals within groups, and to ensure that these needs are met in some way in order that the group achieves its objective. So if these needs appear to be counter-productive, then the demands upon your interpersonal skills will be the greater, because at the end of the day you have to take the group with you. That's what leadership is about.

Activity 7.6

How then do we deal with **group-think** when we identify it in action? Remember, we have been emphasizing all along that good leadership is about taking the group with you in the decision-making processes, having them follow you because they want to, because they feel committed to your goal. But what if the goal involves an element of risk – risk to the group's influence, self-esteem, jobs, future? You have congratulated yourself on building up your team, on creating cohesion, solidarity, psychological bonding – and now, instead of working for you and the organization's goals, that bonding appears to be working against you.

Group-think is flavouring the decision-making process – and it's not the flavour of the month you want! There have been a number of studies of this process of social control in action, the most famous being Irving Janis's studies of 'disasters' in American foreign policy, which led to his creating the concept of 'group-think'. From these studies Janis suggested a number of clear symptoms of group-think. These are as follows:

1. the belief that the group view cannot and will not be challenged;
2. evidence which might contradict the group's views and assumptions is dismissed or explained away as invalid or inappropriate;
3. the 'rightness' of the group's values and goals is unquestioned;
4. those whose views are in opposition to the group are seen as ignorant, weak or sinister;
5. there is seen to be open and direct pressure on everyone to conform;
6. individual members who are known to have or might have opposing views do not make them known;
7. there is apparent unanimity, as silence is read as agreement;
8. the group is denied access by individual members to information which might be of value or which could invalidate the group's thinking.

Imagine that all these symptoms are apparent in discussions you are having with your team about a plan to reorganize the management structure in your contract catering company, Feisty Foods, in order to delegate responsibilities in line with the new concept of **empowerment**, which gives junior staff more control over decisions being made in their department. In the group discussion, each member reflects one of the above group-think characteristics in his or her attitude towards your plan.

For example, member A (point 1) refuses to believe that there is any alternative to the present system in Feisty Foods, which has always 'delivered the goods', evidenced by the company's healthy bank balance.

Member B (point 2) is convinced by the evidence that such a system did not work in a similar company, Exceptional Eating, which has just closed down.

Member C (point 3) stoutly defends the system in Feisty Foods on the grounds that the management team always have the workers' best interests at heart.

Member D (point 4) suggests that any company which has such a system is just revealing the deficiencies of management who don't know what the word 'management' means.

Member E (point 5) states categorically that it is in everyone's interest to keep to the present system, while Member F (point 6) reports that she will go along with the majority, and Member G (point 7) says nothing.

Member H (point 8) argues that it is not necessary to look at how such a system has worked in other organizations because all situations and circumstances are different.

Your reading of the literature from journals like *Personnel Management* suggests that greater productivity and job satisfaction comes from empowerment policies. What communications techniques might you use to persuade your colleagues that it is worth a try, that the risk involved is minimal?

Thoughts on Activity 7.6

I am sure that you can see here the conflict between the apparent advantages of the group, or committee, as a communications channel, and the reality of the manner in which groups may generate ideas, solve problems, come to decisions. Yet again an understanding of the 'human needs' element is of equal importance to that of controlling the formal operational process of the group in question.

Thus it can be easily seen why groups come to decisions which are not of the best, because the group cohesion encourages conservatism and discourages risk-taking, which is what appears to be happening here. So did your dialogue reflect at all the following responses? These will hopefully encourage more open and informed debate, and achieve your objective without your having to 'pull rank' – never a good communication technique for a leader!

Member A believes that Feisty Foods' management structure is perfect; the company bank balance proves that.

Your response: (you want to encourage open expression of doubt) 'I wonder if that is due to our management structure. It may be because our products are very good, or our marketing strategy is highly effective. Would anyone like to justify our management structure on other grounds?'

Member B argues that Exceptional Eating has gone bust because that structure did not work for them.

Your response: (you want to show that there may be useful information even although it contradicts present assumptions) 'Yes, I agree that this system did not seem to work for Exceptional Eating, so I am happy to consider any evidence which shows me their collapse was due to the system being inappropriate.'

Member C takes the moral stance that the present structure is in the workers' best interests.

Your response: (you recognize that senior staff have up to now taken the lead in determining these best interests, but now you feel this is no longer appropriate) 'I think as far as this issue is concerned, I'll leave my opinion and that of the Assistant Manager until last, as we have to a great extent determined the workers' interest previously.'

Member D sees structures such as those being debated just a sign of weak or stupid management.

Your response: (you want to avoid the tendency towards stereotypical reactions within groups) 'Yes, I know that that could be the case. However an organization similar to ours, Gastronomes Inc., has successfully implemented this system, and although they are not quite the same sort of organization as us, I think it would be worth asking them for their opinion on it now that it is up and running. After all they are not our direct competitors, so I am sure they would oblige.'

Member E claims to represent everyone's view that it is in their interest in keeping the present system going.

Your response: (you want to defuse the impact of an unappointed 'spokesperson') 'As this is a tricky issue which requires a lot of thought and analysis, I suggest that we divide into two or three sub-groups to work through the issues and come to some view which can then be presented to the whole group.'

Member F says she has no strong views, but will go with the majority.

Your response: (you think her reticence is due to her desire not to be seen as deviant by the others, not because of her agreement with them) 'I appreciate your support for a consensus within us, but perhaps that might be achieved more effectively if you did some research into the literature I've made reference to, to see what the arguments are in this debate.'

Member G says nothing.

Your response: (you do not want that silence being interpreted as consent) 'Gerry, you have been very quiet in this debate. Have you a strong point of view one way or the other on this? Without holding you to it, let's at least have some initial reaction from you.'

Member H appears to want to control the amount of information the group have at their disposal.

Your response: (you genuinely want as much information as possible in order to come to a considered decision) 'I agree that all situations **are** unique, but it is worth while at least thinking theoretically what might be the pros and cons of such a system. One way would be for one of you to be a 'devil's advocate' and try and argue, for the sake of it, the opposite of what everybody says. Another way would be for us to look at how our rivals might implement such a system, and the possible consequences for us and them. That could get us thinking about the sort of data we need to make our own decision.'

Of course, there are a number of ways in which you could phrase the above. All I have done is to try and show one construction of language, one way of putting your message, which could achieve the objective you desire, that of dealing with the effects of group-think in your cohesive management team. This requires that, in the case of, say, a major policy change, all options are considered, expert opinion is sought and evaluated, individual doubts are not hidden or ignored, and any bias or 'hidden agendas' are brought into the open.

Of course, the exact opposite could have been your problem – a too hasty rush to implement a new policy because the cohesion in your group has encouraged the exact opposite situation, which we noted can be just as counter-productive. That is unacceptable risk-taking, because the group cohesion diffuses the responsibility for any negative results, or individual, and justifiable, cautionary challenges to a possible group decision are not articulated or are censored.

Given the possible negative aspects of decision-making in groups, it is not surprising that one of the classic organizational jokes is that 'A meeting comprises a group of the unfit, appointed by the unwilling, to do the unnecessary in the worst possible way.' Don't let that be the judgement on your group leadership skills!

FURTHER READING

Barron, R. S., Kerr, N. L. and Miller, N. (1992) *Group Processes, Group Decisions, Group Action*, Open University Press: an academic but relatively easily read book which is especially good on the social influences on group processes.

Belbin, R. M. (1981) *Management Teams: Why They Succeed or Fail*, Heinemann, Oxford: one of the classic writers on teambuilding and teamwork in organizations, Belbin lays great emphasis on 'team roles' and the psychological or personality traits which a good team must reflect if it is to be effective.

Douglas, T. (1983) *Groups: Understanding People Gathered Together*, Tavistock: a simple but highly practical approach, good for giving an initial 'feeling' for the subject.

Formal group management | 8

Nothing is so unbelievable that oratory cannot make it acceptable. (Cicero)

Question 8: What communications and interpersonal skills and techniques are of particular importance when we are communicating in formal situations and groups?

Snapshot

Charles, the Finance Director, and Winston, the Rooms Manager, came out of the weekly staff meeting together.

Winston: 'What a poisonous twirp that man Martin is. He does go on so. You would think he was the only person on the staff who knew anything about marketing. Just because he's worked in a yuppie advertising agency.'

Charles: 'Well, it was the one which created that terrific campaign around the "independent traveller" run by the Jordanstone Hotel Group. And that was a very professional report he gave us.'

Winston: 'I admit his report did make a big impact because of its presentation. But why does he have to be so patronizing? And that assistant of his must have a notion for him – she agrees with everything he says.'

Charles: 'Yes, I know what you mean. Mind you, sometimes it's just as well – Michael's so bad at handling arguments in a committee. No wonder his meetings are so often a waste of time.'

Our final snapshot is a brief exchange of words between two people who have just come from a meeting, which, as far as they were concerned, was highly unsatisfactory. Meetings, from the very informal to the highly formal, are the main communicating medium through which organizations pool ideas, encourage participation, solve problems, and make decisions, and research shows that the average middle to senior manager may spend as much as 40% of his or her working day in meetings (*Industrial Society/BBC Education*, 1993).

It has been estimated that in the UK alone 4 million hours a day are spent in meetings, and well over 60 different types of meetings have been identified. But meetings can in fact be very inefficient when it comes to achieving the above objectives. They can also leave the participants frustrated, angry or upset. We have already touched on part of the reason for that in the previous chapter when we looked at informal group behaviour.

Now we want to look at those aspects of formal behaviour which are important in determining the success or otherwise of meetings, and to link that up with thinking about the presentational skills required generally for communicating in a range of formal contexts which could also be called 'meetings' in that they are contexts in which individuals have come together for a formal rather than a social, or pleasure-seeking purpose, for example, to listen to a talk or speech, or which involve written presentations, like minutes of meetings or business reports.

I am sure you have heard of the witticism that 'A meeting is a group of people who keep minutes and waste hours.' An exaggeration, perhaps, but witty because it does often reflect the reality for some of us, and does suggest that perhaps those who have some control over the effectiveness of meetings do need their communications and interpersonal skills honed up!

Meetings within organizations can generally be divided into three types.

- **Statutory meetings**, which usually take place on a set time pattern, are to share information, discuss and take decisions and organize work on a regular and relatively formal basis. These require a fairly clear structure, a clear agenda and authoritative chairing in order that the official business be completed efficiently.
- **Ad hoc or special meetings** do not have a regular pattern, but are called to respond to a specific issue or problem. For example, to organize a one-off occasion, or deal with an emergency. They may be called, led or controlled by someone other than the normal chairperson (the domestic services manager instead of the general manager) have no formal agenda, and usually work through a more relaxed style of leadership.
- Finally, what could be called **support meetings**, often called to deal with stressful personal or human situations, or to create or revitalize high morale. These are deliberately designed to give individuals the opportunity to talk about feelings and emotions, and can be extremely useful in terms of identifying possible problems arising, say, from how the group work together.

Given the different contexts and objectives of these meetings, again it is easy to see that there is no 'one right' package of communications skills for handling them, or taking part in them.

However in this chapter we are not going to analyse the various types of meetings, or to discuss whether meetings as such are essential in organizations, or whether there might be other more satisfactory techniques for achieving certain objectives. We will work on the assumption that organizational structures and formal decision-making processes generally require that certain meetings, or formal committees, must take place, whether one likes it or not.

So we are going to concentrate instead on looking at meetings, and indeed, several other formal communications channels, as vehicles through which we can illustrate every one of the communications and interpersonal skills we have looked at in previous chapters, and which may come into action in a meeting, dependent upon the role, status, or objectives of the communications process.

Meetings or committees are not just about a specified time and place, and a formal agenda to be got through. They also involve the application of the fundamental skills of perception and presentation, which then enhance our self-presentation, our negotiating and conflict-resolution skills, and our capabilities as group leaders and managers. And meetings, however formal, still reflect **informal group dynamics**, albeit it within a 'set piece' formal process and relationship.

Let's look at one simple example of what we discussing. Think about a meeting in which you have been involved – a sports club, the Students' Association, a meeting at work – and award a mark to whomever controlled that meeting. (He or she may not have been formally designated or labelled as chairperson.)

If the 'controller' got a high mark from you, it is more than likely because s/he not only recognized and applied the formal or operational rules, like sticking to the agenda (or issue in question) and speaking through the chair (making sure only one person talks at a time) but also that s/he could, for instance, contain the more dominant participants and draw out the more reserved, or ascertain exactly when it was 'politic' to bring a debate to a conclusion. That s/he in the main saw that the group reached some sort of consensus – even if it was about 'agreeing to disagree!' – rather than being purely dependent upon the potentially divisive technique of calling for a vote. These are examples of good interpersonal skills, and are required just as much as technical knowledge of committee rules.

Of course, being knowledgeable about and being able to apply the formal rules within a committee is worth cultivating as an interpersonal skill in itself, in the sense that we already know that one of the qualities or attributes expected of a leader is that of self-assurance, of being seen to be 'on top of things'. So the technical learning enhances our skills of self-presentation when it is perceived in action by others. If you actually know what is meant by a 'point of order', or what exactly, according to the rules, is the minimum number of committee members required to be present before a formal decision can be made and implemented, then of course you will impress those who are not so sure of the rules, and you will impress if you can challenge others who try to bend the rules to suit their case or position or interests.

'Performing' effectively in committees, through both technical and interpersonal skills, is said to be a major factor in many organizations in determining who is a 'high-flyer'. And of course as many meetings are not of the sort which have formal rules of procedure, good inter-personal skills are even more essential if there are no external mecha-nisms to help achieve the group's objectives.

Keynotes
1. Meetings are the main vehicle through which organizations encourage participation and make decisions.
2. The conduct and outcome of any meeting is highly dependent upon a wide range of communications and interpersonal skills.
3. The individual who leads, or chairs, a meeting is ultimately responsible for that meeting's conduct and outcome.

Let's now examine in some detail the formal or operational and in-formal or interpersonal skills we require if our committee, meeting or group is to achieve its objectives. We will start with those factors which we have to consider even before the meeting takes place. It will help your thinking if you construct a possible scenario based on a situation about which you have some knowledge or experience – the previous example of a Students' Association committee might be a useful one.

First, **where** should the meeting be held? The more formal the com-mittee, the less room there may be for manipulating the more subtle environmental and spatial factors which can affect its outcome. In Chapter 4, in our discussion of the psychology of space, you familiar-ized yourself with thinking about how to manipulate physical sur-roundings in order to offer the most supportive environment for, say, giving a talk, or running a training session. That is, the place, size of group, or furniture arrangements.

The formal atmosphere of a board room for a committee of about 20 members will affect the process of discussion, just as does the informal atmosphere if you and three or four of your colleagues are discussing issues and ideas over a weekly cup of coffee in the general manager's office (and each meeting will require rather different leadership skills). So, initially, how can we improve the communications process, if we do have some control over the physical and spatial environment?

I'm sure you know that one of the fastest-expanding markets in the hospitality industry is that of the 'in-house' business conference in an hotel geographically distant from staff's workplace and home. That change of physical environment is considered to enhance the chances of worth-while outcomes of the communications process, whatever its goals, which may be training, policy-formulation, team skills, or gen-eral group cohesion and identity. The individuals benefit both from the physical isolation from their day-to-day distractions, and the psychological bonding of the isolated group, which encourages a sense of concentration and importance in the group task.

This situation of course is not feasible, or even necessary, for the run-of-the-mill meetings which pepper the manager's week. But there is no doubt that the location of a room, its designation, its decor, its lighting and seating arrangements, the comfort of the furniture and the temperature, all contribute to the mood of the group, individually and collectively, and thus how they will work towards the group goal. 'We will be meeting in the Board Room today, instead of Michael's office' does suggest a greater formality or solemnity attached to the occasion. In your imaginary scenario of the Students' Association committee, this reasoning would no doubt ensure that you decide that a formal 'committee room' setting rather than the Student Union coffee probably would be the most appropriate for your deliberations!

Second, what about the **seating** arrangements? What do we know about spatial behaviour which suggests that certain seating arrangements are more conducive to participation? Think about where you and others might sit in a meeting if you have a choice – that can tell you something about the likely group dynamics even before the meeting starts. Who sits beside whom? Who sits opposite whom? Who are you 'eye-balling'? It is much less easy to be confrontational if your opponent in an argument is sitting beside you rather than across from you.

If you have the chair, can you control where people sit so that you separate those who might combine against you, or so that they cannot easily communicate with one another through body language or eye contact? Do the seating arrangements have to show status within the group – or do the seating arrangements the individuals choose for themselves reflect their views of status within the group? These are just some of the cues which the perceptive group member can interpret in order to understand better the underlying dynamics of the group.

Third, the **timing** of the meeting. How do you feel about lectures at 9 am on Monday morning? Or 4 pm on Friday afternoon? I suspect not very positive, or receptive, for obvious reasons, so I know that I have to put that much more effort into delivering a lecture at these times if I wanted to communicate with you. I would certainly not **choose** to lecture then. But I am sure that you will also recognize that the purpose and format of our 'meeting' in a lecture theatre is not that of a management team meeting to discuss a new marketing idea, or a job specification, or a redecoration plan.

Again and again we can see that effective communications come from recognizing the **transactional** aspect of the process, what those communicating perceive the message to be, and what they expect to gain from the social interaction. It may be that it would not matter when you had to attend a lecture – you do not ever expect to be other than relatively passive – and students quickly cultivate the non-verbal communication skill of **looking** as if they are listening!

But given the choice, you do not as leader choose to have a meeting at what is seen as an inconvenient or inappropriate time, because an initial barrier to communication would be there before you even started the process, a negative feeling in the participants' minds stemming from a perception that you have not considered their needs or priorities. The time factor comes into the process in another way. The length of a meeting in itself is not necessarily a problem, if the group see that the meeting is achieving its objectives. The chairperson must however be perceptive enough to recognize the body language which is saying 'this is going on too long' or the tone of voice which is saying 'my mind is now on other things'.

Fourth, **who** should attend the meeting? We have already noted that the optimum number for effective group work generally is around six people. We have also noted that certain individuals with certain qualities or attributes can be brought together to make the 'perfect' team. And it would be very nice to 'include someone in' if s/he has a particular intellectual or social resource to bring to the occasion, or leave someone out because there is something about that person which will hinder the goal accomplishment.

In our snapshot at the start of the chapter we heard how Martin, the Assistant Manager, appeared to create resentment, despite his obvious talents, because of his way of communicating with his colleagues. But there was no way in which Michael could avoid having Martin at his management team meeting.

So when we are looking at a team or group or committee which is already in existence, we have to be fully aware of the interpersonal skills required to work with those whose organizational position, or status, or self-esteem, will determine their behaviour, or to deal with the political factions or hidden agendas which exist, and the attitudes and perceptions already in place from previous group interactions, all of which may interfere with the group moving towards its goal.

Finally, the **agenda** for the meeting. An agenda is an advance notice of what is to be discussed at a meeting, which allows for those involved to make any necessary preparations. That is why the phrase above – the 'hidden agenda' – is used, to label situations or issues or motives which are likely to have an impact on discussion **without** everyone having knowledge or warning.

An agenda can range from the very formal notification, presented in a conventional business style, to a brief memo merely calling colleagues together – or even a phone call around staff. Very briefly, apart from the operational aspect of 'where' and 'when', an agenda notifies the participants in a meeting not only what is to be discussed, but also the order of discussion. The items may be totally controlled by the chairperson, or may be initiated by or added to by any of the group members. In operational terms, this should allow for more regulated and informed discussion.

The group member who tries to bring up some issue which reflects a personal hobby horse can be brought to order if the issue is clearly not part of the agenda. But again that human element creeps in. The chairperson, in framing the agenda, must assess which items are likely to cause controversy, or challenge entrenched attitudes; which items require detailed fresh thinking; and which items are likely to go through 'on the nod'.

The decision can then be made as to which order these items go on the agenda. You might like to stop here and think for yourself whether discussion and decision are enhanced or limited if a controversial item is at the beginning or the end of an agenda. Where on the agenda of this imaginary Students' Association committee meeting is an item which proposes doubling the honorarium paid to the secretary? What human factors might influence your decision?

Keynotes

1. Before a meeting takes place, consideration should be given to the external structural and environmental factors which can be manipulated in order to enhance the likelihood of the meeting achieving its objectives.
2. These factors are as follows:

   - the time of the meeting;
   - the place of the meeting;
   - the seating arrangements;
   - the decision as to who takes part;
   - the objective of the exercise.

3. Once a meeting is under way, the human element means that the process is **dynamic** and the interpersonal elements require continual review.

Let's look now at the role and function of the leader, or chairperson. There are various procedures through which someone becomes chairperson of a group. It may be that the decision is outside the group's control – for instance, the general manager or the head of a department, by virtue of his/her formal position, is the chairperson. But in circumstances where the group has control over who performs the role, and a decision as to who does take it up could be very heavily influenced by having an awareness of the skills required to undertake the task. We will have a more detailed look at this point in one of the activities.

It is said that the chairperson of a committee is both its 'master and its servant'. Ignore the sexism in that phrase and concentrate on what it means in terms of the role and function of the leader, once the group swings into action. The chairperson has both to be a formal and a 'social' leader.

The formal requirements are basically the same whatever the size or importance of the group or committee. That is, to introduce the meeting, make necessary preliminary remarks, direct the flow of discussion, according to the agenda, while remaining impartial, and allowing equal opportunities for debate for all members of the group, and finally, to follow the appropriate rules of decision-making. We will look at these formal or procedural aspects in one of the activities. And although they may seem to be a matter of rote-learning, rather than the application of interpersonal skills, they still have a connection with the social role which the leader performs.

A leader, or chairperson's style, from the outset, tells members of the group, through his or her verbal and non-verbal communication, whether their contribution will be both welcome and listened to 'without fear or favour'. Thus the chairperson (I think I shall use the word 'chair' from now on, instead of chairperson; haven't we noted that it is a good communications technique to use a shorter word instead of a longer word if the meaning can be seen to be the same?) in theory ensures that there is equal opportunity for debate. But it might not look like happening in practice. Why? Because someone of high status tries to dominate, because someone is diffident about contributing, because prior negotiations (an example of the 'hidden agenda?') have taken place to control the discussion along particular lines?

The chair requires to be very perceptive as to the cluster of motives and attitudes brought by the members to the group's discussions, to the message coming over from the dynamics of the meeting, and to the techniques s/he can use to maintain impartiality in the debate. Our snapshot isolated the example of a committee member who was seen to agree on all occasions with her superior. Did she really? The skilled chair recognizes that the power relationship could be a factor in the debate, and, through careful use of language, could draw out from her what her real views were, without her feeling she might be open to pressure from a higher status member of the organization, if they conflicted with his views.

Remembering what we learned from our discussion on leadership styles, we can appreciate that the general rules of social interaction have to be regularly refined relative to the context and the relationship between the transmitters and receivers in the communications process. Where the chair feels it essential to control a meeting in order to achieve its objective as speedily as possible, then that may be the occasion for the 'task-orientated' approach – the closed question, the injection of mini-summaries to ensure that a debate keeps to the point. When it is considered essential to involve all members as fully as possible, then the style of the chair becomes 'needs-orientated' in order to encourage the reticent or shy to contribute without their feeling they have been 'put on the spot'.

You will see that many aspects of those skills we identified as 'listening skills' are the key to the effective performance of the chair.

Perceiving and interpreting what is said, and what is **not** said, **how** something is said, **who** says it, only comes from productive listening. Directing the flow of communication in order to encourage involvement and discussion also requires that the chair recognizes those important points which should be emphasized, those antagonisms and personality clashes that need to be resolved. This demands not only that the chair gives support without judgement or criticism, but also that s/he encourages difficult issues to be brought up, and shows support through feedback when someone says something about which s/he feared criticism.

And again the perception of the chair is of key importance as the group works together. What can be learned about the individuals through the way they communicate with one another (remember we looked at communications patterns in Chapter 7). Are there particular patterns of communication, verbal or non-verbal, which tell you about on-going or developing relationships within the group? Who is dominant? Who gets listened to? Who is ignored? How is disagreement received? Again, your understanding from Chapter 7 should raise your level of awareness. The chair has to be alert to these processes so that s/he can control them in order that the group fulfils the task set it.

Finally the chair must be able to assess the psychological moment at which s/he can call for a vote or a consensus or the 'feeling of the meeting' to be recorded. Judging the appropriate length of time for a discussion on any issue is a skill in itself – too much time, and the group may lose interest and track of the key points, too little time, and the group may feel cheated. The formal mechanism of allocating a fixed span of time for each item on an agenda may make operational sense, but it has to be tempered by the chair's perception of the dynamics of a discussion and the human emotions involved.

But the effectiveness of the communications process does not depend purely on the chair's control of the proceedings. The secretary also plays an important role in enabling the group to operate effectively. We have seen that leadership **styles** can be divided into task-orientated and maintenance-orientated. Let us now think of these concepts not as styles, but **roles**.

The role of the secretary, who may not necessarily be a formal appointee, but just someone who is there to record any proposals made or decisions taken, could be interpreted as almost entirely task-orientated. However the skills of verbal communication are absolutely essential in a good secretary. S/he must be just as perceptive as the chair as to how words are used, of the tone and register of the verbal communication, because any report of the outcome of the meeting, be it a formal set of minutes or an informal note, requires both the observable actuality and something we call the **sense** of the meeting to come through.

All the non-verbal nuances are denied to the reader of the minutes, so this entails summarizing and putting into the appropriate words not just what was decided, but also the feelings of the individuals involved which must be conveyed as clearly as possible. The record should convey to any who were not at the meeting whether certain items were controversial, aroused strong emotions, produced very conflicting views. So the words have to be chosen carefully – neutral on the surface, but having what we have already identified as a **metamessage**, an underlying communication which is in a sense like putting a 'tone of voice' to written words.

A regular example I have seen recorded in formal minutes is 'There followed a long and intense discussion . . .' – meaning 'There was an extremely heated argument!' (I am sure you all know the journalists' description of someone who is rather drunk as appearing 'tired and emotional!') So we are not just talking about the obvious – the highly developed listening skills the recorder must have during the meeting – but also the less obvious verbal skills of recognizing what is the right **tone** and **register** for this particular type of organizational communication. How do you think Charles's behaviour at the staff meeting will be recorded? **Will** it be recorded? **Can** it be recorded?

Keynotes
1. The chairperson of a committee has both a **formal** role and a **social** role.
2. The formal role is to ensure that the rules of procedure are followed to the letter.
3. The social role is to ensure that the individual needs, motives and behaviour, over or covert, verbal or non-verbal, are directed towards achieving group objectives. This requires particularly highly developed listening skills, skills in giving support and feedback, and skills of diplomacy and negotiation, while remaining totally impartial.

Finally, we have to recognize that although we appear to have concentrated on the role of the leader in this chapter, most of what we have identified as important in terms of perceptual abilities and communications skills are equally necessary for all members of the group. It is said that 'leaders need followers', in this context meaning that some of the responsibility for ensuring that a group or committee fulfils its task lies with the members as individuals. They also have to know how to negotiate alliances, how to be assertive and win arguments without causing offence, how to restrain a tendency to dominate discussion, or overcome a tendency to shyness, in order to achieve their individual objectives.

Their behaviour can be just as important as the leader's. How the various needs, motives, and behaviours are harmonized towards the group goal is, to repeat, a **dynamic** process. We cannot assume that the more formal a committee is on paper, and the more formal its rules of procedure, the more easily we can identify outcomes. The human element will always be there. It can be difficult enough interpreting all the nuances of dyadic communication; the permutations in interpreting the behaviour of people in groups may be said to be infinite, and thus the interpersonal skills required must be far more highly developed.

So far we have concentrated on discussing aspects of formal meetings. Let's move on to thinking about how these ideas relate to 'public speaking' or 'speaking in public' in the widest sense. The ability to communicate effectively through giving a speech, or a talk, which is by definition far more of a one-way process than being involved in a formal meeting, still requires that we employ both these technical and social skills in order that we keep the communications process going and achieve our objectives. A talk can have one or several purposes, and, dependent upon the purpose(s), the technical means and constraints and the interpersonal aspects and factors which have implications for the style, tone and register, are very similar to those we have discussed already.

For example, the objective of a talk may be to inform (new health and safety at work regulations), persuade (changes in shift rota planning), motivate (cheer up staff after a very bad week's takings), and admonish (carelessness in applying food hygiene rules). But these objectives are set within a context in which there is some sort of power or control relationship (your staff), the audience is, relatively speaking, 'captive' (it is not there from choice) and the context of the expectations is such that it is unlikely they think they will be amused, entertained or involved in a discussion.

One can of course argue that, if they are amused, entertained or involved in a discussion, this will enhance the chances of their retaining what you have said. But equally the opposite can be claimed. I can remember some very entertaining lecturers when I was at university. I'm not so sure that I remember anything about the content of their lectures – just their witty jokes and clever timing!

Compare giving a talk in that working context with the manner in which you would plan a presentation which is part of a marketing exercise for your organization to an audience of interested businessmen or potential tourists, and the techniques you might use to get and keep their interest and thus perhaps gain their custom. Now work out whether different communications skills and techniques are required for giving a **speech**, instead of a talk, and if so, what and why!

Finally, let's apply your understanding to another very important channel of business communication – the writing of reports. Once again, you will see the relevance of the theoretical and rather abstract frameworks through which we have been looking at communications and interpersonal skills.

The criteria against which a good report should be judged reflect these general headings we established back in chapters 1, 2 and 3. Who is the 'audience'? What do we know about it? What is the objective of the communication? What barriers might there be which would prevent that being achieved? The formal skills of presentation – visual readability, clarity in language, well-organized information, appropriate grammar and spelling, useful and easily accessible referencing – must be complemented by a style and register which takes into account a number of human elements which will affect the communications process.

The 'encoding' is not just a matter of satisfying the above formal tests, but also that of appreciating that no one reads business reports for fun, that those who are on the receiving end of them may not be prepared to spend too much time on decoding professional jargon or obscure thoughts, which reflect the transmitter's self-esteem rather than the receiver's capacity for understanding.

Additionally, the conclusions or recommendations of reports may have implications for an individual or group's role, status or self-esteem, and thus the evaluation of the report can be affected before it is even read.

Finally, business reports are written for the **eye**, whereas talks and speeches are constructed for the **ear**. What, if any difference, does that make to your encoding, to how you transmit in the appropriate style, tone and register? And how do we transfer all this knowledge and understand of communications and interpersonal skills to the **mass media** – the presentation of messages through the press, radio and TV? Is the toolbox of understanding, skills, and techniques so different?

Thus 'speaking in public', which for the purpose of our discussion also means 'speaking' through some formal written mechanism, may initially be seen as far more dependent upon technical and operation skills, because the need to do so has arisen as a consequence of your formal position or role. But this does not mean that you can ignore the human touch element. It is far more subtle and pervasive, even in business relationships, than has previously been thought, and its link with high productivity, high motivation and good leadership, and thus organizational effectiveness, is now emphatically established.

It is not surprising, therefore, that the most recent research into management styles suggests that those qualities thought to be peculiarly female – ability to empathize, to appreciate emotional needs of employees, to communicate in supportive rather than dominating language – have given us that new label for management style for the twenty-first century, and to which we have already referred. The 'feminine' management style as opposed to the 'masculine' management style – dominating, aggressive, neglectful of feelings, task-orientated. This could be an eye-opener for the hospitality industry, given its predominance of male managers. Are your presentational skills up to it, chaps?

────────────────────── *Activity 8.1* ──────────────

We have noted that the formal leadership role of the chairperson in keeping a meeting on the right track depends very much upon his or her interpersonal skills. The appropriate style and tone of language must be used so that those at the meeting feel their contributions are worth while and the atmosphere of the meeting is maintained at a calm and rational level, even although members may have strong emotions about certain issues. Here are some examples of the words used by a chairperson who does not appear to have the appropriate communications skills! How would you re-phrase these sentences in order to achieve the above 'human needs' objectives?

1. The skill of **encouraging**: 'That's a pretty useless idea. It's far too complex.'
2. The skill of **diagnosing**: 'I wish you wouldn't be so domineering – nobody else can get a word in edgeways.'
3. The skill of **peace-keeping**: 'Would you all shut up and stop complaining. Why do you need to be so obstructive?'
4. The skill of **convincing**: 'I'm absolutely sure I've got this right, so there's no use going on about it.'
5. The skill of **empathizing**: 'I don't know why you are being so dismissive of this change; it can't have much impact on you.'
6. The skill of **resolution**: 'You all seem to be so unenthusiastic about this idea. It's very depressing and off-putting.'
7. The skill of **clarifying**: 'I can't see what's so difficult about this idea. Perhaps you should pay more attention.'
8. The skill of **decision-making**: 'What do you think we should do now?'

The communications problems or barriers here revolve to some extent around what is seen to be assertive, aggressive, passive or manipulative language. That should help you rewrite the above statements.

Thoughts on Activity 8.1

Of course, there are a number of ways in which you could rephrase these sentences. And it is just possible that in certain contexts, you would not wish to rephrase them! The objective of the communication process as far as you are concerned may be exactly to send someone off with what we would call 'a flea in their ear'! But in general, for obvious reasons, you might not want to do that in public.

So let's assume these are public pronouncements you are to be making, and the following are indicative of how you might make them. But at the end of the day, as always, you have to tailor what you say to the nature and objective of the meeting, and what you know of the roles and needs of those involved. You will know yourself that you can seem to insult certain people with impunity – because it is almost taken as a compliment! (You may need to think a minute as to why that can be the case.)

1. The skill of **encouraging**: 'That seems to be an idea worth pursuing. It's obviously very complex, but I'm sure as we work though it, we'll be able to unravel it.'
2. The skill of **diagnosing**: 'I can quite understand why you have such strong views on this issue in the circumstances. Let's see if any of your colleagues feel the same way.'
3. The skill of **peace-keeping**: 'Let's keep our cool, chaps. We don't have much more time to discuss the problem, and it would be much better if we can agree to some solution which could hopefully be in all our interests.'
4. The skill of **convincing**: 'Of course, I realize that I am asking you to take a lot on trust here, but I'd be very happy to go over the arguments again if you feel that is necessary.'
5. The skill of **empathizing**: 'I can sense you are pretty upset about the proposal for change. Let's take a minute or so to assess its particular impact on each of us, and we then might see your fears are needless.'
6. The skill of **resolution**: 'Look, you know that I've not let you down before. I've looked very carefully at all the pros and cons, and I am absolutely confident that the risk is worth taking. Yes, it may seem a gamble to you, but let's see it as a calculated gamble. I want you to trust me.'
7. The skill of **clarifying**: 'The issue is not as complex as it appears initially. I am sure it would help if we unpacked what exactly will need to be the specific contribution made by each department, then an overall pattern will begin to emerge.'
8. The skill of **decision-making**: 'Right, let's bring this to a conclusion. I am sure you feel we have talked around the subject for a sufficient period of time. If there are no other contributions, I propose we put it to the vote, as it looks like we might not get a general consensus, and it is essential that we take a formal stance.'

So the chairperson is both master and servant of a committee. Combining these two roles – responding to the committee's needs and demanding that it reaches its goal – requires that the chairperson has control not just through his or her formal authority, but also as a consequence of being a **facilitator**, the ability to control the **emotional** climate of a meeting.

Activity 8.2

If the chairperson could be said to be the 'prime minister' of a committee, then the secretary could be said to be the 'civil servant'. In larger organizations, the role of secretary to committees is generally carried out by a professional administrator, but however small the organization, or how informal a committee, or meeting, regular or otherwise, the system will work more effectively if a record of some sort is kept of discussions and decisions.

And although it may not seem so obvious a point as with the chairperson, whoever performs the organizational and communication role of secretary, whether formally labelled as such or not, must have the appropriate communications and interpersonal skills for the position. The best of chairing can be hindered or even totally negated if the correct support is not forthcoming from the 'record-keeper'. Task and maintenance orientated teamwork is of the essence.

Basically, records of meetings allow those who were not there to learn what went on, remind those who were of what happened, and to settle any disagreements in the future as to what was decided. On the surface this looks like a pretty straighforward job.

However you have just been reading about the special qualities demanded of the 'recorder's' role. Not only should s/he be aware of the conventional presentational style involved in communicating not only what has happened, but what should happen! In other words, initially setting the agenda in the real sense, as well as setting the agenda in the psychological sense, and then detailing what has happened at the meeting in the formal style, as well as recording the **feeling** of the meeting – the 'reading between the lines' sense.

For example, if you, as a member of middle management, returned after a few days' holiday to find that a decision had been made at a staff meeting to shift staff from weekly to monthly salary payments, and that a new policy with regard to payment for overtime was to be implemented, you would most certainly want to know as much as you could about the mood of the debate, the arguments which were put up, who articulated positive and negative reactions, and just how popular the changes actually were. The fact that the vote went a certain way – and whether it was 85% for, or 53% for – is not sufficient to tell you about the human elements in the process, and you are going to have to work with these people, to motivate them.

This simple scenario illustrates the skills required by the secretary, the skills outlined in this chapter. S/he must be capable in the formal organizational sense of taking and circulating information, which requires listening and writing skills of a high order. And s/he must also be capable of encoding that information in a manner which reflects an understanding of all the human elements in the process.

Take, for example, the British system of government. The 'committee' which runs Britain is the Cabinet, chaired by the prime minister. The prime minister is supported by a top civil servant, the permanent secretary to the Cabinet. It has been argued by a number of political observers that the permanent secretary is actually the most important person in the country, not the prime minister. You may have an inkling why, when you think more deeply about the communications skills required by a secretary. So let's test your understanding.

This activity and the next one reflect two aspects of a secretary in action – an agenda, and an excerpt from an imaginary meeting. For this activity, what comments would you make as to the quality of this agenda, and why?

NOTICE OF MEETING
There will be a meeting next Tuesday to discuss, among other things, some problems which have arisen as a consequence of Head Office's new marketing policy.

Thoughts on Activity 8.2

The prime reason for an agenda is to give the receiver information which is essential if a meeting is to fulfil its objectives. A poorly structured meeting without an agenda can mean time wasted, tempers frayed, lack of participation because of lack of knowledge, debates centred around the interests of dominant individual or groups, issues not given the attention they deserve. If that is the case, what then is wrong with the above agenda? How would you reconstruct it? How about this model?

NOTICE OF MEETING
There will be a meeting of the management team next Tuesday, August 16th, 1994, at 2 pm, in the General Manager's office.

AGENDA
1. Apologies for absence
2. New marketing policy (Head Office: paper attached)
3. Proposed rota changes (MBC: Personnel)
4. Fall in bar takings (AHD: Bar Manager)
5. AOCB

(signed)

Honorary Secretary

Circulation list:
General Manager
Assistant Manager
Personnel Manager
Financial Director
Bar Manager
Food and Beverages Manager
Press and Public Relations Director

Of course, if this was a regular staff meeting, then you would probably have a record of the previous meeting. In which case, the first items on the Agenda would be **1. Minutes of the last meeting (date)** with the question to the group '**are these a true record?**' which allows for clarification or corrections, and **Matters arising**.

Additionally, the secretary might merely have sent out the notice of the meeting with an invitation to submit items for the Agenda. The chairperson and the secretary would then construct the Agenda between them. Thus a properly prepared Agenda lets people know what is going to be discussed, who will lead the discussion, and what information they need to prepare any thoughts or arguments in advance.

By asking for items, people are encouraged to participate and thus feel more responsibility for the content of the meeting and the way it goes. An Agenda also prevents 'fringe' or irrelevant material being discussed, with the item, AOCB (any other competent business?) allowing minor issues to be dealt with, and notice being given of major issues for the next meeting. By identifying who is leading discussion, participants know who to contact for advance information.

Additionally, items on the Agenda can be 'starred' for discussion, for information only, or for decision. The Agenda is thus not only a means of formal control; it is also a means of social control! It can contain the dominant members of the group, ensure a formal hearing for the more timid, and gear up participants to concentrate their minds on the most efficient use of the time. available. Now work out an agenda for 'controlling' a meeting to plan your Graduation Ball.

Activity 8.3

This activity emphasizes the skills involved in presenting the informal **feeling** of a meeting, in addition to the formal recognition of decisions made. How would you present (a) the formal decision and (b) the feeling of the the following spoken words and their implications for action in a written Minute?

> Chairman . . . I mean Chairperson . . . I'm very glad that we seem to have some sense of social reponsibility in this organization . . . there's not a lot of that about these days . . . and I know that the locals are pretty 'anti' more tourists . . . more fool them, when you think of the money they bring in . . . but anyway, if we want our young people educated, which is partly what we are about . . . although I know the income is important . . . given government cutbacks, some of us could be out of a job by this time next year . . . I am certainly of the opinion, and I know some of you are as well, that we continue to offer really good concesssion to school groups visiting the Heritage Centre . . . OK so some people think differently . . . as a matter of fact have we got up to date accounts on this . . . maybe that will convince some of

you . . . although I know that we will have to think about parking facilities for busloads of the brats . . .

Thoughts on Activity 8.3

Yes, we all know committee members like that! Of course a good chairperson will generally not let people 'waffle'. But occasionally one has to – for reasons of status, self-esteem, democratic participation. So the secretary's listening skills have to come into full play here, because the Minutes should then reflect feelings as well as facts. The mood and tone of discussion must be accessible to those who get the Minutes and who were not at the meeting. Unless of course the Minutes were of the sort which recorded only decisions which were taken, or actions which should be taken. In this case, the answer to question (a) might look like this, which is merely a formal, simple record of a decision taken:

5. School visits to the Heritage Centre

It was agreed that full details of the income from concessionary rates for the Centre and of the requirements for bus parking facilities be made available for the committee's next meeting.

Action or 'resolution' minutes are often all that is required in small organizations, and they are certainly easier to produce by the non-professional, or honorary, secretary. However more detailed minutes are the norm in complex organizations. They may be called 'narrative' minutes because they describe as well as record. If the above conversation was to be part of a narrative minute, it might look something like this:

5. School visits to the Heritage Centre

Mrs Clark strongly supported Mr Hart's view that concessionary rates for schoolchildren visiting the Centre should remain, although she did have sympathy for the members of the committee and the local-people's reservations about the increasing number of tourists. She felt that fuller information on the financial and parking aspects of the issue would relieve doubts, and asked that these be investigated and made available to the members.

The narrative minute can reveal attitudes, values, stances, on an issue. When they are circulated in advance of a following meeting, they allow debate to 'take off' with each member of the committee having as much access as possible to the context within which discussion will now take place.

Finally, as a set of minutes should formally record who was and who was not at a meeting, readers of the minutes have access to information which is also useful in establishing the mood or tone, and why decisions went the way they did. Back to the roles that individuals play, or the attitudes or motives which affect the decision-making process!

─────────────────────────────────── *Activity 8.4* ───────

Perhaps the most obvious skill which comes to mind when we are talking about good formal communications is that of being able to give 'a talk'. And however informal that talk may appear to be in its content and context, we all know that it is still a 'formal' presentation in the sense that we are communicating in a manner that we would not be communicating were we sitting in a coffee bar with a group of friends chattering about exactly the same topic or issue. Obviously it helps your presentation enormously if you **know** what you are talking about, but I am sure you have at some time been on the receiving end of a talk given by someone who is extremely knowledgeable, but who for a variety of reasons has not been able to present his or her knowledge in a manner which allows the audience to assimilate it effectively.

And we are not talking just about being interesting or amusing. There may be many occasions when you have to talk to a group where being 'entertaining' is the last effect you are aiming for (although no doubt you will appreciate why formal learning of the most intense kind will take place more easily if you are also interested – it is no surprise that university lecturers are now positively encouraged to learn how to **teach**, a skill which they may not have despite their intellectual powers).

So jot down three or four circumstances in which you might, as a manager, have to give a talk. Then apply your understanding of the human elements we have identified in the communications process to the circumstances and work out what you have to consider **beyond** the specific content of what you want to say. Remember that we are thinking about the human elements involved in both verbal and non-verbal communication. And that we also need to assess the interaction between these and the formal or operational aspects of communicating. Are there enough clues there to get you going? There ought to be!

Thoughts on Activity 8.4

The situations or circumstances which I thought could be appropriate for our purposes were (a) a training session on new food Hygiene Regulations (b) a presentation of a new company pay policy to union representatives, and (c) an outline of local tourist attractions to a group of foreign guests. The questions you need to ask yourself are very general. The answers in each case can be very specific, and will also reflect how **you personally** read the situation, and your communications skills as you see them and how you might use them.

Question 1: Establish the objective of the communication. Is it to inform, persuade, counsel, for interest or entertainment? Is there more than one objective? If so, can you prioritize in terms of importance? In the examples above (a) involves information and persuasion, (b) involves information, persuasion and perhaps counselling of a sort and (c) involves information and interest – and probably interest being even more valuable than information. It might even be that the persuasive purpose in the exercise is to persuade the listeners that you are a good boss, or manager, and that will then take priority in terms of goals to be achieved!

Question 2: To whom are you speaking? Every audience has different needs, so what might seem to be a straight passing on of formal information at a human level may involve you, as a 'leader', a strong element of motivation, as in example (a) or of reassurance, as in example (b) or an ability to engender an air of excitement and anticipation as in example (c).

Question 3: What is it about the audience as individuals I should know? What do **they** know about the subject? In example (a) you are probably building on information and understanding that they have, and it is also unlikely that they will be become 'emotionally involved' in the new information or what is being said to them.

But in example (b) you probably will have an audience with fairly strong views as to what they would consider a good pay policy, and thus you might guess that you are starting from the basis of a group with preconceived ideas, perhaps an element of suspicion, and a very strong group identity, all of which can be a barrier to communication.

However example (c) perhaps encourages us to think about quite different social factors which could affect what you tell the group about the local tourist attractions. What age are they? What sex are they? What appears to be their educational, social and occupational background?

These factors could all affect which specific tourist attractions you suggest or emphasize. However beautiful the view from the top of a local range of hills, or however fascinating the medieval ruins in the town centre, we can assume that the first example is unlikely to appeal to the senior citizens, and the second to the teenagers on holiday with mum and dad!

Question 4: Where will your presentation be given? In a conference suite, a boardroom, an office, a public hall? How much will the physical and spatial arrangements (seating arrangements, lighting conditions)?

In example (a) will the staff take you more seriously if you talk to them in a fairly formal setting rather than just over coffee in a physically relaxing atmosphere?

In example (b) can you win support by trying to avoid the 'us' and 'them' feeling through presenting your ideas in your office, but over coffee and biscuits? (It was no accident that the prime minister of a British Labour government was renowned for his 'beer and sandwiches' working lunches with union leaders at Number 10 Downing Street.)

But of course in example (c) you might rightly feel that you would intimidate guests if you asked to see them in your office – the hotel lounge bar, with the most informal seating arrangements, would no doubt come to your mind.

Question 5: When will your presentation be given? The date, day and time can all affect an audience's attention positively or adversely. The training session needs to be held when the staff's minds are at their sharpest and most receptive – so you don't plan to fit it in at the end of a busy day. Conversely you might positively want to have what could be a contentious discussion at a time when the union representatives are **not** at their most aware, dare I say! And example (c) might be a situation where you would deliberately not bombard new guests with facts and ideas the minute they set foot in the door, but left till they have settled down, and worked out in theory roughly what they would like to do.

The information-giving session then can become a two-way process, in which they can ask questions, with the consequence that you will be seen to be even more helpful! So your ability to give a good talk depends just as much on 'knowing' your audience as knowing your facts. And the more aware you are of both, the more likely you are to be aware of any barriers to communication, and the possibilities that you have of manipulating the variables which will enhance the communication.

Activity 8.5

A business report is a formal, factual communications channel. It is a written document for a specified audience in order to inform and/or persuade. Subject matter includes policy statements, progress summaries, the results of internal research, public relations documents. Reports may be purely for internal consumption, or go outside the organization. And there are many good textbooks which detail the format of a 'model' or 'conventional' report – I have suggested a couple in the references at the end of this chapter.

So why are we looking at the business report in the context of interpersonal skills? Is it not just about grammar and spelling and sensible numbering, sub-dividing, and referencing? Of course not – or I would not be asking you to think about it! Just as you want your voice, dress and body language to present a positive image of you in order to enhance your formal role and status, so also you want any formal report you write to say even more positive things about you than does its formal content.

It is no accident that large organizations go to great expense employing public relations specialists and graphic designers to construct their reports to shareholders, progress reports, etc. Whatever the knowledge content, we recognize that readers of reports also have the human need to be accorded the status of being important enough to receive a glossy presentation, to be properly and appropriately informed, interested, entertained, amused. Just as, whatever the brilliance of your qualifications, you will still 'dress up' for an interview to show the interviewers that you consider the importance of the particular context requires more than just the information that you have a degree.

So the exercise here is not just to look at the general plan of attack for writing a report, but also to look at those other factors which will affect how the reader perceives your intellectual effort, what in this particular context requires an extra bit of attention on your part. In other words, the human element.

Just as in all communications processes, the physical effort of reading a report and the mental effort of understanding can be either enhanced or diminished by the way the reader's **beliefs**, **attitudes** and **needs** are considered by the writer. An untidily written essay which is difficult to read may lose a student marks from me because I cannot easily follow the flow of his argument; it also puts me in a bad mood because it suggests that I am not important enough for him to take care with his writing!

Now go through the following points and note down those which suggest to you that your interpersonal as well as your fact-finding, analytical or word-processing skills have to come into action.

1.   THE FORMALITIES OF THE OPENING PAGES

1.1 Title page: the report title, the name of the author, for whom it was prepared, and date of issue.
1.2 Synopsis: a short summary or abstract, with very brief details as to the problem, the research techniques, conclusions and any recommendations.
1.3 Contents table, with page numbers.

2.   THE TEXT

2.1 Introduction: background, problem and research methodology. This could include why the study was undertaken, the terms of reference, the importance of any findings, previous information which is needed to bring the reader up to date, how data was collected.
2.2 The findings: the complete body of information collected and collated.
2.3 The conclusion: the summary, bringing everything together and highlighting the most important points, and recommendations for action, if any.

3.   APPENDICES

3.1 Supplementary tables, graphs, statistics, diagrams, which support the main body of material.

3.2 Bibliography, book, periodical, media references, categorized and listed in alphabetical order and conventional style (note how my references are presented; there is an alternative method, in which the book or journal title is underlined as opposed to being *italicized*, and the date of publication is put at the end instead of after the author's name).

3.3 Glossary, not essential, but important if there are frequently used but perhaps unknown or misunderstood words, which need to be listed and defined.

4. GENERAL PRESENTATION

4.1 Headings and sub-headings should be used for sections and paragraphs to indicate and separate the various ideas, issues, lines of thought or investigation. These generally are identified also with numbering, the contemporary business practice being decimal numbering, as I have been using here.

4.2 Underlining, use of CAPITAL or upper case letters, or **bold**, careful spacing and indentation all improve clarity, ease of reference, and speed of reading.

4.3 Generally reports are written in the third person. That is '**it was** discovered during the investigation' rather than '**I** discovered during the investigation'. However, the less formal, more personal **I** may be used in reports which are purely for use within an organization where you are likely to be known to the readers.

Yes, despite what I am sure you are thinking, the 'human needs' element can be very powerful here if you want to ensure your report is received favourably. Work on it . . .

Thoughts on Activity 8.5

I have no doubt that by now you will be very well aware of the message you are to draw out of this exercise. That is, the importance of taking into consideration the 'human factor', even in a very formal piece of communication regularly used within organizations, and of recognizing that the formal writing skills required by a business report are not in themselves sufficient to ensure that the report communicates what you would want it to do. Let's look at the formal or business context first.

In business, 'time is money'. Thus the content and presentation of a report should be geared towards its being read and understood as quickly as possible. That is a communications skill – understanding that the format itself will enhance the reading speed. So we have the convention as to what comprises the first few pages (point 1). The reader knows immediately what the report is about, why it was written, and where to find specific material if there is not time to read the complete report. The appendices (point 3) offer supporting information if it is wanted or needed.

The layout generally (point 4) can also facilitate reading and understanding, as it will highlight important points and ensure that the eyes scan the written word with ease. I am sure you must have chosen a textbook on at least one occasion because it **looked** easy to read! And research actually suggests that only 20% of readers reach the most important parts of a report, which is why reports often **start** with the conclusions instead of ending with them!

Secondly, 'money is money!' Typing, paper and printing costs can be saved if you write in good plain English. In Chapter 2 we touched upon the social factors surrounding the use of words; here we are thinking about clear concise and correct language. It is less expensive to write a good report than a bad one, because if you are vague, or ambiguous, or long-winded, further correspondence may be necessary to clarify what you are saying.

Let's now look at that all-important human element. Well, in the first place, we have to recognize that people do not read business reports because they want to in the sense they want to read the latest airport thriller or 'shopping and sex' novel! They want because they have to – or they don't have to – but ought to, so they have to be motivated to read. The formal or technical aspects referred to above will encourage that.

That 'human needs' element however has a number of more subtle ingredients. Perhaps a little scenario will help illustrate this point. Caitlin, the new general manager of the Hebrides Hotel Group, would not admit publicly that she could not understand certain parts of a report in case she was thought to be stupid, especially if she felt that she should understand the words or phrases. This would be a threat to her self-esteem. So this could be a barrier to communication, if the English is not as simple as possible and there is only essential 'jargon'. Caitlin also likes to be communicated with in a manner which she feels reflects the importance of her role and status.

Thus she expects reports to be presented in a style which shows that the writer 'means business', is taking the exercise seriously and that the writer appreciates that he is writing for the general manager, not the chatty staff magazine or the local tabloid newspaper. (My point about sloppy student work . . .?) And Caitlin, being relatively new to the job, is very sensitive to the views of other organizations as to the new, very positive corporate image of the Hebrides Hotel Group she is hoping to project, which is a consequence of her unique managerial skills. The reports, which she commissions, have to reflect this new dynamic business ethos; they have to serve a dual purpose, presentation as important as content.

In this scenario, Eileen, the Marketing Manager, recognizes that her reports have to take into account the human needs of the receiver. So she thinks very carefully about how she encodes her message. She calls on all her knowledge and understanding of the receiver(s), her audience (you can reflect back to Activity 8.2 here) and chooses the appropriate language, tone and register (Activity 3.3).

Finally, Eileen recognizes that through her reports, she has the power to market herself, to enhance the perception of others as to her competence and efficiency. In this case, for her, presentation may be more that content!

So it is obvious that the content and presentation of the written word, whether it is a letter or a business report, is just as important and can be just as effective in communicating our understanding of human needs as well as organizational requirements. By applying our understanding of that through use of our interpersonal skills in conjunction with our formal writing skills of spelling, grammar and vocabulary we will be able to control the communications process, its outcome and our objectives even more effectively.

Activity 8.6

Communicating through the mass media is a highly specialist skill in itself, in that it requires a particular style and use of language. But the essence of that style still depends upon those communications skills which we have identified in all our deliberations – that we encode our message in the appropriate register for the channel of communication chosen. The term 'mass media' means those channels used for the mass or public dissemination of information, such as radio, TV, film, the press, magazines, journals, and advertising.

We cannot cover in detail all aspects of communicating through the mass media, and in a lot of circumstances you would not be doing so anyway because you would have hired a professional to do the job for you. But familiarity with the local media and how to use it often opens up opportunities for extra useful publicity for your organization.

The local press and radio are always hungry for what's called 'human interest' stories, and you do not need to wait for them to come to you if you think that something newsworthy has occurred, or something has happened which could be made newsworthy. The major stories will bring them to you anyway; what you want is to create publicity when it might not be there. The latest addition to the Head Chef's family can be a news story if he creates a special celebration dish in the baby's name! A couple of foreign tourists in themselves may not be very unusual, but then you find out that one of them had an ancestor who lived in the area, and she's come back to trace her roots.

So train your mind to tune in to recognizing the information and events which could be put to good use because they draw attention to your business or service. And of course the local journalists will be very happy to get material from you frequently in the appropriate style and format. It makes their lives a lot easier, so they will begin to look to you for filling columns regularly. And editorial publicity is often far more effective than direct advertising.

Once you have identified something newsworthy, what communications skills are required to get it published, or aired on the radio? Remember the basic checklist. What is the objective of the communication? What about the context? What do you know of your audience? What, if any, are the barriers to communication with which you have to deal? Having answered these questions, what do they tell you about the appropriate style, tone and register for your communication?

Thoughts on Activity 8.6

I am sure that you will have realized that the answers to these questions will vary according to whether you are constructing a piece of news for the local press or for local radio, because basically one medium is to be read, the other to be heard. Therefore in the latter case, the quality of the voice is a key factor in addition to the quality of what is being said. We will come back to that particular point later.

Firstly, your **objective**. This, at a surface level, is to persuade a news editor to use your efforts, and then to persuade people to read or listen to what you want to say. At a deeper level, you want to put over as impressive an image of your organization as possible. The journalist will respond to an interesting story, presented in a professional way (two copies, typed-up double-spacing, on one side of a page only, with a name and telephone number to contact if necessary) and the reader or listener will respond to a snappy title or headline that attracts attention.

Which leads us on to the **context**. Local newspapers are not generally full of items which 'wait around' to be read, and local radio may have to compete with traffic jams, noisy children or vacuum cleaners to be heard! You do not have a 'captive audience', and the audience you do have may only be with you for a few minutes before it is attracted elsewhere. This can be a real constraint or barrier to communication.

Whatever information you want to get over has to be packaged and presented fast. For example, if you were using the news of the Head Chef's new baby to entice customers into your restaurant, you would want to feature the description of this wonderful new dish before you warble on about the happy event which led to its creation.

Then what do you know about your **audience**? Nothing – and everything! The material put out by the local media is designed to attract the whole reading and listening population, irrespective of age, sex, socio-economic or ethnic group. So what you write has to be accessible to them all. So the material most likely to achieve your objective needs to be generally simple and straightforward in its **style** and **register**.

You probably know the word 'journalese'. It is a particular style and register of writing which is associated with the press, and the mass media in general. It has a number of characteristics, the most significant of which are that it usually rejects many of the tenets of good grammar and sentence construction, draws on symbolism and allusion rather than facts to illustrate points, and uses a range of literary techniques in exaggerated ways to draw or keep attention.

This in itself can be a very creative exercise, and the language of advertising draws upon it heavily. It's not for nothing that the *Sun* newspaper is regularly praised for its headlines by people who would have nothing to do with its ideas! For example, compare the following headlines which might be used to lead into a story about an unhappy meal experience:

1. 'Customers voice their objections to the quality of gamebirds served in restaurant.'
2. 'Grillroom grouse gets gourmet guests grumbling about grotty grub.'

The use of alliteration (each word beginning with the same letter or sounds) attracts attention. In other words, to produce a good piece of journalism of the sort your local paper will love, you put aside your crisp business language, the conventional, elegant literary style you learned at school, and in the main, write much as you would talk. Short words. Short sentences. Colourful and imaginative use of language. Not the easiest of communication to encode, but because you take into account the needs of the audience (to be entertained as well as informed in as painless a manner as possible) and the context, then you will achieve your objective.

Finally, back to the point about quality of voice when communicating on radio. You may find that even though you have constructed a press release, it is a professional newsreader who presents it, in which case you have no control, but probably no worries anyway, about voice quality. Alternatively, stories are often given over radio in the form of a 'question and answer' session. But even then the material is usually scripted, so you can practise the appropriate language. However this is one of the occasions where you think about 'horses for courses'.

As the voice quality is so important, and the metamessages given off by the voice are part of the overall encoding process, then why not use the member of staff (who may or may not be you, or even someone at your level in the organization) whose voice will reinforce or embellish in some way the message being transmitted to the listener. For instance, can you think of 'human' reasons as to why you might choose a woman to do the job? Or when you might go for someone with a fairly strong local accent instead of what is called Standard BBC or Received English? Or when a member of a minority ethnic group might be more likely to be listened to? The social factors perceived in the voice itself can set a scene for positive feedback – or create a barrier to communication if it conveys negative cues to the listener.

FURTHER READING

Janner, G. (1989) *Janner of Chairing*, Gower Publishing, Aldershot.

Higham, M. (1979) *A Businessman's Guide to Report-Writing and Making Speeches*, Wellingborough, Kent.

Two books which are especially useful for their highly practical 'tricks of the trade' approach, and both very readable.

Open University (1990) *Better Meetings: A Handbook for Individuals, Groups and Trainers*, Open University Press, Milton Keynes: an exceptionally well-presented book which is very interesting to read and full of good ideas for improving formal communications within organizations. It has many practical exercises, with easily adaptable scenarios, which can be used in staff training sessions at any level.

Conclusion

I do not object to people looking at their watches when I am speaking. But I strongly object when they start shaking them to make sure they are still going. (Lord Birkett)

Are you now shaking your watches? Perhaps I have not convinced you that communicating is more than common sense, and thus there is nothing here for you. But if you are prepared to agree with me, after reading this book, that the general theories, ideas, findings, explanations, do seem to offer a range of techniques or solutions for a particular communications process or problem, then our 'transaction' is complete.

It's back to that omelette again. Theories from chemistry or physics show us not only how to make an omelette successfully, but also how to present the egg in a thousand different ways (recipes) in a thousand different contexts (breakfast, lunch, dinner, soup, main course, pudding). So then theories from social psychology, sociology, socio-linguistics, help us communicate in a thousand different ways in a thousand different contexts.

'Common sense' does not tell us how to present an egg, when to present an egg, except in the sense of how we are used to seeing eggs presented, which may or may not be what other individuals and groups are used to. Indeed some groups would not even consider eating eggs in the first place, and it is just as well that you know which groups and why, if you are catering for them. 'Common sense' does not tell us how to present ourselves, except in the sense of what we are used to doing, like recognizing what is acceptable and unacceptable language in our home or work scene. But we have to think in terms of sociological theories to understand why this is the case, and to help us deal with new and unfamiliar contexts in which we cannot call on experience, on what we are 'used to doing'.

I'm sure you have no doubt that you will be able to train staff when you are a manager. I'm sure you have no difficulty in understanding that it's their actions or behaviour you are interested in when you evaluate their competence at silver service, or at handling a computerized booking system, or a sophisticated new piece of equipment. They may resent the 'new- fangled' equipment, disapprove of the 'impersonal' system, think silver service is an outdated concept. You don't really care **what** they think, because you are not attempting to change what they **think** of the system system or the equipment, only their **behaviour** with regard to it.

So I hope I have not suggested to you in this book that I personally can make you feel a more friendly, or more confident or more authoritative or more dynamic person. You may turn out to **be** one as a consequence of new or improved social skills, but that's not the object of the exercise, only to be **seen** as one.

Nor, I hope, have I suggested that you can acquire such skills that you will never be involved in a communications breakdown again. However good you are, however much time you invest, there may be those individuals who you will never 'get through' to.

For instance, your success as a communicator is dependent not only upon yourself, but also upon your customers' expectations and assumptions about the nature of service, or your staff's expectations and assumptions about the nature of leadership. And controlling perceptions of service and leadership and what is 'quality' in these contexts is both difficult and complex. As another author put it, 'Good service has nothing to do with what the provider believes it is; it has only to do with what the customer believes is true' (Davidow and Uttal, 1989).

People cannot be manipulated so easily, or if they could, there never ever would be any communications breakdowns and everybody would go around getting on with everyone else all the time! However recent research in the USA suggested that 94% of the population wanted to get on with each other, and thus would normally respond positively to the appropriate communications. That leaves only 6% who are real problems, and you may never meet them!

Michael Argyle (1965, 1968) referred to social skills as 'those interpersonal behaviours that contribute to the individual's effectivness as part of a group of individuals'. **Your** 'effectiveness' will relate to, depend upon, what you want to achieve, what the context or situation is, your own attitudes, values, beliefs, cognitive abilities, and your unique personal style.

Your effectiveness also has to be measured in terms of a particular group or cultural framework, and a particular framework and particular pattern of communication. The combinations and permutations of all these variables are infinite, so at the end of the day it is up to you to decide what is appropriate. A Chinese philosopher argued that 'You can never step into the same river twice.'

Just as the the swirls and ripples of water never repeat a specific pattern of movement, so every piece of social interaction is unique in its own way, because people's minds can 'swirl' or 'ripple' according to circumstances of the moment which cannot be predicted or controlled. I hope that you now at least have the ideas and the confidence to deal with whatever ripples – or floods – come your way.

> *The interest in life does not lie in what people do, nor even in their relations to each other, but largely in the power to communicate with a third party, antagonistic, enigmatic, yet perhaps persuadable, which one may call life in general. (Virginia Woolf)*

Bibliography

ACAS (1985) *Workplace Communications*, ACAS, London.

Adair, J.(1984) *The Skills of Leadership*, Gower, Aldershot.

Adair, J. (1987) *Effective Teambuilding*, Gower, Aldershot.

Adair, J. (1989) *Great Leaders*, Talbot Adair Press, Guildford.

Alderfer, C. P. and McCord, C. G. (1970) 'Personal and situational factors in the recruitment interview', *Journal of Applied Psychology*, **54**, 377–85.

Allan, J. (1989) *How to Develop Your Personal Management Skills*, Kogan Page.

Argyle, M. *et al.* (1973) *Skills with People: A Guide for Managers*, Hutchinson, London.

Argyle, M. (1975) *Bodily Communication*, Methuen, London.

Argyle, M. (1981) *A Handbook of Social Skills*, Methuen, London.

Argyle, M. (1981) *Social Encounters: Readings in Social Interaction*, Penguin Modern Psychology Readings, London.

Argyle, M. (1981) *Social Situations*, Cambridge University Press, Cambridge.

Argyle, M. (ed.) (1981) *Social Skills and Work*, Methuen, London.

Argyle, M. (1991) *Co-operation: the Basis of Sociability*, Routledge, London.

Argyle, M. (1994) *The Psychology of Interpersonal Behaviour*, 5th edn, Penguin, London.

Arnaldo, M. (1981) 'Hotel managers: a profile', *Cornell Quarterly*, November, 53–6.

Arnold, J., Cooper, C. and Robertson, I. (1991) *Work Psychology: Understanding Human Behaviour in the Workplace*, Pitman Publishing, London.

Atkinson, J. (1984) *Our Master's Voices: The Language and Body Language of Politics*, Methuen, London.

Atkinson, P. E. (1983) 'Developing cohesive workgroups', *Hospitality*, **29**, 19–23.

Baron, R. S., Kerr, N. L. and Miller, N. (1992) *Group Processes, Group Decisions, Group Action*, The Open University, Milton Keynes.

Belbin, R. M. (1981) *Management Teams: Why They Succeed or Fail*, Heinemann, Oxford.

Berger, F. and Vanger, R. (1986) 'Building your hospitality team', *Cornell HRA Quarterly*, February, 83-4.

Berne, E. (1984) *Games People Play: the Psychology of Human Relationships*, Methuen, London.

Bernstein, D. (1988) *Put It Together, Put It Across: the Craft of Business Presentation*, Cassell, London.

Binstead, D. (1986) *Developments in Interpersonal Skills Training*, Gower, Aldershot.

Blake, R., Shephard, H. and Mouton, J. (1964) *Managing Intergroup Conflict in Industry*, Gulf Publishing, Texas.

Boddy, D. and Buchanan, D. (1992) *Take the Lead: Interpersonal Skills for Project Managers*, Prentice Hall International, London.

Boella, M. J. (1987) *Human Resource Management in the Hotel and Catering Industry*, 4th edn, Hutchison, London.

Bolton, R. (1987) *People Skills: How to Assert Yourself, Listen to Others and Resolve Conflict*, Simon & Schuster, New York.

Bremner, M. (1990) *Inquire Within: the Ultimate Problem-Solver*, Random Century Group, London.

Brotherton, R. (1993) *Hospitality Management Education and Training in Britain and Europe*, Blackpool and the Flyde College.

Brownell, J. (1992) 'Hospitality managers' communications practices', *International Journal of Hospitality Management*, **11**, 111–28

Bryman, A. (1992) *Charisma and Leadership in Organisations*, Sage, London.

Buchanan, D. and Huczynski, A. (1985) *Organisational Behaviour: an Introductory Text*, Prentice-Hall International, London.

Bull, P. (1983) *Body Movement and Interpersonal Communication*, Wiley & Sons, Chichester.

Burton, G. and Doubleby, R. (1988) *Between Ourselves: an Introduction to Interpersonal Communication*, Edward Arnold, Sevenoaks, Kent.

Carnegie, D. (1937) *How to Win Friends and Influence People*, Simon & Schuster, New York.

Cartwright, D. and Zander, A. F. (eds) (1968) *Group Dynamics: Research and Theory*, Harper & Row.

Casse, P. (1992) *The One Hour Negotiator*, Butterworth-Heinemann, Oxford.

Clark, M. (1993) 'Communications and social skills: perceptions of hotel managers', *Employee Relations*, **15**, 51–60.

Commission for Racial Equality (1991) *Working in Hotels*, CRE, London.

Corner and Hawthorne (eds) (1982) *Communications Studies: An Introductory Reader*, Edward Arnold, Sevenoaks, Kent.

Coulson-Thomas, C. (1983) *Marketing Communications*, Institute of Management/Heinemann, Oxford.

Coutts, M. and Maher, C.(1980) *Writing Plain English*, Plain English Campaign, Whaley Bridge, Stockport.

Dainow, S. (1988) *Developing Skills with People: Training for Person to Person Direct Contact*, John Wiley, Chichester.

Dann, D. (1990) 'The nature of managerial work in the hospitality industry', *International Journal of Hospitality Management*, **9**, 319–34.

Davidow and Utal in Bowker, R. (1987) *Total Customer Service: the Ultimate Weapon*, HarperCollins, London.

Davis, K. (1953) 'Management communication and the grapevine', *Harvard Business Review*, January/February.

Day, P. (1977) *Methods of Learning Communications Skills*, Pergamon, Oxford.

Donohue, W. and Kolt, R. (1992) *Managing Interpersonal Conflict*, Sage Publications, London.

Douglas, T. (1983) *Groups: Understanding People Gathered Together*, Tavistock.

Douglas, T. (1978) *Basic Groupwork*, Routledge, London.

Drucker, P. (1988) 'The coming of the new organisation', *Harvard Business Review*, January/February, 45–53

Duck, S. (1991) *Human Relationships: An Introduction to Social Psychology*.

Dunkel, J. and Parnham, E. (1984) *The Business Guide to Effective Speaking*.

Ferguson, D. H. and Berger, F. (1984) 'Restaurant managers: what do they really do?', *Cornell Hotel and Restaurant Administration Quarterly*, **25**, 26–36.

Fiedler, F. E. (1967) *A Theory of Leadership Effectiveness*, McGraw-Hill, New York.

Fisher, A. (1990) *Impact: A Guide to Business Communications*, Prentice-Hall.

Fletcher, J. and Gowing, D. F. (1987) *The Business Guide to Effective Writing*, Kogan Page, London.

Fontana, D. (1990) *Social Skills at Work*, BPS Books, Leicester.

Forbes, R. and Jackson, P. R. (1980) 'Non-verbal behaviour and the outcome of selection interviews', *Journal of Occupational Psychology*, **53**, 65–72.

Forte, C. (Lord) (1986) *Forte: The Autobiography of Charles Forte*, Sidgwick & Jackson.

Fowler, A. (1990) *Negotiating Skills and Strategies*, Institute of Personnel Management, London.

Gardener, K. and Wood, R. C. (1991) 'Theatricality in food service work', *International Journal of Hospitality Management*, **10**, 267–78.

Gilbert, D. C. (1989) *Advertising and the UK Hotel Industry*, University of Surrey, Monograph.

Goffman, E. (1959) *The Presentation of Self in Everyday Life*, Doubleday Anchor, New York.

Goffman, E. (1967) *Interaction Ritual: Essays on Face to Face Behaviour*, Doubleday Anchor, New York.

Goffman, E. (1981) *Forms of Talk*, Blackwell, Oxford.

Gordon, J., Mondy, R., Sharplin, A. and Premeaux, S. (1990) *Management and Organisational Behaviour*, Allyn & Bacon, Boston.

Gowers, Sir Ernest (1980) *The Complete Plain Words*, Penguin, London.

Guirdham, M. (1990) *Interpersonal Skills at Work*, Prentice Hall.

Gudykunst, W. (1992) *Readings on Communicating with Strangers*, McGraw-Hill.

Hackman, J. R. (1987) 'The Design of Work Teams', in Lorsch, J. W. and Hargie, O. (eds) (1986) *A Handbook of Communications Skills*, Croom Helm, London.

Handbook of Organisational Behaviour, Prentice Hall, New Jersey.

Hargie, O., Saunders, C. and Dickson, D. (1987) *Social Skills in Interpersonal Communication*, Routledge, London.

Hayter, R. (1993) *Careers and Training in Hotels, Catering and Tourism*, Butterworth-Heinemann, Oxford.

Hicks, L. (1990) 'Excluded women: how can this happen in the hotel world?', *The Service Industries Journal*, April, 348–63.

Higham, M. (1979) *A Businessman's Guide to Report-Writing and Making Speeches*, Wellingborough, Kent.

Hind, R. A. (ed.) (1972) *Non-verbal Communication*, Cambridge University Press, Cambridge.

Hodgson, P. and Hodgson, J. (1992) *Effective Meetings*, Random House, London.

Holladay, S. J. and Coombs, W. T. (1993) 'Communicating visions: an exploration of the role of delivery in the creation of leader charisma', *Management Communication Quarterly*, **6**(4), 405–25.

Hollin, C. (1986) *Handbook of Social Skills Training*, Pergamon, Oxford.

Honey, P. (1990) *Improve Your People Skills*, Institute of Personnel Management, London.

Hotel and Catering Training Company (1992) *Meeting Competence Needs in the Hotel and Catering Industry – now and in the future*, HCTC.

International Journal of Hospitality Management (1990) 'Survey of industry expectations of competences for management trainees', **2**(4), 47–58.

Janis, I. L. (1982) *Victims of Groupthink: A Psychological Study of Foreign Policy Decisions and Fiascos*, 2nd edn, Houghton Mifflin, Boston.

Janner, G. (1986) *Janner on Meetings*, Gower Publishing, Aldershot.

Janner, G. (1989) *Janner on Chairing*, Gower Publishing, Aldershot.

Jay, A. (1971) *Effective Presentation: The Communication of Ideas by Words and Visual Aids*, British Institute of Management, London.

Johnson, D. W. and Johnson, R. T. (1987) *Joining Together; Group Theory and Group Skills*, Prentice-Hall, New York.

Kay, M. (ed.) (1980) *The Relationship of Verbal and Non-verbal Communication*, Mouton, the Hague.

Keegan, B. M. (1983) 'Leadership in the Hospitality Industry', in Cassee, E. and Reuland, R. (eds), *The Management of Hospitality*, Pergamon, Oxford.

Kennedy, G. (1987) *The Pocket Negotiator*, The Economist Publications, London.

Kleinke, C. L. (1986) *Meeting and Understanding People: How to Develop Competence in Social Situations and Expand Social Skills*, Freem & Co., New York.

Laver, J. and Hutcheson, S. (1972) *Communication in Face to Face Interaction*, Penguin Modern Linguistic Readings, London.

Lawton, P. and Rigby, E. R. (1992) *Meetings: Their Law and Practice*, Pitman, London.

Lee, R. and Lawrence, P. (1991) *Politics at Work*, Stanley Thornes Ltd, London.

Ley, D.A. (1980) 'The effective general manager; leader or entrepreneur?', *Cornell Hotel and Restaurant Administration Quarterly*, **21**, 66–7.

Locke, M. (1980) *How to Run Committees and Meetings: a Guidebook to Practical Politics*, Macmillan, London.

Ludlow, R. and Panton, F. (1992) *The Essence of Effective Communication*, Prentice Hall, New Jersey.

Lurie, A. (1981) *The Language of Clothes*, Heinemann, Oxford.

McCann, D. ( ) *How to Influence Others at Work*, Heinemann Professional, Oxford.

McKay, M., Davis, M. and Fanning, P. (1983) *Messages: the Communications Skills Book*, New Harbinger, California.

March, R. M. (1992) *Working for a Japanese Company: Insights into the Multicultural Workplace*, Kodansha International.

Margerison, C. (1973) *Managing Effective Work Groups*, McGraw-Hill, Maidenhead.

Mars, G. and Nicod, M. (1984) *The World of Waiters*, Allen & Unwin, London.

Martin, D. (1993) *Tough Talking: How to Handle Awkward Situations*, Institute of Management/Pitman Publishing, London.

Martin, R. and Lundberg, D. (1991) *Human Relations for the Hospitality Industry*, Van Nostrand Rheinhold, New York.

Maslow, A. (1943) 'A theory of human motivation', *Psychological Review*, 50(4).

Mayon-White, B. (ed.) (1986) *Planning and Managing Change*, Open University, Milton Keynes.

Mintzberg, H. (1980) *The Nature of Managerial Work*, Prentice-Hall International, New Jersey.

Morris, D. (1977) *Manwatching*, Cape, London.

Mullins, L. (1992) *Hospitality Management: A Human Resource Approach*, Pitman, London.

Murdock, A. (1993) *Personal Effectiveness*, Butterworth-Heinemann, Oxford.

Myers and Myers (1982) *Managing by Communication*, McGraw-Hill, London.

Napier, R. W. and Gershenfeld, M. K. (1981) *Groups: Theory and Experience*. Houghton Mifflin, Boston.

Nebel, E. C. and Stearns, K. (1977) 'Leadership in the Hospitality Industry', *Cornell HRA Quarterly*, **18**, 69–76.

Newman, H. (1982) 'The sounds of silence in communicative encounters', *Communication Quarterly*, **30**, 142–510.

Nofsinger, R. (1991) *Everyday Conversation*, Sage, London.

Open University (1990) *Community Education: Better Meetings: A Handbook for Individuals, Groups and Trainers*, Open University, Milton Keynes.

Open University (1991) *Plain English*, Open University, Milton Keynes.

Parkinson, C. N. and Rowe, N. (1979) *Communicate: Parkinson's Formula for Business Survival*, Pan Business Management.

Paxton, J. (1986) *Dictionary of Abbreviations*, 2nd edn, Dent, London.

Peel, M. (1990) *Improving Your Communications Skills*, Kogan Page, London.

Pfeiffer, J. W. and Jones, J. E. (annual) *A Handbook of Structured Experiences for Human Relations Training*, University Associates Publishers and Consultants, San Diego, California.

Phillips, K. and Fraser, T. (1982) *The Management of Interpersonal Skills Training*, Gower, Aldershot.

Pickard, J. (1993) 'The real meaning of empowerment', *Personnel Management*, November, 28–33.

Rasberry, R. and Lemoine, L. (1986) *Effective Managerial Communications*, Kent Publishing,

Richards, M. (1993) *Effective Meetings*, Fairman Training Ltd, Ely, Lincs.

Robbins, S. P. (1989) *Training in Interpersonal Skills: TIPS for Managing People at Work*, Prentice- Hall, New Jersey.

Singleton, W., Spurgeon, P. and Stammers, R. (1979) *The Analysis of Social Skills*, Plenum Press, New York.

Smith, P. (1985) *Language, the Sexes and Society*, Blackwell, Oxford.

Sommer, R. (1969) *Personal Space*, Prentice-Hall, New York.

Sparks, B. (1994) 'Communicative aspects of the service encounter', *The Council on Hotel, Restaurant and Institutional Education*, **17**(2), 39–50.

Spender, D. (1980) *Man-made Language*, Routledge & Kegan Paul, London.

Spradley, J. and Mann, B. (1975) *The Cocktail Waitress: Woman's Work in a Man's World*, John Wiley, New York.

Steinberg, R. and Shapiro, S. (1982) 'Sex differences in personality traits of female and male Masters of Business Administration students', *Journal of Applied Psychology*, **67**(3), 306–10.

Stevens, M. (1987) *Improving Your Presentation Skills: A Complete Action Kit*, Kogan Page, London.

Stewart, J. and D'Angel, G. (1988) *Together: Communicating Inter-personally*, Random House.

Stewart, R. (1988) *Managers and Their Jobs*, Macmillan, Basingstoke.

Stone, G. (1988) 'Personality and effective hospitality management'. In *Proceedings of the International Association of Hotel Management School Symposium*, Leeds.

Sunday Times (1993) 'Chin out, you chaps! Young leaders falter at Sandhurst', 18 July.

Sydney, E., Brown, M. and Argyme, M. (1973) *Skills with People: a Guide for Managers*, Hutchinson.

Tannen, D. (1991) *You Just Don't Understand: Women and Men in Conversation*, Virago, London.

Thorne, B., Kramarae, C. and Henley, N. (1983) *Language, Gender and Society*, Newbury House, Plymouth.

Tourism for All Advisory Committee (1994) *The Last Untapped Market*, ETB/STB/WTB/NITB/Holiday Care Service, London.

Turner, C. (1983) *Developing Interpersonal Skills*, Bristol Further Education Staff College.

Wainwright, G. R. (1987) *Meetings and Committee Procedure: Teach Yourself*.

Wilkinson, J. and Canter, S. (1982) *Social Skills Training Manual: Assessment, Programme Design and Management of Training*, John Wiley, Chichester.

Wittgenstein, L. (1967) *Philosophical Investigations*, 3rd edn, Blackwell, Oxford.

Wood, R. C. (1994) *Organisational Behaviour for Hospitality Managers*, Butterworth Heinemann.

Worsfold, P. (1989) 'Leadership and managerial effectiveness in the hospitality industry.' In *Proceedings of the International Association of Hotel Management Schools' Symposium*, Leeds.

Yukl, G. (1989) *Leadership in Organisations*, Prentice-Hall, New Jersey.

Index